D1556931

Scarlet Memorial

Scarlet Memorial

Tales of Cannibalism in Modern China

ZHENG YI

Translated and edited by T. P. Sym
with a Foreword by Ross Terrill

 WestviewPress
A Division of HarperCollins*Publishers*

Copyright © 1996 by Zheng Yi

Published in 1996 in the United States of America by Westview Press, Inc., 5500 Central Avenue, Boulder, Colorado 80301-2877, and in the United Kingdom by Westview Press, 12 Hid's Copse Road, Cumnor Hill, Oxford OX2 9JJ

Library of Congress Cataloging-in-Publication Data
Cheng, I, 1947–
    [Hung se chi nien pei. English]
    Scarlet memorial : tales of cannibalism in modern China / Zheng I;
    translated and edited by T. P. Sym ; with a foreword by Ross Terrill.
        p. cm.
    Includes index.
    ISBN 0-8133-2615-X (hc). — ISBN 0-8133-2616-8 (pb)
    1. Kwangsi Chuang Autonomous Region—Politics and government.
2. China—History—Cultural Revolution, 1966–1969.   I. Sym, T. P.
II. Title.
DS793.K6C4413   1996
951.05'6—dc20   96-33948
                                                                                  CIP

10   9   8   7   6   5   4   3   2   1

For All the Victims

Contents

Illustrations

Foreword

Ross Terrill

Scarlet Memorial is one of the saddest books ever written about the People's Republic of China and also one of the most important. In the following pages Zheng Yi pieces together and reflects upon fearsome cruelties of the Cultural Revolution of 1966–1976, in particular the practice of cannibalism against class enemies in the autonomous region (really a province) of Guangxi. If verified and extended by further research, as I believe it is likely to be, this work will be a landmark in the history of totalitarianism.

The author carried out his investigation as a journey and the reader feels a sense of a shared adventure with Zheng Yi as he collects facts and seeks to put them in historical, anthropological, and political context. Zheng Yi is a writer, not a political scientist, and his book is at once subjective and broad-reaching. In clear and simple prose (extremely well translated) the book presents candid and daring thoughts and wrestles with the most difficult issues of Chinese culture's interaction with dictatorial politics.

In the late 1960s China experienced an internal political fight that in scope, intensity, violence, and dislocation is without parallel in the life of major nations in our time. The convulsion began from above, and to the degree that it comprised "rebellion," this was mostly the fake variety of rebellion-on-instructions. Supreme power did not change hands in Beijing during the Cultural Revolution; it had been Mao Zedong's beforehand, and it was still Mao's when the storm subsided, so there was no "revolution." All the cruelty and suffering in the pretty hills of Guangxi, as in a score of other provinces, was at once politically triggered yet without any tangible, sustained political outcome.

A full explanation of the Cultural Revolution must combine traits of dictatorship, Chinese political culture, and the cumulative effect of Communist organization and propaganda on the Chinese people from 1949. Between the supreme leader's views and those of the grass roots, there were few intermediate levels on which ideas were tested, debated, or assailed. As a dictator in the tradition of the Chinese emperors, the late Mao tended to view the Chinese masses, whom he once called "blank" as well as poor, as actors with a fixed role in the political drama, not as participants with thoughts of their own. This seems to have been the central pathology of the Cultural Revolution; Zheng Yi has laid bare its consequences in five counties of Guangxi.

In *Scarlet Memorial* the Cultural Revolution takes on the horror of Pol Pot's killing fields and the Nazi Holocaust. Hatred was licensed, annihilation quotas were laid down, and old vendettas found their moment of opportunity. Knives went in, flesh flew through the air, and the gates of hell opened wide. As the enemies' corpses became available for consumption, the elite chose the hearts and the livers, whereas the masses were allowed to peck at the arms and the soles of the feet. Probably more than 100,000 people in Guangxi died in the political violence. Just in the five counties investigated by Zheng Yi, hundreds of "class enemies" were eaten; thousands joined in the eating.

No one can make the tortured whole or bring the dead back to life, and we in the West are not in a position to directly deter or restrain those who in the name of Chinese communism might torture and kill and devour again. But if we can understand what happened, and especially if the Chinese people can do so, the chance of recurrence may be reduced. Such an understanding must begin with the fact that the politics of Communist China triggered the Guangxi cannibalism. It was a manifestation of ideological frenzy—extreme but intrinsic.

The Beijing investigative reporter Liu Binyan, asked by Zheng Yi during a chance encounter on a train why he had not tackled the topic of cannibalism in Guangxi, replied, "Too evil." Indeed there was an initial tendency on the part of Zheng Yi to turn away from the subject out of delicacy. Likewise for students of China and the world public, there may be an impulse to shy away from this grotesque slice of contemporary history. It would be a grave intellectual and moral mistake to do so.

Readers are likely to begin with skepticism and go through shock, puzzlement, and despair as they accompany Zheng Yi on his dark adventure in the southern region of Guangxi. One must get used to scenes like this one: "Strolling down the street, the director of the local Bureau of Commerce carried a human leg on his shoulder, which he was taking home to boil and consume. On the leg there still hung a piece of a man's trouser" (p. 3). This appears to be totalitarianism's ultimate expression. We are familiar with totalist ideology and total organizational control; in the Cultural Revolution in Guangxi we also confront total elimination of the enemy to the point of devouring him.

In the golden sunshine of Guangxi, among the charming Zhuang people, the most numerous non-Han race in China, Zheng Yi in his investigations—carried out during the mid- to late-1980s—at first felt like a jaded cynic and even doubted whether what the documents and interviews made plain could be believed. It is true that Chinese intellectuals, not excluding Zheng Yi, have a tangential and plaintive relation to the public life of their nation. Attached to a self-image of high purpose and unfailing influence, they are cast into despair by repeated revelations that both are in short supply. As Zheng Yi studied written accounts of cannibalism and interviewed people who had eaten others, he broke out into a cold sweat and became ill.

The maneuvers that preceded the killing of class enemies in Guangxi were the standard ones of Chinese Communist campaigns: from "class analysis," to struggle sessions, and on to "sentencing." But the extent of physical annihilation and the barbarous triumphalism were unusual. This book is almost too painful to read in places. Take the case of a woman from a landlord family, Zou, who was on the list of enemies ("a spy") because her husband had gone to Taiwan (pp. 41ff). She and her 32-year-old son were hung from a tree and beaten with sticks in an attempt to obtain a confession of their links to foreign enemies of China. They refused and were led to a freshly dug pit to be buried alive. The woman, breaking her calm, cried to her son, "Are we going to die like this?" The son said, "We should not confess to things we never did. Let's die." But as the dirt was shoveled in, the son stood up and through his tears called out, "We should not die like this. It's too harsh." A militiaman stabbed him in the chest with a spear. The mother rose and she too received a spear in the chest. As the spears were pulled out, pieces of the lungs came out too. The murderers insisted that as the earth was piled in, the son had to lie on top of the mother. The son blurted out, "Oh God, how can you make me do this?" The burying alive continued and concluded. Afterward the murderers celebrated with a feast.

One of the most terrible things about *Scarlet Memorial* is that most people faced death like lambs. As the sticks and knives were wielded, the innocent "just knelt down silently, no begging, no cursing, no arguing, and not the slightest show of a willingness to resist" (p. 16). Even in these rural areas of Guangxi, where most of the killers knew most of the victims, people did not dare shed tears for murdered friends and family, much less collect the body parts for burial.

Not one act of direct physical heroism is recorded by Zheng Yi; he learned of no one who jumped up as a killing began and said, "This is wrong, this is too much, I am going to try to stop it, and if you kill me in the act of trying, so be it!" A few people are recorded as not submitting, crying out to the heavens against the evil that was being perpetrated, and committing suicide. But apparently no one died in a physical attack on a murderer.

The Han people regard Guangxi as a slightly dubious border region—
Zheng Yi himself uses the term (p. 10)—and one view of the cannibalism
of the 1960s is that Zhuang culture was once more revealing its dark side.
It is true that in Zhuang history there is a thread of cannibalism. To a degree, to invoke the Zhuang tradition of cannibalism would be to put the
central focus on hatred and cruelty in Guangxi rather than on the nar-
rower pathology of cannibalism. If one goes back far enough there is cannibalism also in the Han tradition; the great statesman Liu Bei, who
founded the Shu State after the fall of the Han Dynasty, ate human flesh.
Zheng Yi faces the reality that all peoples evolved from primitive ways;
he seeks to trace this evolution in Guangxi and to identify the circum-
stances in which cannibalism as an atavism can spring back in a modern
context.

What kind of politics reinforces human altruism and what kind under-
mines it? In the brief and destructive history of totalitarianism we have a
display of the latter. In no sense is human altruism a Western monopoly
alien to China; the Chinese ideas of *ren xin* (human feelings), *ren dao* (hu-
manitarianism), and *ren qing* (human sympathy) are old and powerful. It
was totalitarian politics that removed from Chinese public life the values
of compassion and civility and replaced them with the theory and practice of the end justifying the means. (In the West we have been touched in
recent times by the icy wind of group hatred, but fortunately it has been
counterbalanced by law, a free press, and a strong sense of individual dig-
nity and responsibility; there were no such counterbalances in Guangxi.)

When one of the guilty officials tracked down by Zheng Yi declared,
"Wrongly killing one hundred is better than letting one guilty person escape" (p. 166), this was the quintessential obliteration of law by ideology.
Here we get to the heart of the matter: lack of restraints upon the tribe
and its sense of its own rectitude; this is the marshland where Marxism
and fascism and extreme nationalism meet.

It would be wrong to insist on a sociopolitical explanation for every
shred of evil on display in the Guangxi killings. Evil has sprung from the
human heart in every epoch of history, every corner of the globe, and
every social stratum. In the end some readers may conclude that the
frenzy lay deeper than Communist politics; do people eat human livers
just because they are ordered to do so or because they are offered a promotion for the act? But Communist policy set the stage for the cruelty; it
inspired, licensed, and later covered up the frenzy. Livers were boiled and
eaten as red flags fluttered and Maoist slogans rent the air. And it does
not seem an accident that one of the few heroes in *Scarlet Memorial*, a senior cadre named Wang Zujian, was a former rightist. Wang wrote a petition to Beijing about the cannibalism in Wuxuan County, achieving a
speedy result, which proved that the killing could have been stopped

much earlier had there been more people like Wang and more courage at the grass roots. Stopped but not necessarily exposed; only when the boss of Guangxi, Wei Guoqing, finally fell foul of Deng Xiaoping in 1983 was the path cleared for even Zheng Yi's limited access to the cannibalism story.

Behind the frenzy, normally there was planning. "Those who were about to be beaten were announced by name from a list," Zheng Yi reports (p. 15). Communist officials were the traffic cops for the flow of cruelty, and so in the end a political cause, if a wildly distorted one, was being served by the torture, murder, and cannibalism.

This is not to deny the complicity of many ordinary people who jumped with alacrity to perform the hellish tasks at hand, especially in the county of Wuxuan. Or of those who neither enthused nor resisted but, feeling guilty about the act of cannibalism, took the human flesh mixed in with pork, to modify the effect. Yet basically the violence was a method of so-called class struggle, initiated by Mao's Communist Party, with the people as stage props. That "four elements" types—the lowest stratum of society in the People's Republic of China—were marshaled for the nastiest jobs clinches the point that Communist politics and the Communist worldview were the framework for the killing and eating. The very term for being beaten to death was "subjected to dictatorship."

In Guangxi the genuine class struggle of land reform after 1949 saw far fewer victims than the contrived, atavistic, cynical "class struggle" of Mao's duel with his supposed enemies in the 1960s. The reader of *Scarlet Memorial* may also come to reflect on the parallels between the imperatives of nationalism and those of Communist politics, for cannibalism was justified in the war against Japan by considerations analogous to those invoked amidst the "class struggle" in the 1960s. Unlimited hatred of the enemy was the connection between the two. Time and again in his interviews on the Guangxi violence, Zheng Yi heard the refrain, "The person I killed was the enemy." In other words, what could be wrong with that? "Didn't Chairman Mao say, 'Kill or be killed'?"

As a political inquiry *Scarlet Memorial* does not always pin down answers; and indeed the mixture of Zhuang culture, Han culture, totalitarian politics, the class analysis of Marxism-Leninism, and the personality of Mao is a devilishly complex one. Zheng Yi leaves untouched some tantalizing points. Why didn't some threatened people flee the county or the province? How should the term "murder" be handled when often in the People's Republic of China no clear distinction has existed between state execution and "private" murder?

Over the years there have been a number of interpretations of the Cultural Revolution and I am not sure that any of them will stand the test of time and further access to evidence. For example, the upheaval cannot be explained by the "impact of the West" approach, by China's reaction to the Vietnam War, or by Chinese utopianism. All of these approaches were common when I was a graduate student at Harvard during the Cultural Revolution. All underestimated the role of the personal dramas of Mao and Jiang Qing in the Cultural Revolution and took insufficient account of the role of Chinese fatalism and collectivism. We can only say in broad terms that the keys to the upheaval are to be found in the age-old ways of Chinese culture, the modes of Communist dictatorship, the pent-up energy of people denied political participation, and Mao's personal quest for untrammeled power and a phantom of perfect socialism. Zheng Yi's attempt to interweave these four themes is a major achievement.

Zheng Yi has his own theory of "Two Cultural Revolutions"—one from Beijing and one from below. It gives *Scarlet Memorial* an extra fascination that Zheng Yi believes one level of the Cultural Revolution was a democratic struggle from the grass roots against "seventeen years" of Communist rule itself. But his argument (p. 129) that "political immaturity" and "perpetual divisions, instigated by Mao," derailed this struggle and produced factionalism is not the full answer. Why is factionalism so prominent in Chinese politics? Surely it has something to do with the Chinese people's way of defining themselves less by individual traits than by membership in a group. And not everyone will follow Zheng Yi to his conclusion that "cruelty during the Cultural Revolution (including cruelty among the masses) was an expression of rebellion and wrath in response to the violent politics of the 'seventeen years'" (p. 130).

The task of punishing the cannibals, torturers, and murderers in Guangxi was not tackled vigorously. I agree with Zheng Yi that a "thorough settling of accounts under Communist Party rule . . . is impossible" (p. 115). In a Communist system punishment is often a case of using law for a political purpose, rather than subjecting reprehensible acts to the judgment of law. The huge task of assessing the role of Communist ideology in the Cultural Revolution must await a post-CCP rule historiography.

Meanwhile, even if we set aside the fringes of Zheng Yi's case that are based on rumor, the essential, solid core of his story is a major contribution to the identification of the pathology of Mao's China. One saving grace is found amid the blood and shame: Some of the barbarity was recorded by observers and the record lived on to provide the basis for some punishments—and for this book.

The story of Zheng Yi is one of a leftist driven to the Right by realities. He had once been a Maoist believer and *Scarlet Memorial* has a strain of appalled shock that "our revered god [Mao] was none other than a murderer who was shoving us into the abyss of poverty and death" (p. 29). He wrote the book in the aftermath of the democracy movement of 1989, in which he was a participant and while he was on the run as a wanted counterrevolutionary. Part of the book is a trenchant reflection on the nature of Communist dictatorship.

China today still is ruled by a Communist Party exercising a monopoly of political power as it was in the 1960s. Unfortunately, there are observers of China who write as if politics does not exist anymore in China and who believe that post-Mao China has become exclusively an economic phenomenon. This school of "China exceptionalism" projects upon the Chinese an extraordinary immunity from any desire for political life. If there is one conception of Deng's China that is wrong and will set us up for a shock if embraced, it is the death of politics. An implicit contribution of Zheng Yi's book—which was researched and written in the Deng era, in the face of much obstruction and harassment—is to warn us of this point.

Read *Scarlet Memorial* and weep. Only if one condescends to China, or, worse, puts the Chinese race in a separate exotic category, would it be possible to take this material lightly. To care about China as a substantial part of the human race is to find this book deeply troubling. Of course, the "China exceptionalism" school avoids the agony by declaring that China is so different from any other culture that common values do not exist. But Westerners who feel a universal bond with the Chinese cannot remain human beings and *not* face what happened—this stain on China will never go away, even as its full explanation may never be grasped.

Note from the Translators and Editors

Scarlet Memorial (Hongse jinianbei) by Zheng Yi was first published in Taipei, Taiwan, in 1993 by the Huashi Cultural Publishing House. Sections of the original text that document the incidents of cannibalism in China's Guangxi Autonomous Region have been translated in full (with minor modifications by the author and translators) as Chapters 1 and 2. Zheng Yi's analysis of the political and cultural context of the events in Guangxi, and his recounting of similar abuses during the Cultural Revolution (1966–1976) in other regions of China, have been compressed into Chapters 3 and 4 and the Epilogue. Extensive lists of names, dates, and places are provided throughout the volume as part of Zheng Yi's effort to provide an extensive documentary record of the Guangxi cannibalism.

The notes at the end of each chapter are Zheng Yi's. The editors have added a series of footnotes to explain important historical events in China and to elucidate obscure Chinese terminology. Documents on the cannibalism in Guangxi compiled by Zheng Yi will be published under separate cover. The editorial assistance of Peter Rand (John K. Fairbank Center for East Asian Research, Harvard University) is gratefully acknowledged. Thanks also to Susan McEachern (formerly of Westview Press), Ross Terrill (John K. Fairbank Center for East Asian Research, Harvard University), and several individuals who must remain anonymous. Above all, we wish to extend our respect and admiration to Zheng Yi and his wife, Bei Ming, for their indefatigable and courageous work.

"T. P. Sym" is the pseudonym used by a team of Chinese and American writers.

Historical Chronology, 1950–1989

1950	Guangxi (formerly Kwangsi) is "liberated" by Chinese Communist forces.
1955	Wei Guoqing is appointed governor and Party secretary of Guangxi Province.
1957	June: Anti-rightist campaign leads to widespread persecution of intellectuals and writers throughout China.
1958	Guangxi is established as one of five "autonomous regions" in China.
1958–1960	The Great Leap Forward is launched by CCP Chairman Mao Zedong.
1960–1963	The "three bitter years" of famine and privation sweep the nation as a consequence of Mao's irrational and grandiose Great Leap policies.
1962–1965	The Socialist Education Movement is launched in the Chinese countryside against cadre corruption and the abuse of power.
1965	March: Large-scale U.S. bombing of North Vietnam begins near the Guangxi border.
1966–1976	The period of the Cultural Revolution.
1966	May: First big-character poster appears at Peking University (Beida) initiating a mass campaign among students.
	July: First Red Guard organizations appear in Beijing.
	August: A series of massive Red Guard rallies begins in Beijing. Eleventh Plenum of the CCP Central Committee authorizes formation of the Revolutionary Committees.
1967	January: The first Revolutionary Committee is established in Heilongjiang Province as left-wing radicals decide to seize Party and state power.
	April 22: "Small Faction" of Red Guards is formed in Guangxi leading to a two-year period of intense factional fighting.

	July: Wuhan incident brings China to the brink of civil war as PLA units in this central China city directly challenge central authority.
1968	January: Mao denounces the factionalism and anarchism of extreme Left.
	March: Extreme Left regains the initiative as Jiang Qing, Mao's wife, strengthens her control of leftist elements.
	April: The Left is encouraged to step up attacks on powerholders in the Party and government.
	June: Violence intensifies throughout China.
	July 3: CCP Central Committee, the State Council, and Central Military Commission issue "July 3 Bulletin" warning against disruption of railway communication in Guangxi and attacks on PLA organs and troops. The bulletin provokes vicious battles in the region among various factions that result in incidents of cannibalism.
	August: Provincial-level Revolutionary Committee established in Guangxi headed by Wei Guoqing.
1969	April: Ninth Party Congress selects Lin Biao as Mao's official successor.
1970	Effort to rebuild CCP apparatus in China is inaugurated.
1976	September: Death of Mao Zedong brings an end to the Cultural Revolution.
	October: Members of the Gang of Four, including Jiang Qing, are arrested and imprisoned.
1978	Deng Xiaoping emerges as China's paramount leader and inaugurates a period of reform.
1983–1984	Following Wei Guoqing's fall from power in Guangxi, CCP investigations of abuses during the Cultural Revolution unearth evidence of cannibalism there.
1986	May: Zheng Yi travels to Guangxi to investigate reports of cannibalism during the Cultural Revolution.
1989	April–May: Pro-democracy movement breaks out in Beijing and one hundred other Chinese cities.
	June 3–4: Democracy movement is crushed by the Chinese army. Zheng Yi and his wife, Bei Ming, escape arrest and ultimately flee to the West.

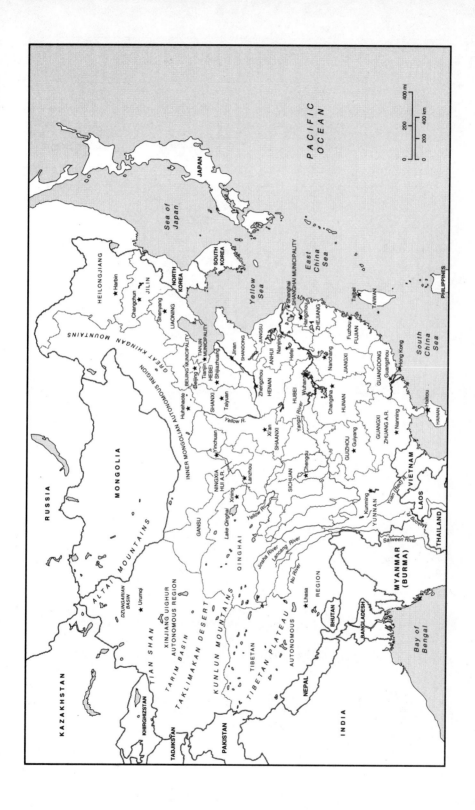

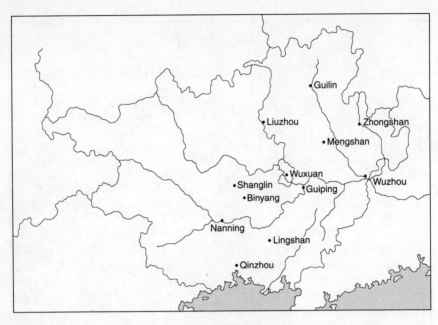

Guangxi Zhuang Autonomous Region (places mentioned)

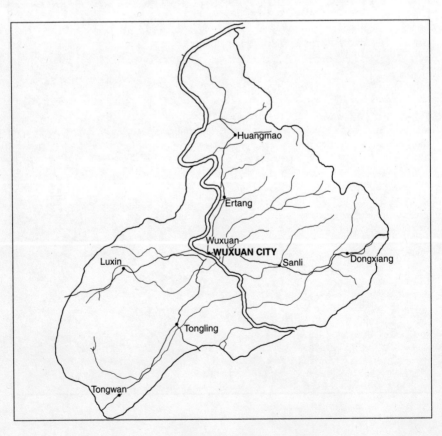

Wuxuan County

Introduction

In the midst of the Cultural Revolution, I decided purely by accident to head off to the city of Guilin in the Guangxi Autonomous Region.* It was 1968. Although I had nothing of any real importance to do there, I went there anyway and, to my great surprise, discovered that Guilin was at that time an encircled city. The faction called the Guilin Grand Alliance, which held to the "April 22" view, was retreating to the central part of the city. It was on the verge of defeat at the hands of the powerful faction of the United Headquarters of the Proletarian Revolutionaries (lianzhi), which was supported and armed by elements of the military.† Like the battlefield in Chongqing, in Sichuan Province in 1967, there were no boundary lines demarcating the territory occupied by the two factions, and it was very hard to distinguish exactly which buildings belonged to which group. In order to deal with sudden attacks, members of both factions were trained to shoot on a moment's notice in the direction of any

---

*The Guangxi Autonomous Region was set up in 1958 and is one of five such "autonomous" administrative regions heavily populated by non-Han minorities in China. Theoretically, these regions are organs of self-administration, but under Communist rule they have generally enjoyed no more than mere paper autonomy since the 1950s. See Thomas Heberer, *China and Its National Minorities* (Armonk, NY: M. E. Sharpe, 1989), p. 41.

†The Guangxi Autonomous Region was wracked by some of the most intense conflict in 1967 and 1968 during the Cultural Revolution. On one side stood the United Headquarters of the Proletarian Revolutionaries, which was also known as the Big Faction (Dapai) and was headed by Wei Guoqing, a member of the Zhuang minority and a veteran army officer and CCP official who had ruled Guangxi singlehandedly since 1955 and was backed by the army. Like many provincial leaders during the Cultural Revolution, Wei defended his political position while seeming to obey Mao's directives by dismantling the conventional Party structure and establishing the system of Revolutionary Committees. On the other side, stood the Grand Alliance (laoduo)—also known as the Small Faction (Xiaopai)—headed by Wu Jinnan, who had been sent to the region in 1957 to force greater Sinification of the Zhuang minority and who, during the Cultural Revolution, mobilized Red Guards to challenge Wei Guoqing's formidable authority. Members of this group, which was formed on April 22, 1967, are described by Zheng Yi as adhering to the "April 22 view." Large-scale battles between these two groups broke out throughout 1967–1968 as Wei Guoqing secured from the central authorities in Beijing the order to use the army to suppress the April 22 faction. See Stanley Karnow, *Mao and China: From Revolution to Revolution* (New York: Viking Press, 1967), pp. 434–440.

1

individual activity taking place in the city. One particular young lad I happened upon told me that he kept a rifle wrapped in an old newspaper hidden under his arm so that it looked like a book or a package of fried pancakes. He was very quick on the draw. Although I was a Red Guard member of the Qinghua University *Jinggangshan*, affiliated with the Congress of Red Guards in the capital *(Shoudu hongdaihui),** which itself was involved in student movements all over the country, I had no particular ax to grind with either of these two factions in Guangxi.

For that reason, I decided to seek out some peace and quiet in the midst of this chaotic situation and to enjoy the many famous scenic spots around the area. Unfortunately, since most of the scenic sites in and around the city were occupied by the military, the only place I actually managed to visit was Elephant Trunk Mountain. Bearing in mind the old saying that the scenery in Guilin is number one in the world and that Yangshuo is number one in Guilin, I had also planned to take a nice boat ride down the Li River to the scenic spots of Yangshuo. People whom I had befriended in the city were astonished by my plans. They tried to persuade me not to leave Guilin, warning of grave dangers. Unrestrained slaughter was taking place nearby on a daily basis, and it was said at the time that a decision by only three armed militiamen was all it took to arrange an immediate execution in the name of the proletarian dictatorship. To some people, of course, nothing seemed in the least wanton about any of this; it was simply a special legal procedure, implemented during an extraordinary period, which was formally known as the special tribunal of the poor and lower-middle peasants. But the ominous sound of the term *special tribunal* gave me a funny feeling in the pit of my stomach, and I soon decided to cancel my trip to Yangshuo.

As a result of this experience I started to give some attention, once I had returned to Beijing, to the course of the Cultural Revolution in Guangxi, which had never before interested me. At this point, the Qinghua University *Jinggangshan* Red Guards were still submissive, and Mao Zedong had not yet decided to abolish them. News reports flew onto the Qinghua campus via a nationwide network that had been established by Red Guards over a period of two years; it was during this time that I learned

*The *Jinggangshan* Red Guards were organized at Peking and Qinghua Universities in early 1967 and took their celebrated title from the mountain stronghold in Jiangxi Province held by Communist guerrilla forces in the late 1920s. The Congress of Red Guards in the capital was a citywide organization in Beijing composed of students from the city's colleges and universities. The formation of the Congress of Red Guards was followed by the formation of congresses of Red Guards all over the country. For an account of Red Guard battles at Qinghua University, see William Hinton, *Hundred Day War: The Cultural Revolution at Tsinghua [Qinghua] University* (New York: Monthly Review Press, 1972).

more about the slaughter going on in various parts of Guangxi. I also got wind of these events from Liu Jianxun, the chairman of the Henan Revolutionary Committee, who once commented, apropos of the events in Guangxi, "Well, what's so great about Wei Guoqing?" Wei was then chairman of the Guangxi Revolutionary Committee. "All he ever did was give the order to mow down the opposition with machine guns." The sarcasm was quite noticeable. If these were but mere rumors and exaggerations, then further evidence could be found in the huge slogans, draped atop Tiananmen Square, that proclaimed "Hold Wei Guoqing Accountable for the Slaughter of One Hundred Thousand People in Guangxi!" and "Guangxi Is Bathed in Blood!"

Finally, more astonishing and incredible news swept Beijing: cannibalism in Guangxi! This was too absurd, far beyond anything most people could even allow themselves to imagine. Probably very few people even paid attention to this desperate call for help. But the unimaginable certainly was burned into my own memory as a possibility I half believed and half doubted. Now, after all these long years, these few stories from a certain place, from a certain time, when an entire city was engaged in cannibalism, are still fresh in my mind.

> Strolling down the street, the director of the local Bureau of Commerce carried a human leg on his shoulder, which he was taking home to boil and consume. On the leg there still hung a piece of a man's trouser.

> A peasant who was being chased by a crowd ran to the commune office of the Armed Police *(Wuzhuangbu)*, knelt down and begged for help from the commander. "Help me!" he cried. "They want to eat me!" The obese commander, unmoved, replied, "Let them do what they will." The peasant was immediately executed and then cut up and eaten.

> The principal of a school was smashed to the ground. Each person present ripped off a piece of flesh, and together they started an impromptu campus barbecue.

Years later, sometime in 1984, I happened to meet up with Li Hong, author and deputy editor-in-chief of the magazine *Guangxi Literature (Guangxi wenxue)*. Both of us were staying in the guest house run by another journal, *Contemporary (Dangdai)*, which was published by the Beijing People's Literature Publishing House, then in the midst of editing a selection of our short stories to be reprinted in the journal. Soon, we became good friends. We had been talking to each other about everything under the sun when the topic of the slaughter in Guangxi more than a decade earlier came up. To my great surprise, Li Hong became livid, which once and for all cleared away any doubt in my mind that these horrible events had in fact occurred. He also told me that not long before, a special work team had been sent by the Guangxi Autonomous Region to clear up leftover cases from the Cultural Revolution *(wenge yi'an)*, some of which involved cannibalism. One of Li's friends, who had participated in the work team, had seized a collection of dehydrated human gallbladders (a "delicacy" hoarded over the years by the killers) as criminal evidence and brought them back to Nanning city, where he delivered them to the appropriate authorities. Li Hong was an outspoken friend and a serious writer. I trusted what he had to say.

Again, quite by accident, on a train heading south, I happened to bump into Liu Binyan, the investigative journalist. When I asked him whether he knew anything about the human slaughter and cannibalism in Guangxi during the Cultural Revolution, Liu replied that he did. A moment of silence passed between us. I then ventured to ask him why he hadn't written anything on the subject. "Too evil!" he replied. At that moment, I decided that I would write about it. Quite apart from the fact that I lacked material evidence, I knew that it would not be an easy and simple matter to investigate this story. What would it all mean? About this I had no idea. But I did know that the answer might be serious and profound. From that moment on, I started to shoulder the heavy cross of the Guangxi incident. For, based on my understanding of Communist authority, I knew that I would be stepping into a perilous forbidden zone, a black forest within which the bloody crimes were buried.

1

Searching Out the Criminal Evidence

STRIKE WHILE THE IRON IS HOT

On May 17, 1986, I once again stepped onto Guangxi soil. Accompanying me was my literary friend, Bei Ming, who specializes in literary theory and has a fervent interest in cultural anthropology. She intended to learn about the carefree and romantic southern culture, for which she has great respect, and, of course, she would help me in my explorations to understand Guangxi. A longing of mine was finally to be realized; I was excited and yet at the same time I felt a sense of absurdity. How dramatic—here we were, on a fine sunny day in the 1980s, at the end of the twentieth century, planning to investigate the occurrence of cannibalism. *The Thousand and One Nights!* The tragedy had already been verified, but the beautiful sunshine of southern China made me feel like a jaded cynic, a victim of neurosis.

Since this was our first trip to Nanning, the capital of Guangxi, Bei Ming and I were total strangers. We hailed a three-wheeled pedicab and decided to look for a place for Bei Ming to stay. I had no such concerns for myself, since I had already presented the local authorities with an official letter of introduction that was supposed to provide me with an official residence. The pedicab was very reasonable and the driver was very friendly. When he saw that we weren't satisfied with the hotel that he had recommended, our driver offered to help us look for another place. Somewhat afraid that he might be trying to cheat us out of money—such was the typical reaction of people from hard-edged cities like Beijing—we politely turned him down and began to search on our own. But as we walked along the streets the driver followed us and from time to time offered his counsel, all for free. It seemed that he was not interested in our scant supply of money, but somehow we could not relax. The ancient saying, "Measuring the gentleman's mind with a petty man's heart," well describes our attitude. It was indeed embarrassing. He was the first Nanning local we encountered.

The public transportation system in Nanning also left a deep impression on both of us. Passengers got on and off the bus in two distinct, orderly lines through a narrow door. This was not at all like the crazy, maddening scene in other big, crowded cities. One rainy day, when we were on our way to an interview, we noticed that all the bicycles lined along the streets were covered with the raincoats of their owners: red, blue, and green. Such a scene was rarely seen in other places. On the narrow paths in the villages, Zhuang women of the local minority nationality, especially the young women, politely stopped at a distance as we approached to let us pass by.* This modest and courteous tradition made us almost feel that we were in a kind of wonderland. We were so moved that we even thought that perhaps the slaughter and cannibalism during the Cultural Revolution were nothing more than rumors. Maybe they were part of some historical myth that never could be resolved.

Once Bei Ming settled down, I went to look for a local reporter for the *China Legal News (Zhongguo fazhi bao)* named Wei Huaren, who had been recommended to me by friends in Beijing.† Little Wei, as he was known, was a Guangxi local. In a rather authoritative manner he immediately confirmed the dire rumors about cannibalism. As soon as he had reserved a room for me in the local Public Security Bureau guest house, Little Wei immediately arranged a meeting between myself and Wang Guanyu, deputy Party secretary of the Political and Legal Committee of the Guangxi Autonomous Region. Then, on the afternoon of May 19, he accompanied me to Wang's office. I produced my journalist's credentials, the letter of introduction from the central offices of the *China Legal News* under the central Ministry of Justice, plus an additional letter of introduction from the All-China Writers' Association. I also explained the purpose of our trip, just as I had discussed it with Bei Ming in advance: I intended to collect historical materials on various ruthless incidents during the Cultural Revolution and to analyze the poisonous effects of ultra leftism from a psychological perspective.‡ Although it was true that the psycho-

---

*The Zhuang are China's most populous minority, who in 1990 numbered about 15 million and who constitute approximately one-third of the population of Guangxi. They speak a Sino-Thai language and have dwelled in territories under Chinese control since the thirteenth century. Guangxi is also populated by the Yao minority, who in 1990 numbered about 2 million. Han migration into Guangxi has gone on for centuries and was intensified after the Communist takeover in 1949. See Colin Mackerras, *China's Minorities: Integration and Modernization in the Twentieth Century* (New York: Oxford University Press, 1994), p. 238.

†A specialized newspaper on China's legal system, *China Legal News* led the effort in the mid-1980s to bring to light the enormous abuses of the legal system during the Cultural Revolution and after.

‡*Ultra leftism* is the catch-all political term for the Cultural Revolution radicals led by Jiang Qing, the wife of Mao Zedong. See William A. Joseph, *The Critique of Ultra-Leftism in China, 1958–1981* (Stanford: Stanford University Press, 1984).

logical perspective could not be ignored, I intentionally couched my plan in somewhat casual terms so that I would not arouse any suspicions. The Chinese Communist Party has always been sensitive about its mistakes, and it is especially fearful that writers or journalists might uncover some buried truths.* Cover-ups and distortions had become standard operating procedure among cadres at various levels.

My official status and the introduction by Little Wei allowed me to present my main topic to Wang without difficulty. As soon as I mentioned the Cultural Revolution in Guangxi, his anger burst forth. He picked up a document from his table, slapped it down, and declared that the head of a certain county's People's Armed Police who had initiated the slaughter of numerous people had been given the relatively light sentence of suspended capital punishment. The document, which I quote from later, notes that the sentence had been based on the fact that the suspect had killed more than fifty people but that a more recent investigation had proved that the total number of victims was only twenty-six; the criminal had therefore requested a retrial. As he told me this, Wang Guanyu didn't know whether to laugh or cry. "The Central Committee insists time and again that historical issues should be handled in a lax manner, ignoring the details.† As for leftover cases from the Cultural Revolution in Guangxi," Wang added, "those who should have been sentenced to death were allowed to live, and those who deserved stiff sentences went free. It could not have been more forgiving. Of course, the more generous you are, the sorrier they feel for themselves! Ninety thousand innocent victims were slaughtered, while only a dozen criminals received capital punishment. Even though this guy killed twenty-six, rather than fifty, this murderer has the gall to claim that he is being treated unfairly! What kind of reasoning is that? No way!"

Secretary Wang seemed like an honest person, with no blood on his hands. At the end of our conversation, he signed my letter of introduction: "To the Party Reform Office of the Guangxi Autonomous Region: Please take care of all matters involving the work of this journalist." Wang let me in on the information that the Party Reform Office was actually the former work team that cleared up leftover cases from the Cultural Revolution. Upon leaving his office, I was ecstatic. How fortunate I had

---

*The genre of "investigative journalism" that has since the Cultural Revolution revealed the political and historical secrets of the Chinese Communist Party and its leaders was led by such journalists as Dai Qing, Liu Binyan, and Zheng Yi.

†This phrase was first uttered by Chinese reform leader, Hu Yaobang, during the period in the late 1970s and early 1980s when Party cadres victimized during the Cultural Revolution were rehabilitated. Zheng Yi argues that it allowed the CCP to gloss over its enormous crimes against the Chinese people.

been to get so much information from the senior cadre in charge of legal affairs. Even more important was that I had been given a green light to conduct interviews throughout the entire Guangxi region.

Strike while the iron is hot! I immediately asked Little Wei to accompany me to the Party Reform Office, where I was initially welcomed by Huang Xiangheng and Huang Shaobin. Later, I was directed to talk with Comrade Yu Yaqin of the group handling and verifying leftover cases *(chuyi heshizu).* I now had the holy sword of the political and legal committee of the autonomous region in hand. Equipped with this weapon, I had the courage I needed to bring up the incidents of slaughter and cannibalism that had taken place during the Cultural Revolution. Unassisted by notes, in one breath Yu described quite a few famous cases and mentioned the following counties: Wuxuan, Rongan, Binyang, Shanglin, Zhongshan, and others. Yu also advised me that in order to investigate these incredibly cruel cases thoroughly, I would have to go to Wuxuan County.

Now that the events friends had told me about had been verified by local officials, I immediately proposed that I conduct a series of interviews in counties located in the Nanning, Wuzhou, and Liuzhou Prefectures where some of the most intense factional fighting and barbarism had occurred during the Cultural Revolution. And because this plan accorded with the official clearances I had been given, the various cadres of the Party Reform Office added their signatures, below that of Secretary Wang Guanyu, with instructions addressed to the Party reform offices in Nanning, Wuzhou, and Liuzhou to "please make all the necessary arrangements for interviews by this journalist." I had passed, yet again, a major obstacle. Although I could have obtained most of the information by reading relevant Party documents and materials in official files and archives, I knew that in China, the higher the bureaucrat, the tighter his mouth. I believed, therefore, that it would be more fruitful to focus on the local level, on the counties, towns, and villages, assisted by official signatures, and telephone instructions from higher-ups whom the locals would not dare to challenge. I would be able to get my hands on the original documents and sift out evidence in a completely legal way. In addition, I would be able to meet with various types of people and get firsthand material and information. And, of course, I would also be able to learn more about local history, traditions, and customs. Although this method surrendered the near for the distant, it later proved to be the only effective way for me to break through the various obstacles, bureaucratic and otherwise, to obtain the most important and reliable information.

On day two, I showed up at the headquarters of the Prefecture Party Committee of Nanning; Deputy Secretary-in-Chief Li contacted the authorities in Binyang and Shanglin Counties to set up the interviews.

As a reporter for the only major newspaper in China that serves the legal profession, Wei Huaren would have been more than willing to accompany me during the interviews, but he was preoccupied with work at his own newspaper and simply couldn't find the time. As we parted, he warned me once more to heed my personal safety and never to act on my own. Wei also advised me that when I traveled to the scenes of earlier crimes, I should always make sure to register with the local authorities first and always conduct my interviews in the presence of a local official.

My investigation and interviewing was to begin in Binyang County, where, it was said, cannibalism had been widespread. Word had it that the residents, long experienced as they were in the business of eating people, had concluded that outsiders were tastier than locals. Consequently, it was said that they would first drug the unsuspecting traveler into a stupor and then start cutting and consuming. When the effects of the drug began to wear off, they would hold a mirror to the victim's face and force him to watch while his own body was being consumed. This seemed too bizarre. (In fact, such events never came to light in any of my later interviews; perhaps it had been merely a rumor after all.) Upon discussing this possibility with Little Wei and considering his warning to me, I was in the mood for a bit of comic relief. "Isn't it true that no writer has ever been consumed before in Chinese history?" I asked him. Neither of us could help but laugh.

The next morning I took off for Binyang by myself. Bei Ming returned home. Since my name alone appeared on the letters of introduction, her presence possibly could have caused some unexpected trouble. Heavy rain the night before brought a cooling freshness to the air. The green fields along my route were extremely refreshing to the eye. At about 10 A.M. I arrived at the town of Luxu, the site of the county seat, and later that afternoon I met with Li Zengming, the Party secretary of the local Party Discipline Inspection Commission, the CCP's internal disciplinary organ. At the very mention of the killing that had occurred in Binyang, the secretary became outraged. Before I could even ask him specific questions, he provided the most vivid and explicit description of the collective act of slaughter. His description pretty much coincided with the following account, taken from a post–Cultural Revolution edition of the *Binyang County Gazette:*

> At the end of July 1968, Wang Jianxun, director of the county Revolutionary Committee (and concurrent deputy division commander of the 6949 Unit), and Wang Guizeng, deputy director of the same committee (also deputy political commissar of the County Armed Police), in the name of executing the "July 3 Bulletin," mobilized vicious assaults on so-called class enemies. Total dead and injured came to 3,883 people. Together with the sixty-eight people who had been beaten to death before the July 3 Bulletin, the total number of casualties came to 3,951—a great act of injustice.[1]

Just what was the "July 3 Bulletin"? After I was on the run in 1989 after the June 4 Beijing massacre, I was unable to obtain the original document. But as someone who had lived through the Cultural Revolution, I could still remember its general gist. Issued jointly by the Central Committee, the State Council, the Central Military Commission, and the Central Cultural Revolution Group controlled by Mao's wife, Jiang Qing, this document had whipped up a frenzy of killing and carnage. According to the original declaration, Liuzhou, Guilin, and Nanning in the Guangxi Autonomous Region had purportedly suffered widespread disruption of railway communication, robberies of weapons caches bound for Vietnam, and outright attacks on PLA units, among other things. As a reaction to these events, the bulletin called for tougher measures to be taken against all class enemies. Although it contained no explicit reference to indiscriminate killing *(gesha wulun),* the entire document was suffused with an air of killing and vengeance.

Soon after the "July 3 Bulletin" was issued, the Binyang County Revolutionary Committee held a mass rally of 7,000 people under the banner of "Marching in the Name of 'Loyalty' by All the Poor and Lower-Middle Peasants in the County." At about the same time, the national campaign to create a god was inaugurated, in which everyone "asked for instructions in the morning and reported back in the evening," engaged in "loyalty dances," and promoted the "three loyalties and four devotions." With the erection of the statue of a god, Mao Zedong by name, wholesale slaughter could then be carried out. The history of China at this time is replete with such cases, and border regions like Guangxi were no exception.

On July 22, 1968, a telephone conference was held by the county Revolutionary Committee in which instructions went out to fully implement the "July 3 Bulletin."

Then, on July 23, a rally of 10,000 people was held by Wang Jianxun, the director of the county Revolutionary Committee, who gave a mobilizing speech. Yu XX, the deputy director, also gave a speech, in which he proclaimed that the "July 3 Bulletin" was part of Chairman Mao's ingenious strategy and the most powerful weapon for carrying out attacks on the small handful of class enemies.

On July 24, the "Leading Group for Executing the 'July 3 Bulletin' in Binyang" was established. It was composed of four leaders, all military men.[2] The potential for killing was now set up. Within three days, all the arrangements had been put into place for carrying out a mad slaughter throughout the entire county.

July 25.

Not a flag or drum was to be found anywhere—it was the silence before the slaughter.

July 26.

The Military Control Commission of the public security organs of Binyang County held a meeting and issued the order to all local Party committees, public security personnel, and to local public security precincts at the district and township levels to commence the killing. On the same evening, the Revolutionary Committee of Xinbin Township held a mass dictatorship rally, in the course of which two people were beaten to death on the spot. The bloodshed had begun.

July 27.

Market day in Xinbin Township. Fourteen people were labeled "four elements social dregs" *(silei fenzi)*,* subjected to street criticism parades, and then beaten to death. The practice was thus launched to kill select groups of people all at one time.

The same day.

The local office of the armed police of Binyang County ordered cadres to visit the sites where these killings had taken place. At the same time, the commander of the militia battalion *(minbingying)* of Jianghe commune, Wu XX, and others, immediately ordered the militia company commander of the various villages to send all "four elements" to commune headquarters. That evening, twenty-four people were murdered in cold blood.

July 28.

Market day in Luxu. In order to create a "red terror" and push the slaughter to its zenith, Wang Jianxun issued an order that subjected to criticism in the market square a large contingent of so-called "twenty-three category social dregs" *(ershisan zhong ren)*.† A local mob, stirred into a frenzy, bludgeoned to death eighty or ninety people on the spot with clubs and stones. Their victims included personnel from the county hospital: the executive and deputy executive directors of the hospital and directors of the various departments: interns, surgeons, gynecologists, and pharmacists.

---

*The "four elements" were landlords, rich peasants, counterrevolutionaries, and bad elements who had been targeted for persecution during the rural Socialist Education Campaign in the early 1960s.

†A catch-all category for people accused of being spies, ex-Kuomintang officials, rightists, and an odd assortment of twenty other politically pejorative labels issued over the years by the CCP. The term *rightists (youpai)* refers to intellectuals, writers, and journalists who had been purged during a political campaign in 1957, prompted by Mao Zedong and executed in full faith by Deng Xiaoping.

July 29.

On this particular morning, Wang Jianxun held a meeting of political and legal cadres from the county Military Control Commission. He spoke in a shrill voice about the indiscriminate beating that had occurred in Xinbin Township. He also laid out concrete measures regarding the targets, the time, the methods, and the quota for beating and killing people. The first phase of this battle, he instructed these cadres, would take place from July 26 to August 15, and would target various traitors, spies, unrepentant capitalist roaders,* unreformed landlords, rich peasants, counterrevolutionaries, social dregs, and rightists. The lesser targets will be those who are presently engaged in profiteering, gambling, and people who had attempted to divide up production teams into private farms. Wang also announced that Xinbin and Luxu Townships would be their primary targets. As of now, he told cadres, the campaign had already started in Xinbin. Try to get used to the new situation. People should be encouraged, not discouraged. In carrying out this endeavor, we must not make too much noise; we should just proceed quietly and individually. Those whom the masses earmark as bad people must be subjected to dictatorship. "Do not bind the hands and feet of the masses," he said. He added, "Once the campaign has started, everything will be okay, even if activists use guns to carry out their killing. They should, however, be encouraged to use their clubs, fists, and stones. Only by so doing can the masses be educated in a relatively more efficient way. Altogether, there are more than four thousand 'four elements,'" he told the assembly. "Despite the ideological remolding of the past four years, nothing has changed. The masses have also spent a lot of time and energy carrying out surveillance of the 'four elements.' Why waste time and energy? Why can't we devote our time and energy to agricultural production and development? If we just leave those dregs to the masses, after no more than three days, they will be finished, without a single bullet being fired. This task must be carried out, and completed, in three days. The bottom line is this: One-third or at least one-fourth of the social dregs must be bludgeoned to death during this campaign."[3]

On the same day, the county Revolutionary Committee held an emergency meeting with the commanders of the armed police from the county and district levels and the militia battalion commanders of the small com-

---

Capitalist roader was the term of opprobrium used by the radical leftists against Mao's reputed "enemies" in the CCP who had advocated less radical approaches to China's economic development. They were led by former State President Liu Shaoqi, who later died ignominiously during the Cultural Revolution.

munes. At this meeting, Wang Jianxun put pressure on those who were reluctant to engage in killing:

> In some units nothing has happened, and so you have to begin to execute the order right away. To achieve our goal, we must mobilize the masses to unmask the enemies, and then torpedo them. Those who deserve death will be handled by the masses, but the battalion commanders should volunteer to go out and capture a few bad people on their own.

In this way, the door of hell was opened wide. In no time, the entire county was in a scarlet frenzy, hurled into a terror of unprecedented slaughter. On the afternoon of July 29 and throughout July 30, "model demonstrations of killing" (*sharen yangbanhui*) were held all around. Following that, as many as 172 brigades* (so-called small-scale communes) became involved in the killing frenzy. The slaughter now reached its climax.

During this period, a herd of public security cadres scurried all over the county as official "observers," to supervise the killings and to submit daily "progress" reports. Cadres on the county and commune levels kept up a telephone campaign to pressure those units whose "progress" was lagging. Everywhere, instructions rang out: "Don't use bullets, use fists, clubs, and stones!" Thousands upon thousands of innocent people were ruthlessly slaughtered. Under the blows of stones and clubs, bones broke and flesh flew through the air. Blood was everywhere.

Now that the air reeked of blood, there was no way to hold back the vampire-like mobs. Kill! Kill! Kill! People went crazy in their killing spree. The more they killed, the easier it became, the more exciting it got, and the more cruel. The killing went on until even its prime promoter, Wang Jianxun, grew a bit hot under the collar. On August 2, the Binyang County Revolutionary Committee held an emergency meeting, where even as the progress of the campaign was reported, local leaders called for a halt. It was too little too late, however. There was no way to halt the vehicle and so, even after the meeting, the killing went on and on. In the expectation that the killing would soon be prohibited, in many places the progress was accelerated under the guise that such an opportunity would never arise again. In effect, the meeting to halt the vehicle served as a mobilization meeting for even more killing.

Only nineteen years later did people have an opportunity to take an overall look at the killings in Binyang County. Back in 1968, during the

---

*The brigade was the second intermediate level of socialist agricultural organization in the Chinese countryside, which generally encompassed an entire village. At the highest level was the commune, incorporating several villages, and at the lowest, the production team, incorporating 10–20 households within a single village. The 1978 agricultural reform in China effectively dismantled this structure.

short period of eleven days (July 26 to August 6) when the "July 3 Bulletin" was fully implemented, the "achievement" was indeed magnificent!

Throughout the entire county, 3,681 people were beaten or persecuted to death. Among them, fifty-one were state-level cadres, twenty-seven state workers, seventy-five workers in collective units, eighty-seven teachers, and 3,441 were either peasants or township residents. The greatest number of victims killed in one group was thirty-four; they were killed by the cruelest of means. Either they were shot, or else they were stabbed, strangled, poked with pitchforks, beaten with clubs, drowned, or pelted with stones. Some were even buried alive. In three families, each with three brothers, all the male members, a total of ten people, were beaten to death. One hundred seventy families suffered the loss of a spouse and children. Fourteen families were totally wiped out. One hundred ninety-one households lost more than two family members, for a total of 435.[4]

I was suffocated by the bloody smell emanating from my interviews and documents. One night, I went for a walk after dinner through the streets and alleyways of Luxu, which were crowded with snack stands selling liquor and meat. The town is famous for its dog fare, a common delicacy in the south. The shorn dog is roasted in its whole skin. Once on display on the food stands, the whitish meat is somewhat difficult to identify as cooked dog. I bought one half jin [a jin is equal to one-half kilogram] of the dog meat and sat down along the side of the street. I started to eat as I sipped the local liquor and took in the street scene. The town was actually an important materials supply depot, with a very well-developed transportation system and local economy. In fact, it was one of the four most renowned townships in Guangxi. At present, the collective economy was prospering, especially the small commodity sector (particularly garments), where the wholesale market was thriving. In front of me, the entire street, on both sides, was lined with stores. Market day was every three days, but now every day the street was quite clamorous. There were also all kinds of fruit stands, restaurants, and vegetable stands. At night, the streets were lit up with kerosene and calcium carbide lights, which, along with regular electric lights, added their glare to the racket of selling and buying goods.

This was downtown Luxu, as also described by Party Secretary Li Zengming. So where were the bodies stacked so high that they once blocked traffic? Where were the blood stains that could not even be washed away with lime? Today's prosperity seemed to mask the nightmare that had occurred years earlier, and which now seemed beyond human understanding. Numbers and simple descriptions of events could be used to reveal only certain problems. What I intended to find out more about were the people: the ruthless people, the desperate people, the killed, the killers, those who were instigated, and the instigators, the obedient ones, and those who resisted. In my opinion, only by learning more about those people and about their thoughts and their feelings could one gain at least a modicum of understanding about the otherwise inexplicable frenzy that had taken over this town.

With Secretary Li Zengming's help, I interviewed a certain Director Wang of the county court; a cadre by the name of Huang Huashan, who had been punished by the Party's disciplinary organs (an activist at the time in the Binyang Middle School Red Guards, Huang personally had killed four teachers from the school and nine captives of local factional battles); and a prisoner named Lu Deqi (who had been involved in cutting open a victim's stomach under the guise of avenging another victimized youth.) Their descriptions helped me recreate some sense of the terror that had been felt.

At that time, "the most sublime instruction" of Chairman Mao Zedong, that "dictatorship meant dictatorship by the masses," had already completely supplanted an already frail sense of legality among the Chinese people. Indeed, not one person in Luxu had opposed the idea of indiscriminate slaughter. The only exception to this was the director of a certain propaganda group who lived in a local commune. He had said, "Yes, dictatorship means the dictatorship of the masses; but it does not mean complete slaughter." Unfortunately, the indiscriminate killing did not follow any specific charges. Later, among the fifty-two people convicted for this crime, only four were accused of having engaged in revenge killing against particular individuals, even though revenge among different clans is very common in rural areas.

During the killing frenzy, mass "criticism meetings" had been held on the streets. Representatives from every household were required to join in. Those who were about to be beaten were announced by name from a list, along with their criminal acts, as they were pushed to the front of the crowd. These "criminal acts" were extremely simple: So and so was a rightist, so and so was a counterrevolutionary academic authority, so and so was involved in profiteering. The "most sublime instruction" was recited (it was the legal basis): "According to Chairman Mao, 'dictatorship means dictatorship by the masses.'" In the end, in a voice one octave higher than all the others, the organizer asked for the opinion of the masses. "What shall we do with these ghosts and snakes? You people decide," he called out. The masses would inevitably shout back, "Kill them!" Thereupon, everyone surged forward, throwing stones and beating the victims to death with clubs. In the beginning, the onlookers and curiosity seekers were quite numerous. Later, as the killings grew routine, none of this was particularly surprising anymore. Besides, the accumulation of rotting bodies on the street drove most of the onlookers away. But the situation was never out of control: Those singled out for beating were always selected ahead of time. Nobody was grabbed from the crowd, willy-nilly, to be beaten to death. Despite the random appearance of the beatings, no "innocent people" ever got hurt, because a distinct line was still being drawn between the convicted and the masses.

Ordinary people who joined in the beating could not defy the dictates of conscience. Despite their expressed hatred, most could not continue beyond the first few token strikes of the club. Bachelors were the cruelest ones. These were social dregs from the old gangs, hooligans, and small capitalist roaders, who were now expected to "achieve merit even after a verdict of guilty" *(daizui ligong);* there were also converts from the old pre-CCP opposition parties, such as the Kuomintang (KMT), who, along with various people who were not politically active, were now afraid of being victimized themselves. Of the ordinary masses who took part in the beatings, most were young lads, some in their twenties, some of them teenagers. Generally, though, the masses could not find within themselves the intestinal fortitude to initiate beatings; four elements types were forced to do it. Then, after the four elements types stopped beating victims, they themselves became victims and were beaten to death. During one incident, when thirty-four people were thrown into a watery coal pit to be buried alive, cadres forced the people in the rear of the crowd to push those at the front into the water. Four elements types were ordered to bury the bodies. Afterward, they themselves were beaten to death. Most of the four elements types, knowing that there was no way for them to escape, committed suicide.

The victims, in general, were not bound with ropes because they had no place to which they might escape. Once their names were called, they faced death like lambs. Their faces betrayed no feeling as they knelt on the ground in the course of being beaten. They just knelt down silently, no begging, no cursing, no arguing, and not the slightest show of a willingness to resist. Beaten to the ground the first time, they were commanded to rise and to kneel again. Beaten to the ground once more, again they were forced to get up. This procedure was followed until the victims lost all consciousness. The only examples of resistance I found in my interviews involved two cases in which people used their bare hands. Even though their resistance was hopeless and purely symbolic, the effects were quite cruel and pathetic:

> On the evening of July 31, 1968, local resident Xiong Shilun was beaten to death at the entrance to South Bridge in Xinbin Township. Some suspected that there were guns hidden in Xiong's household, and so the militia ordered that Xiong's house be searched and its contents confiscated. The Xiong family resisted, and threw a homemade bomb out onto the courtyard, although it never exploded. Informed of this incident, Dong Yongxing, commander of the local 6949 unit, led two squads of militia men and surrounded the Xiong

residence. At 3:00 A.M. the next morning, the militia, using hand grenades, machine guns, and rifles, initiated an attack. Two males and one female were killed. Although no guns were ever found, the Xiong family's resistance was considered intolerable. In order to frighten the rest of the town, their three bodies were hung at the entrance to the bridge.[5]

On the same day, the Zhongxing commune in Luxu held another criticism rally. A local farmer named Wu Risheng, whose name was on the "death list," refused to show up. Instead, holding a knife, he took up a position behind the gate to his house. On hearing this, Lai Zengjie,[6] director of the Luxu District Armed Police, led a group of armed militiamen, who charged Wu's home and escorted him to the rally.

The course of Wu's persecution was described by one of his killers, Wu Rixun:

At the meeting, Wu Dexin listed the names of those who were to be subjected to dictatorship (beaten to death): Wu Risheng, Lü Shaoying, Huang Fengying, and her mother. After Wu Rilin read off the "criminal acts" of the four people, the militiamen dragged the four to the rally, where they were verbally assaulted, beaten, and kicked. I myself cut off Wu Risheng's ear (using Wu's own knife). After the beating, I accompanied the armed militiamen who took the four to the entrance to New Bridge. As we approached Stone Drum pond, Wu Risheng jumped into it and attempted to flee. I jumped in, captured him, and led him over New Bridge. On our way, I bumped into Li Guide, the commune Party secretary, and said to him, "We are imposing dictatorship on Wu Risheng, do you have any objections?" He replied, "I completely agree," and then he returned to the commune. Once we were actually on the bridge, I pushed Wu into the river, and pelted him with stones. Just then, Wei Qingcai, Wu's wife, showed up, carrying her baby on her back, and with two other children in tow. She immediately jumped into the river. As a result, all of them were stoned to death (with the exception of the baby). I was not the only one involved in the killing of all four members of the Wu family. There were also the militiamen, Wu Dexin (who has since succumbed to an illness), Wu Rihuan (later himself beaten to death), and others. They had joined in the stoning of the Wu family. Lü Shaoying, Huang Fengying, and her mother were also stoned to death by the militiamen. After finishing off Wu Risheng, I felt very happy and ran back home to cook some food. After eating my fill, I returned to the bridge to take a look at the dead bodies.[7]

After these cases of hopeless resistance were taken care of, no one dared to follow their act in Binyang. Despair and horror crushed all the victims whose names were on the fated "other list":

In Tongde commune, after hearing of a "wind calling for a halt to the killing," eighteen people, who had already been targeted for dictatorship, were contacted by phone and ordered to show up with a rope. After their "criminal acts" were read off, they were bound up and summarily beaten to death and thrown into Stone River. Qin Caiyun, a cadre in a production team, was working in the fields when she was told to report to commune headquarters. She immediately returned home and left for the commune in no time, carrying Mao's Little Red Book of revolutionary sayings and a rope—without even changing clothes or taking a drink of water. While she was being bound up, she pleaded with the commune cadres. "I did not commit any crime. Please let me go and I'll simply work to raise my children," she beseeched them. Of course, her importunings were in vain. She suffered the same fate as all the others.[8]

In great despair, many victims committed suicide. Among them, the Huang Yingji case was the most cruel. After his brother Huang Ningji was strangled, a second brother, Huang Chaoji, was also beaten to death. And then after his wife, Luo Shuxian, hung herself, Huang Yingji fell into deep despair. When his first effort at suicide by smashing his head against the wall failed, he chopped at his own head with an ax. But this second attempt also failed to do the trick. Eventually, he succeeded in hanging himself.[9] The atmosphere of terror was such that no one, not even family members or relatives, dared to go and collect the corpses, nor did they even dare to shed tears. In one case, a widow in Wuliang town was crying over the body of her murdered husband when the baby on her back was pulled to the ground and beaten to death with a shovel. Another widow, crying for her dead husband, was accused of showing sympathy to a class enemy. She was also beaten to death. At the beginning of the indiscriminate beatings, none of the onlookers showed any fear, not even the children. Yet once the streets began to fill up with corpses, people started to be afraid, so much so that important transportation routes were blocked, and all of Binyang County was bathed in streams of blood. After dark, not a soul could be seen on the streets. Killers and families whose members had been killed alike shut their doors in fear at night. An unnamed terror settled upon the entire county. Everyone knew the awful truth that there was no escape.

Over the course of several days of interviewing in Binyang, I came to understand what was behind the insanity in the county, and thus the killing became a bit more comprehensible. In fact, the situation reminded me of the "Red August" (*hong bayue*) that had occurred in 1966 at the beginning of the Cultural Revolution in Beijing. What a similarity! Both were instigated by Mao Zedong, supported by the local authorities, and assisted in their execution by the upholders of the law. Both aimed at "executing dictatorship" against "class enemies." Both made the victims go absolutely berserk in just a few days' time, while draining them of any desire to resist. Both lasted for only a brief period but were executed with extreme viciousness. And in both incidents, the instigators indiscriminately "mobilized the masses" and, later, when frightened by the uncontrollable momentum of the indiscriminate killing, they hypocritically issued new policies that called for greater discrimination, and so on. If a slaughter like the Red August could grip the capital of the country, why should anyone be surprised that mass killings had taken place in the Guangxi border region around Binyang County?

It can be comprehended but never excused. Because of the Binyang slaughter, that year the Binyang "abnormal death" count was the highest for the entire province of Guangxi. As Mao Zedong reminded us, "Without comparison, there is no discrimination, and it is impossible to learn the incompatible advantages of socialism." During the War of Resistance (1937–1945), the death toll at the hands of the Japanese for the entire county was just a few hundred. And that was a national war. At the beginning of liberation in Guangxi in 1949, the number of people suppressed in Binyang amounted to 300 bandits, and they were armed enemies. How was it that in a time of peace, and virtually within a few days, more than thirteen times that number could have been killed? This is a question worth pondering, and it should not be ignored.

Exactly fifteen years after the Binyang incident, in 1983, the Binyang County Party authorities rehabilitated *(pingfan)* virtually all of the 3,951 victims and, in the name of the county government, released a written report regarding the rehabilitation to the victims' families and relatives. Is it possible that this piece of paper was adequate to console the thousands upon thousands of innocent souls who were now buried?

Even more pitiful, only fifty-six people in the entire county were ever convicted of any crime, and only one received the death penalty in accordance with the nonlaw law of the Chinese Communist Party. The nonlaw law, itself, had been superseded by political decisions. (The Guangxi regime was repeatedly instructed by the central authorities that "historical issues should be handled in a lax manner, ignoring the details.") In effect, one life was worth all 3,951 dead. What contempt for society and the law!

Before I had even recovered from what I had learned about the perpetrators of the Binyang slaughter, Party Secretary Li Zengming mentioned yet another, more astonishing, fact: Most of those convicted had demanded fairer treatment. The lax law is not lax enough! Wang Jianxun, the primary criminal behind the Binyang slaughter, is to this day still free! The very person who had meticulously planned and organized the entire slaughter, and whose hands are stained with the Binyang people's blood, was promoted again and again, until he reached the position of first deputy commander of the Canton Garrison Command. Later, he retired with honors and is now taking leisurely walks in a luxurious courtyard behind high walls. No wonder those who were convicted demanded greater fairness. Their rationale was simple: Without the instigation and support of Wang Jianxun, we never would have killed so many people. It was for this reason that the convicted voluntarily submitted notebooks, telephone records, and minutes from various meetings as evidence of Wang's crime.

With a heavy heart, old Li handed me a document entitled *Facts Relating to the Case of the Numerous Killings Planned and Directed by Wang Jianxun.* At the bottom of the document was the signature of the Binyang County Communist Party Committee. I immediately felt that something was out of order here because regular Party committees rarely handled such incidents. Functional units within the CCP, such as the Party Discipline Inspection Commission, were responsible for them. If the Party committee had taken on this task, it indicated a certain feeling, a certain grim determination on its part. Indeed, although this indictment, on the surface, was couched in rather controlled tones, within it was embedded great wrath. This time, the local Party committee, which had always been submissive to higher authorities, stood up, and decided to resist, by confronting all the blood, and the ridicule, and the shame. Despite the subdued tone of the report, it was full of meticulously detailed information about time, place, precise crime, witnesses, evidence, and individual cases. After laying out all the criminal facts, the twenty-eight-page document asserted with a tone of affirmation:

> September 15, 1984:
> The aforementioned facts prove beyond a doubt that Wang Jianxun is the prime criminal behind the slaughter. The number of victims and the cruel methods aroused the anger of the masses. We believe this person should be considered a premeditated murderer.

At the end of the statement, contrary to the usual humble tone that characterizes such documents, it made several unconditional demands:

> It is our opinion that arrests should be made in accordance with the law and that severe punishments should be meted out in order to assuage the wrath of the masses.
>   Binyang County Party Committee

How is it that punishment for these crimes was so light and that the primary criminal (suspect) was granted such protection? "Our own people!" These killers wantonly murdered thousands and thousands of people—yet they were "our own people," of Mao Zedong and of the Chinese Communist Party. All the crimes they committed were either silently agreed upon or were simply the consequence of holy orders. They were at fault merely for being too enthusiastic, too loyal, and too zealous, overdoing a "good deed," and distorting the "bible." There was no way to sentence them to jail or decapitation; at most, they would get a slap on the wrist. As for those who were not "our own people," not one word was spoken about their violation of any laws; thousands upon thousands were summarily convicted of being rightists, all on the highest authority, and in clear violation of their rights as protected by China's state constitution. That is why those killers with blood on their hands— "our own people"—have acted with such daring and have always demanded lenient treatment.

Consider the case of the fascist "alliance" *(liandong)* and Tan Lifu, who frantically advocated "the theory of family lineage" *(xuetonglun)*.* Many years later they wrote letter after letter to the newspapers, complaining about mistreatment that amounted to no more than a slap on the wrist. Such people assume that if they pretend to suffer from mistreatment, people will then forget all about their crimes. Although, unfortunately, Chinese people often do suffer from amnesia, they haven't become as forgetful as these criminals would like to think they have. After all, they were the same criminals who provoked the fascist violence in Beijing in the summer of 1966. That violence quickly spread throughout the entire country and involved vast numbers of people in an unprecedented spilling of blood. Of course, the kindhearted masses would not take revenge, but, in the name of the blood of the victims, the people have a right to nail the criminals to the column of shame in history forever.

When Secretary Li Zengming passed me the "indictment," I noticed that the document had actually been signed a year and a half earlier. During that whole time, this official document, passed by the Binyang County Party Committee, had been virtually ignored by the higher authorities. I did not have the guts to look directly into old Li's eyes, which were heavy and full of inquisition. As a powerless intellectual, in a country where there is no freedom of press, publication, and speech, I didn't have the influence to change anything. All I could do was to record carefully all these facts for later generations, who, I am sure, will one day put this bloody deed on trial.

I said to myself, indeed, I have stepped into a dark forest full of evil, and I have uncovered a scarlet memorial covered with human blood.

---

*The theory asserted that position and power in China's revolutionary social strata were inherited from parents of "good" class backgrounds—workers, peasants, and revolutionary martyrs. This was generally propounded by sons and daughters of veteran cadres who tried to protect their privileged positions from the more radical Red Guards who often came from "bad" class backgrounds—the four elements and twenty-three category types—and saw the Cultural Revolution as a way to break out of the CCP's rigid class structures.

RED SOIL
May 23. Shanglin County.

On that evening, Wei Kequan, propaganda director of the Shanglin County Party Committee, invited me to dine at his home. The dinner was quite lavish and consisted of mixed slices of white chicken and duck, which is a local Guangxi delicacy, along with grass fish, string bean soup, bitter melon with pork, black glutinous rice wine, and double-brewed rice wine. The director of the local cultural bureau, Huang Shoucai, was also present. I recalled that my literary friend from Nanning had told me that I could ask the locals for help; and right off the bat my Zhuang hosts mentioned the incidents of cannibalism. Not only had cannibalism occurred in Shanglin County, but this particular outbreak of cannibalism had involved the consumption of the victims' livers. Many of the cases they cited were unofficial, which is to say that only a few had been formally investigated. One particular incident was mentioned by old Wei right smack in the middle of our meal. A man was walking about carrying a human liver, old Wei told us, when he happened upon an old acquaintance who asked, "Did the victim give you permission to eat his liver?" Startled by the question, the man replied, "How could the man possibly have agreed to such a thing?" The old acquaintance pursued the matter. "You should know," he said, "that in the absence of the victim's consent, the liver is virtually ineffective." (The locals believe that consuming the liver gives them courage; in addition, it is considered a tonic.) Upon hearing this, the man went out and captured a second victim and forced him to grant the necessary permission to allow his liver to be eaten. Once this was done, the man proceeded to cut out the victim's liver while the victim was still alive. The man then presented the liver to the victim's mother and said, "Look, your son's liver!" The mother, of course, fainted. This sounds like an old myth, and a subsequent examination of the documents revealed no such case. However, since my dinner companions recounted these events so earnestly, I wrote them down for later reference.

After several glasses of hard, white liquor, I cautiously asked my friends whether, in fact, cannibalism was a tradition in these parts. I asked this question because history books frequently recount cases of minority people engaging in cannibalism in the Lingnan area of China.* Without the slightest irritation, my friends willingly admitted that historical

---

*Lingnan refers to Guangdong and Guangxi Provinces. For a complete historical review of cannibalism in Chinese history, see Key Ray Chong, *Cannibalism in China* (Wakefield, NH: Longwood Academic, 1990).

records clearly indicate that Zhuang and Yao minority peoples had indeed practiced cannibalism. Even today, "I feel like eating your liver" is a common saying. How did the custom originate?—I wanted to know. After an intense discussion, my friends came to the conclusion that both the Zhuang and Yao are people of great honesty and passion, an extremely hospitable people who gladly invite strangers to dinner and provide them shelter. If they love you, they will offer you everything; if, however, they happen to resent you, they then feel like eating your liver. That explanation seems a bit simpleminded. Still, it is an explanation. In order to guard against revealing any kind of great Han chauvinism, however, I decided to avoid such unsophisticated explanations until I had learned the whole story. If this naive explanation does indeed contain some truth, then the Chinese Communist Party should be held accountable for the horrible events that occurred in this minority region. For, despite the presence of some uncivilized features and primitive emotional elements in the local minority culture, there also exists something that can be characterized as quite admirable and loving. Surely it was the philosophy of struggle under the proletarian dictatorship that suppressed their capacity for human love and promoted the hatred that eventually pushed these honest and simpleminded people into the abyss of revenge and killing. At the time, I quickly extricated myself from these flights of fancy. Experience warned me that without quantitative facts, any theory can be founded on castles in the sky.

The next morning, Mo Shumou, who was the deputy secretary of the Party Discipline Inspection Commission, came for an interview about the case that involved the large-scale slaughter that had occurred in a relatively small region of Shanglin County after July 1968. During a period from the end of July to the beginning of August 1968, the Big Faction ordered 400 militiamen to march on Nanning city to join in attacks on the bases of the various elements of the Small Faction. Four people died during the battle. On August 2, a large-scale rally was held to mourn one of the dead militiamen killed at Dafeng (the county seat). Right there, twenty-four class enemies were swiftly beaten to death. (Twenty-four lives in exchange for one life!) The angry crowd forced the four elements and twenty-three category types, along with those holding to Small Faction views, to kneel down in front of the coffin of the dead militiaman. Immediately afterward the beating commenced. Fortunately, a few people with a conscience secretly drove some class enemies away from the spot; otherwise more people would have died.

On the following day, another gathering to mourn a militiaman was held at Xiangxian commune, and there forty-three people were beaten to death. (Forty-three lives in exchange for one life!) On August 7, yet another funeral gathering was held at Mushan brigade, Qiaoxian commune, and seventy-two people were beaten to death (seventy-two lives in exchange for one!). The largest collective slaughter took place in Sanli District. There, on August 17, at a mass rally held to "Assault the Small Handful of Class Enemies for Bombing the Red Political Power," 167 people were beaten to death, the record for collective killing in the entire autonomous region. Over the entire Cultural Revolution period, a total of 1,906 people were beaten to death (of whom more than 1,100 were killed in July and August 1968). In that small county, with a population of only 206,000, yet another record was set for the region: Seven out of every 1,000 people were beaten to death. Another scarlet memorial.

As for cannibalism, Mo Shumou mentioned that quite a few incidents had occurred. However, since the schedule of the work team for handling leftover cases from the Cultural Revolution had been extremely hectic, no really meticulous investigation had ever been attempted. Secretary Mo also mentioned three cases from the Mushan, Longlou, and Longxiang brigades. In the Longxiang case, the victim held to the views of the Small Faction and thus was accused of running an assassination team. This particular victim was first stabbed with a knife and then later cut open, alive. As they cut away the liver, his predators also accidently cut his lung. When the murderers once again attempted to remove his liver, the victim's eyes were still moving. (A CCP member was the lead murderer in this case; he was subsequently sentenced to eight years in prison.)

A case in the Gaochang brigade was also notable for its particular cruelty. In this case, the brigade leader, and director of the Public Security Bureau, Zhou so-and-so, also held to Small Faction views. Thus, together with Zhou, five Party members from his family were beaten to death. His youngest daughter was hung from a post in a tool storage room, stripped naked, and her pubic hair was torched with a gas flame. The killers also crushed her hands and feet and ordered a militiaman to rape her. (In this case the lead murderer was sentenced to twenty years in prison, but he is now on residential probation because of illness.)

Secretary Mo told me as much as he could and promised to provide help and assistance for my interviews. I felt that he must have had experiences similar to those of Secretary Li, of Binyang County, who was once accused of being a rightist and was persecuted for several years. I was not surprised therefore when old Mo smiled, and admitted that yes, indeed, he also had endured a life-and-death experience. Following the outbreak of the Shanglin slaughter in 1968, his name was also put on the list of those to be killed. He was deputy director of the district at that time, but he was not involved in Small Faction activities. Even so, he was accused of being one of its supporters and a "backstage director of various snakes and ghosts." Fortunately, the Big Faction was less than unified on this issue. On the morning of August 18, old Mo was working in the fields with eighteen other people. All eighteen were ordered to the criticism meeting, and not one returned. Old Mo was the only one left in the field. Not knowing what had happened, he asked the militiamen if perhaps he, too, should follow along. The militiamen hesitated for a while. Finally, they decided that since old Mo was a cadre from the district, he was outside their jurisdiction. They were only supposed to take people away from their own brigade. After he related this story to me, old Mo smiled again. "Had I followed along that day," he said, "I too would not have returned."

Before my departure, old Mo sadly recounted another aspect of this story. Director of the County Revolutionary Committee, Shang Xingqiao, who served as county Party secretary both before and after the Cultural Revolution, should have been held accountable for the Shanglin slaughter. This is not exactly what happened. Quite the contrary. Instead of being punished after the Cultural Revolution, Shang was promoted to the position of deputy assistant director of Nanning Prefecture. He is now retired, but during the period when matters left over from the Cultural Revolution were being investigated, so many people had reported on his activities that he ended up getting an internal Party warning. To this day, however, neither the cadres, nor the masses, not to mention the murderers of Shanglin County, are really satisfied. As in Binyang, I could find nothing to say. Silently, I wrote down the name of Shang Xingqiao.

That afternoon, I went to the county archives and read about five additional cases. All of them involved the consumption of human livers. The confessions and information provided by a dozen witnesses depict a series of dark images. The following is my documentation, as I recorded it in my journal:

All of these events occurred at night. After lighting their kerosene lamps, the hunters searched for their victims, all the while shading the lamps with their hands to block out the wind. Once they had seized their prey and indulged in some small talk, one of them would sit on the body of a victim, while another tightly held his arms and legs, and yet another cut open the stomach with a five-inch knife. The liver always popped out with a little squeeze or kick. As soon as they had cut out the liver, the hunters fled with their provender. They were always so nervous that the lamps blew out. Usually, after having returned home, the hunters discovered that they had cut off part of the lung by mistake. Cutting away the lung and some other adjacent body parts, they then searched for the gut. At that point, someone always went home to fetch some garlic and rice wine. After boiling the human liver just as they would cook a pig's liver, seven or eight people sat around a table in the dark and silently consumed the liver by the light of the stove. Some used chopsticks, and some simply ate with their hands. After they had eaten for a while, they often found that the food was too bloody, and so there were leftovers. On the morning of the next day, they either fooled others into believing that they were eating the leftover pig's liver, or else they simply announced, out loud, that human liver was tasty. The cry went out, "come get it while it's hot!" Some visitors asked if they could have a piece of raw liver to take home to dehydrate, and then consume. Once, a woman came with her weakened son, hoping to get a share for some medicinal purpose.

I spent one entire morning in the archives. The more I read, the more I began to break out in a cold sweat. In these five cases, the consumption of human liver was mentioned at least fifty or sixty times. Accompanied by the confessions of the murderers, along with evidence from the witnesses, and bolstered by information contained in the legal appeals filed by relatives, these cases shall forever be burned into history. The pity of it is, however, that not one murderer involved in these five cases has been punished under the law. The killers merely lost their Party memberships. The file of a certain Lan Denggang actually reveals how he managed to avoid punishment. In July 1968, Wei Yankang and Su Guoan, of the Longlou brigade, Baixu commune, were both murdered. Their livers were consumed. Huang Suzhong and another person were directly involved, both in the killing and the cutting out of the liver. Lan Denggang, along with nineteen other people, joined in the cannibalism. Lan, also, was one of those who ordered the murders of twelve people, and another group of seven, and took part in the rape of a relative of one of the victims. On June 21, 1984, Lan was sentenced to thirteen years in prison. On July 21, 1984, to assuage the people's anger, the Party Discipline Inspection Commission of Shanglin County withdrew Lan's Party membership. Then, on March 12, 1985, the Political and Legal Committee of Nanning Prefecture, "in accordance with document Number 54 issued by the district committee (1983)" regarding the method that "historical issues should be handled in a lax manner, ignoring the details," decided not to prosecute Lan Denggang.[10]

On May 26, accompanied by the deputy director of the local Appeals Office *(xinfangke)*, I headed for Mushan brigade.

I took numerous pictures at the famous killing field in Sanli in the area near Feishui Bridge (Photo 1.1). There, a slaughter had taken place on August 16, 1968. "On that same day, 167 people were beaten to death (among whom, six were state cadres or workers, 137 were peasants from the commune, and twenty-four were four elements types). With extreme cruelty, it became an unprecedented tragic slaughter."[11] I went over to the area below the bridge and walked back and forth along the bank. Many details I had read in the files flashed back into my mind. Perhaps the river, the bank, and the wandering innocent souls at the site of the tragedy would summon forth the ruthless scenes.

*   *   *

PHOTO 1.1   Feishui Bridge, Sanli Township, Shanglin County where on
August 16, 1968, 167 victims were slaughtered.

In the early morning of August 16, 1968, a huge explosion rocked the area. Before the crack of dawn, loudspeakers awakened the commune with astonishing news. A small handful of class enemies, aiming to overthrow the newborn leftist political power, had bombed the Commune Revolutionary Committee during the night! The next day, an emergency mass rally was called to "Assault the Small Handful of Class Enemies for Bombing the Red Political Power." There, the decision was announced to immediately carry out dictatorship against the class enemies. The entrance to Feishui Bridge, where red flags fluttered and where people milled about was the designated site of carnage. Cadres and masses who held to Small Faction views, along with the unfortunate four elements types, were forced to kneel down on the bank. The Party secretary of the district (township), the chairman of the district, and the chairman of the Women's Affairs Office were all among those earmarked for execution. The slaughter was launched under the direction of, among others, Wu Futian, who later was given the relatively light sentence of suspended capital punishment. The victims were forced to move toward the riverbank, line by line. The mad crowd then started beating them with their hands, feet, and with stones. Immediately, blood and flesh flew in the air, numerous people slipped and fell in the pools of blood. When the murderers got tired of beating, they simply pushed everyone into the river, and guards manning machine guns, set at the entrance to the bridge, then opened fire on the victims.

Lan Xiufei, the twenty-year-old director of women's affairs in the district, did not die with the first shot. She yelled out, "Long live Chairman Mao! Long live the Communist Party!" The sight of blood dispelled the victims' hopes of living. Chanting "Long live Chairman Mao," they walked down to the river's edge on their own and confronted death with ease. In no time, the air was filled with their raucous slogans. Yet the collective killing was not, it seems, such an easy matter. A resilient will to live enabled the victims to struggle for a while in the river. If they could pull themselves to the riverbank, they could avoid death. Some people called out to the victims who were still alive to pull themselves over to the riverbank so they could be helped. To these victims, they threw out a hope, like a lifeline, that they could evade death. These promises were a swindle. Moreover, the climax had been decided in advance. When the kindhearted young four elements types pulled the victims onto the bank so that the masses could finish them off, their own fate was no better. Apart from a small number of them who were to be returned to the brigade for further criticism (as it turned out, they too were all beaten to death on the way back), no one escaped death. One victim swam away from the site, but he was chased by the killers for two miles and later murdered. The river turned red, and its banks were covered with blood.

Those at the site had to throw their blood-soaked shoes away. Blood cannot be washed away—whether it is blood at Feishui Bridge or blood on Tiananmen Square. It cannot be washed away no matter what is used: water or soap. And blood stains in the minds of the people are especially indelible.

As our vehicle left Feishui Bridge, the chant rang in my ears, "Long live Chairman Mao!" One inexplicable sorrow was haunting me. What would I have done if I had been at the site? Yes, I too would have confronted death blurting out the strongest slogans of our generation. How could we have divined, during that last moment in life, that our revered god was none other than a murderer who was shoving us into the abyss of poverty and death? Could we suddenly have understood that the enterprise to which we devoted our lives was nothing more than a machine of self-destruction? I never would have surmised that. My last flash of life would have been the red flag, flying above the Kremlin and the White House. I would have seen the glorious, smiling face of that "old beloved"—what a tragedy!

Soon, we arrived at the government office of Sanli town. According to a relevant file, the explosion at the Commune Revolutionary Committee had only created a small crater. To execute 167 people because of an explosion that never hurt a soul was by itself a ruthless act. Yet what people didn't realize was that all of this was no different from the Reichstag fire in Germany. In order to create a rationale for crushing the Small Faction by wanton murder, the three leaders of the Big Faction decided to bomb themselves. This became the infamous case of Bombing the Red Political Power. Given their limited education and the lack of publications in that region of China on historical matters, I doubt that these people were all that well-informed about modern German history. But conspiracy is a creative act; you don't have to learn it from some master. Unfortunately, I couldn't really inspect the actual site of the alleged bombing incident; the cadres from the town simply pointed to a place "over there," outside some newly built houses. All of a sudden, I realized that this incident had taken place eighteen years ago. Alas!

In Qiaoxian town, Wei Huaichang, the head of the township, and the secretary of culture of Mushan brigade, Zhou Luguang, accompanied me to Xinpu village. In front of a big, tiled house, I met one of the murderers of the Mushan massacre, a man named Xie Jinwen. Back then, Xie had been head of the Revolutionary Committee, and later he became Party secretary of the agricultural brigade. He looked just as I would envision a killer to look. In his two demonic eyes, there shone a conspiratorial glint. I could imagine how vicious he must have been. As he squatted on a simple wooden stool, he started to recall some of the good old days. And from time to time, he looked at me obliquely, as though he were trying to

figure out what I was up to. When his own crime came up, he kept repeating over and over that back then there were "historical reasons" for
what had happened. He also mentioned that at the beginning of the Cultural Revolution, a high-level document had explicitly stated that dictatorship should be imposed on the twenty-three category types, that it had
been this document that had brought about the indiscriminate killing.

As soon as Xie discovered that I was more interested in the details of
cannibalism than anything else, he suddenly relaxed and began to brag
all too willingly about his glorious feat of gobbling up those class enemies. Xie had participated in the Chinese Communist guerrilla movement. In 1948, when a local spy led a group of KMT police into the area,
Xie and his comrades had killed the spy and then consumed his liver.
(According to the historical files, in the Jinggang Mountain area of Jiangxi
Province, in the 1930s the hearts of Red Army soldiers, especially the
newly recruited, were also cannibalized by their own troops. Like Xie's
prey, they, too, fell victim to a belief in the tonic powers, both physical
and mental, of other people's body parts.) As he related these past events,
Xie grew ever more relaxed, as if he were having an after-dinner chat.

Criminal elements who had not yet been sentenced under the law really didn't like having their pictures taken. Now that the pressure to confess was off, they were even more reluctant to be photographed. Before I
entered Xie's house, I had removed the cover of my camera, and because
the room was quite dark, I had set it at a wide aperture and a relatively
slow speed. Soon after we began talking, I chose a place to sit and pretended that I was carelessly playing with the camera, while in reality I
was getting ready to snap a few surreptitious pictures by calculating the
distance between myself and Xie. From time to time, Xie became so engrossed in his reminiscences that he ignored me and I would press the
button (Photo 1.2). All of a sudden, my imagination ran wild and I began
asking questions like, "Is liver tastier when tile-barbecued than when it's
boiled?" To that, Xie replied, "Of course, barbecued liver is delicious. But
at this particular time during the Cultural Revolution, it tasted quite
bloody."

Although I felt extreme disgust, physiologically and psychologically,
toward this cannibal, at one and the same time I was grateful to him, because he had pointed out to me that the cannibalism that had occurred
during the Cultural Revolution was, in fact, a continuation of history. It
had been acceptable to consume the liver of a spy during the Civil War,
and therefore it was okay to consume the livers of twenty-three category
types in the 1960s. If it was all right to consume the livers of KMT agents,
then naturally it was also permissible to consume those of the political
opposition and of capitalist roaders. If the Red Army and guerrilla forces
could consume human body parts, then of course the revolutionary com-

PHOTO 1.2   Xie Jinwen, former CCP guerrilla fighter and cannibal during the Cultural Revolution in Guangxi.

mittees, the poor and lower-middle peasants, and the revolutionary masses could follow suit. Anything was acceptable as long as it was in the name of class struggle and proletarian dictatorship. Over the past few decades, all ruthless incidents fomented by the Chinese Communist Party originated from a rejection of common morality. Humanism was ignored, love was scorned.

After our interview with Xie, we walked to the house of another criminal, who had also been involved in the gruesome practice of cutting out human livers. Unfortunately, he wasn't home and so I simply took a few snapshots of the surrounding Xinpu village and returned to the township government guest house. Later, I went to Mushan Junior Middle School and took a few pictures there, at the site of a documented killing field. According to the local archives, on August 7, 1968, a funeral was held in the school playground for a militiaman. At the same time, in the woods surrounding the playground, crowds of people were ruthlessly beating up innocent victims. The green leaves must somehow have screened out the effects of the nearby mourning. On that day, seventy-two people were lynched. The frenzy continued well into the next day. In the course of forty-eight hours, over 150 people were killed. That event is now known as the "Mushan massacre." Eighteen years later, the only thing left for me to gaze upon was a beautiful forest. The blood stains and body parts from the past had long since been covered by the fallen leaves. And yet, I still felt compelled to snap the shutter of my camera, to record this scene (Photo 1.3). Although I knew that this "site" or that "site" could not be used to prove anything, that it would not constitute evidence to prove the occurrence of the Mushan massacre, or of the Sanli slaughter, I snapped away. These pictures might not mean anything to other people, but in my emotional world they are important. They express my deepest sympathy for the victims. I would tell the world what these unfortunate people could no longer relate, even at the risk of sacrificing my fame and my life. For, despite being surrounded by the most powerful regime in Chinese history, one that was willing to go to any length to cover up this ugliness, I still possessed my mouth and my pen to counter the cover-up.

Qiaoxian town officials treated me to lunch. On that day, the main course was sautéed pig's liver. I tried very hard not to vomit as I swallowed two pieces. I then quickly turned away from the table. Fortunately, some bean curd and green vegetable soup were also served. During the previous few days, I had encountered nothing but stories about the cutting out of human livers, boiling human livers, consuming human livers, and barbecuing human livers. My tolerance had reached its limit.

After lunch, I returned to Mushan Junior Middle School to interview the son of one of the victims. Deputy Secretary Mo Shumou had described that case to me, and so, on my way over, I opened up my journal:

PHOTO 1.3   The basketball court of the Mushan Junior Middle School where the Mushan massacre occurred. Here, over the course of two days, 150 victims were beaten to death.

ZHENG JIANBANG OF MUSHAN BRIGADE, QIAOXIAN COMMUNE

Veteran guerrilla fighter, later accused of being a rightist, and prior to his death a cadre at a labor reform facility. Also accused during the Cultural Revolution of being the political director of an anti-CCP salvation army. After fleeing the area for a few months, he was arrested, and on his way back to Mushan he was beaten to death. His body was thrown into a pit. For having shown some resentment, his elder son [Zheng Qihong] was criticized during the day and had his liver cut out at night while still alive. More than ten people divided it up for consumption, claiming that the liver of the unmarried was even better to strengthen one's innards and to cure diseases. Two Party members involved in the case were later subjected to internal CCP discipline. The commoners who had been involved could not be punished, and so they merely apologized to the family, and paid some money (about a hundred yuan [$30]).

Had Xie Jinwen been one of the two Party members involved in the consumption of Zheng Qihong's liver? I checked my journal. Yes. (Photos 1.4 and 1.5).

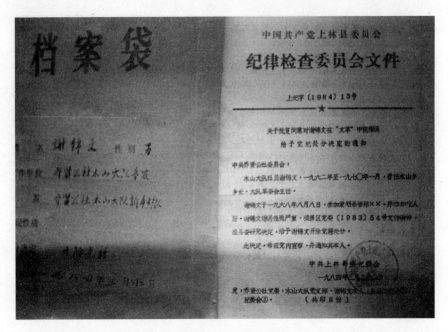

PHOTO 1.4   The official document of the Shanglin County Party Committee indicating the removal of Xie Jinwen's membership in the CCP.

We entered a shabby hut and saw Zheng Jianbang's younger son, Zheng Qiping, a short and courteous young lad (Photo 1.6). He recalled the past events in a rather low voice and from time to time appeared to be uneasy. It was all very abnormal. Zheng Qiping hung his head in sorrow, so much more like one would think a murderer would act than had the boastful criminal, Xie Jinwen.

> Two days after my father was killed, they also killed my mother and pushed her into the river, claiming it was a suicide. The reason for beating my mother to death was that she had used a piece of paper with Chairman Mao's image on it to make a simple paper figure. "What kind of paper figure?" I asked. It was a scarecrow made out of old newspaper. It just so happened that Chairman Mao's image was on it. My second uncle was also beaten to death during the Mushan massacre. On the same night, my elder brother was also beaten to death and had his liver eaten. My second elder brother was handicapped and could not walk. He died of hunger. My paternal grandmother turned to my aunt for help. Knowing that the situation would deteriorate, my father had sent me to my elder sister's place. After five members of my family were murdered, the situation became extremely tense. The murderers searched for me everywhere in the hopes of cutting out the roots of our family. Fearing that something might happen to me, my

PHOTO 1.5   The site of the kitchen of the Mushan Village Committee Office where Xie Jinwen et al. boiled and consumed the heart and liver of victim Zheng Qihong.

elder sister sent me away to my relatives in Sanli. At that time, the Sanli slaughter had just occurred, and so there were bloody footprints everywhere. I can still recall seeing the blood and dead bodies on Sanli Bridge. Many families were there searching for the bodies of their kin. I had no choice but to return to my elder sister's. I was only six years old, and I missed my parents badly, so I was always whining to go home. I had only fear, as I had no idea of what was going on and what had happened to my parents and two brothers. Not until the leftover cases were dealt with in 1983 did I learn that my elder brother's liver had been consumed. Later, when I enrolled in school, I was looked down upon by classmates. At the very mention of the Cultural Revolution, I could not find a place to bury my head. To this day, we have not yet found the bodies of my family members. The more than one hundred dead from the Mushan massacre were indiscriminately buried by four elements types. Most of them are gone. As for an apology—I've never received one. I don't think so. No one has ever come to us to apologize.

As he recalled these painful events, Zheng Qiping continued to wipe away his tears. Yet somehow he silently managed to suppress his sorrow, and he continued to describe the bloody events in a monotone. Tears streamed down his face, but he kept on with an expression that was as

PHOTO 1.6   Orphan Zheng Qiping. Five members of his family were slaughtered.

flat as a stone. Over the course of my interviews, I tried very hard to suppress my own emotions, silently to record and document the facts and information in my journal. But the self-control of this young lad caused tears to swell in my eyes. I sat there as if before a stone sculpture, with sentimentality written across my face. But without revealing my inner thoughts, I merely let the cold tears stream down my face. Time and again, whenever he paused in his narrative, perhaps in accord with the wishes of the cadre, perhaps following his own logical train of thought, Zheng Qiping mentioned the concern shown to him by the Chinese Communist Party and the government—he had been given a position at the Mushan Junior Middle School. This made his moving account even more unbearable.

During the course of this interview, two township cadres mentioned another cruel event. Among the victims of the Mushan massacre, they told me, was another twenty-year-old named Pan Zhancai. On that day, Pan was plowing the fields. An order suddenly came for him to participate immediately in a meeting. He left his water buffalo and tools in the fields and walked off to his death. His aged parents, who were sixty and seventy years old, pulled a shabby cart to the village center and collected his body. They returned to the fields he had just been plowing in order to bury him, but the burial of bodies in communal fields or even in private plots was prohibited. Death, but no place to bury the dead. What crime had their son committed? He merely had held to Small Faction views. With no other alternative, Pan's poor parents lugged his body off to a barren mountain, along with some kerosene, and four jin [two kilograms] of soybeans. (The soybeans would help burn the body thoroughly, even convert the bone into ashes.) After they had buried their son's remains, the two poor parents could not help but wail for their son. Who has ever seen parents burning their own son? God! God! Open your eyes! We are the first!

With the burning of the ashes, a young life was brought to a final conclusion. Alone in the fields, the water buffalo waited for the return of the young cowherd, standing there, not moving a bit.

As Zheng Qiping saw us off, he and I walked shoulder to shoulder in silence. I held his shoulder with one hand and felt a powerful young life run like a current through my entire body. He was the same age as his elder brother had been when he was killed. The sorrow of both families, and the beautiful current of life, made it hard for me to repress my feelings. Gritting my teeth tightly, I tried to prevent myself from crying out. The cadres from the county and the township seemed to understand what was happening. They slowed their steps to let the young lad and me walk a short distance ahead. After we got into our car, I could no longer hold back my tears. Then, amazingly, a storm developed. On both sides of the road grew slender lemon trees, as pure and fresh as naked maidens. Alas, the beautiful lemon tree! The sudden, violent wind tore off its twigs and ripped open its reddish bark and scattered its pieces across the road. Big rain drops spattered the windshield and raced in rivulets over the glass surface like streaks of tears. The whole sky was pouring forth tears. Sorrow filled the heavens.

All of a sudden, I thought I could see Pan Zhancai's buffalo out in the middle of the fields. Why did that image shake my soul? Perhaps it symbolized the innocent and kindhearted working people, so subject to oppression. Perhaps it symbolized unawakened freedom, restrained by a muzzle. Perhaps it symbolized a force not submissive to suppression, one that would burst forth at any moment. Or, rather, perhaps it symbolized a silent expectation.

Indeed, it was more like an expectation. But then who was doing the expecting? And what was being expected? When the wind and storm died down at dusk, the scenery along both sides of the road became simply poetic. Only the soil of southern China after a heavy rain could look so deeply red. All of a sudden, it seemed to be filled with human blood. The sun shone through the leaves, creating dappled images in the wind. I felt as though I could see many of the eyes of the victims, staring silently at me, smiling, accompanying me as we drove past the soil soaked in their blood. From that moment on, even though I was merely sitting in the Beijing jeep, passing by lemon trees and buffalos in the fields of red soil, I could not help but confront those eyes full of expectation. No sorrow, no begging. There was only expectation. Nothing but expectation. I was confronting them in silence. However, I knew that they trusted me. I also understood their thoughts.

Lie in peace, my thousands of fellow countrymen! As long as I can still breathe, I will tell the rest of humankind everything that you would like to relate but cannot.

SO BASE AND SO OBSCENE!
May 28. Guilin.

Guilin was on the way to the next site of my interviews in Zhongshan and Mengshan Counties in Wuzhou Prefecture. At the same time, Bei Ming had returned from northern China. Based on the information I had received, Wuxuan County was to be the focus of our most important interviews. But first we decided to interview in other counties in order to accumulate more information and then focus all our energy on Wuxuan. Before heading off, however, we decided to tour the countryside around

Guilin, which has some of the best scenery in the world. Having been immersed in the subject of blood for so long, I felt smothered and I wanted to try to forget the Binyang and Shanglin killing fields, at least for one day.

I decided that we should tour Yangshuo by boat and swim in the Li River. A young lad I became acquainted with on the riverbank loaned us an old inner tube so that we could float in a leisurely way down the river. The day before, we had equipped ourselves with food, a map, and plastic bags and had started out before dawn. At a construction site, we helped ourselves to some pieces of wood, and with them and the inner tube, we made a raft. At dawn, in a light rain, we set off. Of course, the raft was not big enough to support people. We merely placed our clothes, food, and camera on it in secured plastic bags. On the river, I pulled the raft with a plastic rope as Bei Ming swam alongside. We were so at ease that we even sang a few country songs. At peace, we observed the scenery along the river. We saw water buffalos munching away and cormorants resting on a branch of a tree, like a chorus line of black-tied gentlemen. At about four or five in the afternoon, we arrived at a small village that had a big banyan tree. Looking over the map, we realized we had swum 40 li [20 kilometers], only one-fourth of the way from Guilin to Yangshuo. Should we spend three or four more days swimming to Yangshuo? No need, we decided. We'd had enough relaxation. It was time to get back to work. Psychologically, I was ready once again to confront the blood. We tore apart the raft and headed toward Yangshuo by bus.

Since Bei Ming did not have the requisite letters of introduction, she could not assist me in the interviews. Once again we parted company. She returned to Shanxi Province, I went on to Wuzhou Prefecture. At the Party Reform Office, I contacted the director, whose name was Tao, and asked him to telephone ahead to Zhongshan and Mengshan Counties. The next morning I was on my way to Zhongshan.

June 3, 1986. Zhongshan County.

The director of the Party Reform Office, Li Zhiqiang, greeted me. By his account, *only* 625 people had been killed in Zhongshan County during the Cultural Revolution. Twenty-eight killers had been sentenced after 1983. There were two high points in the killing. One was October 1967, when locals were influenced by the killing of landlords and rich peasants in Dao County, in Hunan Province, just north of Guangxi. The second came after the "Xiwan battle," when a large number of those captured were killed. Xiwan is the place where the Coal Bureau at Guiping was located. There, the Small Faction was in a leading position, and the Big Faction could not touch them. The leaders of the Big Faction decided, therefore, to mobilize "physical struggle" teams from several counties, including Zhongshan, He, Fuchuan, and others, to surround Xiwan and to cut off its supplies of grain, water, and electricity. Within fifteen days, the forces in Xiwan were defeated. As a part of their revenge, the leaders of the Big Faction selected a large number of captives to be "criticized" and "sacrificed for the martyrs who had died at Xiwan."

As I was perusing the county archives at the local Chinese Communist Party History Office, a comrade specializing in local history mentioned to me an incident of mass slaughter that he personally had witnessed:

> The scene is forever burned in my memory. The first indiscriminate killing took place in the center of the Zhongshan County seat. Under a Chinese scroll with the title "The Supreme Tribunal of the Poor and Lower-Middle Peasants," two victims were pulled up onto a stage to be criticized. Without knowing what was going on, more and more onlookers gathered. Suddenly someone appeared and, after reciting an instruction from Chairman Mao, read out the criminal act committed by the two victims: involvement in a secret meeting that conspired to overthrow the Communist Party. Then the announcer called out: "Should they be killed?" Still in the dark about what was going on, the assembled onlookers responded in unison, "Kill! Kill!" Immediately, the two convicted conspirators were yanked offstage and dragged to the side of the road. In no time, two heads were brought back and hung from the trees. Among the onlookers there was a cadre standing next to me who was in charge of political and legal affairs. In a state of shock, I asked him, "How can they kill like this?" Fatalistically, he replied, "Mass movement." He could not do anything about it.

At the behest of Director Li, I busily searched through the archives and came upon several typical cases he had mentioned. The first was the case of Pan Qingyang and Pan Qiurui, father and son, who were buried at Songgui stockaded village, Shilong Township:

TIME: October 18, 1967 (lunar calendar).
PLACE: At the foot of stone bamboo hill, Songgui village, Shilong commune.
VICTIM: Pan Qingyang, middle peasant.
CRIME: Instead of selling sesame seeds to the state, he sold them on the private market.

Once the mass movement began, Pan was accused of profiteering. Later, accused of being a member of an assassination squad, he was half strangled to death and, still breathing, buried alive, together with his son.

The next evening, the poor and lower-middle peasants of the entire village set up twenty tables to prepare for a feast. After collecting chicken blood, a local named Pan Hongzhi read out an oath, warning people not to follow the example of the Qingyang faction and not to collude with the "April 22" faction of Shanhu (the name of a place). People who followed the example of Qingyang, Pan warned, would perish like the Xianxiang faction. Having said that, Pan Hongzhi put a handful of incense into a wine bottle.[12] More than two hundred people thereupon set about indulging themselves in raw chicken blood wine, which, locally, is known as "victory wine." The rich peasants, of course, footed the bill for the entire feast.

The second case involved Zou Qinghua and Pan Huixing, mother and son, who were also buried at Songgui village, Shilong Township. This is their story, as recounted by one Pan Xiangfu:

TIME: November 23, 1967 (lunar calendar).
PLACE: Behind the mountain in Songgui village, Shilong commune.
VICTIMS: Zou Qinghua, 54 years of age, female, landlord class. Graduate of a famous university in Beijing; prior to the 1949 liberation, her husband had gone to Taiwan.

This "overseas connection" was the sole reason for her persecution. Her son, Pan Huixing, high-school graduate, 32 years of age, was buried at the same time. Before their deaths, mother and son were hung from a tree and subjected to nonstop criticism, during which they were bullied to confess their crime of "colluding with foreign spies." But mother and son both refused to confess. Leader Pan Lianzhao then retorted, "Dictatorship means dictatorship of the masses. If these two culprits continue to refuse to confess, bury them alive!" A squad of armed militiamen then force-marched the mother and son to a barren field where, as darkness fell, they were led to a freshly dug pit.

> The mother asked her son, "Huixing, are we going to die like this?" The son replied, "Even God cannot save us now! We should not confess to things we never did. Let's die." The militiamen ordered them to go down quickly into the pit. The mother wept. Although bound up, their limbs were limp from all the beating. Before the dirt was shoveled over them, the son stood up, crying and breathing heavily, "We should not die like this. It's too harsh," he cried. Peixing (a militiaman) stabbed him in the chest with a spear, causing his blood to spurt out. The mother also stood up. Yihong (another militiaman) then stabbed her in the chest with a spear. When the spear was extricated, it pulled out a piece of lung. The victims moaned. The militiamen screamed at us to shovel on dirt quickly and warned us that if we weren't quick about it, we would follow mother and son into the pit. Greatly frightened, we dumped on the dirt until it was piled one foot high.

Pan Xiangfu obviously had been on the "other name list," because, although he was not a four elements type, he could not escape being one of the twenty-three categories. He continued his recollection:

> Coming back from the burial, we pigged out. The militiamen called it a "feast celebrating victory." The pork they purchased themselves, whereas the chicken and rice were taken from the house of the victims.[13]

In my journal, I wrote the following line: "Cases in Zhongshan County (Wuzhou Prefecture) occurred in which the grandson was ordered to take the grandfather to the death tribunal and in which mothers and sons were buried together. The means employed were extremely base and obscene." This was a quote from Madam Yu Yaqin of the group handling leftover cases in the Party Reform Office of the Guangxi Autonomous Region. During my interview with her, I wrote down the words *base and obscene (xialiu canren)* without really considering their exact meaning. I assumed that burying a mother and son together violated local traditions and therefore was considered base and obscene. But to my great surprise, as a comrade at the Zhongshan County Party history archives was providing me with a detailed description of the events, he happened to mention an important detail that had been left out of the documents. Evidently the murderers had insisted that the son lie on top of his mother. The son could not bear it and he blurted out, "Oh God, how can you make me do this?" Only then did I realize the meaning of this word *base*, something that the locals were hesitant to tell me. So base and so obscene! No wonder this case was known all over Guangxi.

The killing of the renowned engineers, Zhou Shaochang and his wife, was equally well known in the region.

At the end of May 1968, forces from several counties joined together to encircle and attack the Coal Bureau at Guiping, the base of the Small Faction. After several battles, it was discovered that Liang Binsheng, a militiaman from Huangfeng brigade of Gongan commune, Zhongshan County, had been killed. In response, the victors indiscriminately selected three prisoners to accompany the dead soldier. Among the three was Zhou Shaochang, an engineer at the smelting plant at Guiping and a 1937 graduate of Qinghua University.* According to a few comrades from the autonomous region and from the Zhongshan County government, Zhou was famous both at home and abroad. His inspection of ore sand for export was so thorough that further inspections were unnecessary. His wife, Lu Yiqian, had also graduated from Qinghua University in 1937 and was a lab engineer at the Guiping Smelting Plant. In addition, she was a dele-

---

*Qinghua is China's premier technical university in Beijing.

gate to the Third National People's Congress in Beijing. During the encirclement operation against the coal district, the couple had failed to escape, and they were arrested by the Big Faction. According to the file, "On the morning of June 6, 1968, Zhou Shaochang and his wife, along with others, were sent to participate in the funeral of some members from the ninth regiment production team of Huangfeng brigade, Gongan commune. Later, all three were killed in front of the newly constructed burial site at Jigongkou."[14]

I arrived at Gongan Township, hoping to take a look at their murder site. However, all the local township cadres claimed that they "had no idea where it was located," nor "could they recall it clearly." Such a huge site, could they forget it that soon? Eventually, I "caught up" with a deputy leader of the village Party committee. He had no choice but to take me to the site.

A grassy area next to the road had been the main site of the "funeral."

> Murderer Tao Jingfu conducted the funeral himself. Murderer Yang Qunliang spoke on behalf of the commune armed police units. After the funeral was over, the deceased's family members accompanied Liang's coffin to Jigongkou. At the same time, the militiamen ordered Zhou Shaochang and the others to follow the procession.[15]

As I walked the mile or so distance from the grassy area to Jigongkou, I stepped on the same road traversed by the three victims. As we arrived at Jigongkou I noticed a tomb covered by weeds. (Liang's coffin has since been removed.) It was after Liang's burial that the slaughter began.

> Liao Shoufeng read off the "criminal acts" committed by the three: "the two engineers from the Guiping Smelting Plant earned 135 yuan a month. The woman had been a member of the Kuomintang and was once a branch secretary. This couple were leaders of the 'coal mine bandits.' They had designed the defensive trenches and pillboxes at the smelting plant. The third was head of the Xiwan Small Faction. (Zhong Fangfu, a member of Wanggao commune of Xiwan brigade [comment by Zheng Yi].) Liang Binsheng was killed by the three of them." "Everyone! Should we kill people like them?" At this moment, Zhou Shaochang demanded to speak to the masses.[16]

What had he intended to say? I was sure he would have begun by explaining that they had never been involved in battles, that they had not designed the trenches and pillboxes. After all, he would have protested, they weren't civil engineers. He would have tried to explain away that criminal label, "secretary of a Kuomintang branch," which had been imposed on his wife. He would also have mentioned the itinerary she had made from "secretary of a Kuomintang branch" to "delegate to the Third National People's Congress." Finally, he would have declared that as delegates to the People's Congress, they enjoyed legal immunity. After all,

"Public Security units cannot arrest or kill delegates without the express approval of the People's Congress." But he ended up saying none of these things. Commander Liao so-and-so did not give him the chance to speak.

> Unaware of the truth, and provoked by Liao Shoufeng, the masses began yelling, "kill!" Later, the murderer Yang Qunliang stood in front of Liang Binsheng's tomb, fired two shots into the sky, and at the same time ordered the killing. Immediately, the three victims were chopped to death with knives and spears by Liang so-and-so, Liang so-and-so, Liang so-and-so, Liang so-and-so, Dong so-and-so, Liang so-and-so, Liang so-and-so, and others who joined in the fray. The situation was beyond human imagination.[17]

What the documentation failed to mention was that as soon as Yang Qunliang fired the two shots, the first to rush forward and start the chopping were two young girls. (Even more unfathomable was that people usually encouraged young girls to do the killing, and later they would address them as "sister nine" or "sister ten" based on the number of people they had killed!)[18] (Photo 1.7). Standing on the soft grass, I inquired about the victims' remains and was told that they had been secured by relatives in 1983 during the period when leftover cases were handled. The

PHOTO 1.7   Lengshuiyan village, Daan Township, Zhongshan County where a young girl took the lead in beheading a world-renowned engineer couple.

son of Zhou Shaochang and his wife had come all the way from Beijing and had carefully recovered the bones of his parents, wrapping them piece by piece in coarse paper. Deep knife wounds in the father's cranium were still apparent.

At dusk, herds of buffalos carrying their cowherds slowly meandered by. There was serenity in the fields. The lush present covered over the dire frenzy of the recent past. As I boarded the bus, I turned around and took one last look at Lengshuiyan village and the lime peak pointing toward the sky behind the harmonious houses. What a beautiful picture it made. It was early summer, and the lush countryside was so beautiful that it brought sorrow to my heart. This is my land, these are my people. Ugly? Beautiful? I cannot tell. I cannot tell.

KILL OR BE KILLED!
June 5, 1986.

Yang Xusong, the head of the standing committee of the County People's Congress, came along for my research into the killing of Deng Jifang. On that day we arrived first at the office of the Huilong Township government to talk with Party Secretary Zhu Minsheng. Formerly, Zhu had been director of the local Leftover Cases Group. He had also been a deputy Party secretary of Qingtang Township, where the Deng murder had taken place. Zhu had been personally in charge of the case and therefore was in a position to provide me with a detailed description. Vice Chairman Tao Youhua also attended the interview. He agreed to send along the township secretary of culture, Zhong Yongwen, as a sort of go-between with the murderer, Yi Wansheng of Sishao natural village. Yi was reluctant to utter a word, or so it was said, but although I felt that I had already obtained ample information, I still wanted to visit the original site of the crime and get a feel for it myself. Long before we reached the village, our vehicle was forced to halt in front of a shabby wooden bridge, and we had to walk the rest of the way. The sun blazed in the sky and the ground seemed to be steaming. We were sweating so furiously that we took off our shirts. After we had walked 2 or 3 kilometers, we still seemed to be no closer to the village. Blisters began to burn on my shoulders, back, and arms. Before we finally entered the village, we stopped and took pictures at the place where the murderers had sliced open their victims' stomachs and foraged about for their livers. The site was a sloping bank on the edge of the Siqin River, located about 10 meters from the rice mill.

During the killing frenzy, the murderers had cut open the victims when they were still alive. Li Shangwu, then Party secretary of the district (and later the deputy director of the Legal Affairs Office of Wuzhou Prefecture), just happened to be passing by at that moment. Li noticed that someone was holding something down and trying to kill it and he assumed that the person was killing a water buffalo. It was not until later that he discovered that a murder had been committed right out in the open.

We headed directly for the house of Yi Wansheng in Sishao natural village. Based on accounts from several sources, I had already gained a good grasp of the case.

Victim Deng Jifang's father had been a landlord in Sishao village. During the Land Reform period, 1948–1953, old Deng had resorted to banditry with his two older brothers. Later, all three of them were killed. Deng Jifang, who was the youngest of his father's children, had gone up into the mountains with his father and his two uncles, but later, due to his youth, he was only sentenced to two years in prison. After his release, when he returned to the village, he found out that his mother, some time before, had hanged herself. Seeing that he had no place to put down his feet in Sishao village, Deng Jifang moved to a nearby village named Kangping brigade, and there he was adopted by a poor and lower-middle peasant by the name of Tao so-and-so. Then, quite beyond anyone's expectation, the Cultural Revolution was launched. In Sishao village no one seemed to meet the criteria for a killing, but then suddenly people remembered the young son of a landlord who happened to be living in the nearby village. Huang Paoci (one of the three names used by this man), the Party secretary, ordered a detachment of militiamen to go and arrest Deng. But it turned out that the nearby village hadn't forgotten about class struggle—they had already arrested Deng and shut him up in the brigade office. As soon as he saw the militiamen coming from Sishao village to arrest him, Deng figured that his end was at hand. In order to avoid suffering death by ruthless torture, he tried to hang himself. The cadres and militiamen swiftly overpowered him, however, and escorted him back to Sishao village. Halfway there, even though he was being beaten, Deng refused to go any further. The militiamen then put Deng in a bamboo cage and carried him that way back to the village, where they hung him from an electricity pole. People immediately started to beat him with ruthless ferocity, but this punishment did not adequately slake the crowd's thirst for revenge, so they resorted to "using a burning-red spatula to scorch his face and chest."[19] The very cruelty of these acts threw the crowd into such a frenzy that it seemed to be totally out of control. Veteran Party members, cadres, land reform activists, and the poor and lower-middle peasants all joined in calling for Deng's death. Someone even voiced a demand to disembowel Deng. Once the victim had passed

PHOTO 1.8   The arrow points to the rocky bank stretching into the river where Yi Wansheng et al. dug out the heart and liver of victim Deng Jifang.

out, he was pulled to the side of the river, and with five or six people pressing down on Deng's arms and legs, Yi Wansheng cut open his chest with a sharp butcher knife. (Photos 1.8 and 1.9).

*   *   *

Was this Yi Wansheng? This short and skinny old man? In a dark and shabby hut, I finally came face-to-face with the famous murderer. When we entered the room, he was having a good time playing cards with two old cronies.

"What drove you to kill someone at an age when you should have been enjoying life?" I inquired of him.

PHOTO 1.9   The beautiful and peaceful site in Sishao village where Deng Jifang, the son of a landlord, was consumed.

The old man's reply was, I thought, quite gutsy. "Yes," he declared. "I admit everything! I am already 86 years old. I've lived long enough. Why should I be afraid of going to prison?"

After uttering his comment, the old man glared at me with a somewhat confrontational mien. Instead of reacting to him, I just sat there and listened to his long-winded talk.

Why was he killed? Deng, his father, and two uncles had gone up to the mountains and had become bandits, disrupting the stability of the entire village. At that time, roughly 1949, I was a militiaman. My shoulder was permanently scarred from standing for long stretches of time at the post with my gun. What crime did his father commit? One spring while still a landlord, instead of lending grain to us, his own villagers, he loaned grain to people in other villages. Later, he became a bandit and led his brigands in attacks on our village. Ultimately, the PLA defeated the bandits and saved the entire village. A soldier named Qian (Qianhai) was killed during the battle, and during the fighting Deng's father had ordered several thousand jin of grass to be burned, so we had no fuel to make any lime! Yes, I killed him. No matter who asks the question, I have the same answer suggested to us by Chairman Mao. Fear nothing! Everyone supported us and what I killed was the enemy. Fear nothing! Will his ghost return and seek revenge? Ha! To engage in revolution, my heart is red! Didn't Chairman Mao say "kill or be killed"? If I live, you must die. Class struggle! (Photo 1.10).

The only mistake we made was that we should have let the government kill him, rather than us. I laid the first knife on him. But that knife was too dull, so I threw it away and I used a sharper knife to do him in. I was not involved, however, in cutting out his heart and liver. (According to a local file: "Yi Wansheng attempted to cut out the heart, liver, gall bladder, and kidneys, but the blood in the victim's chest was so hot that he couldn't touch the body parts. Yi then poured some river water over the victim and, as his chest cooled off, Yi extracted the organs, cut them into pieces, and laid everything out on a board.") The heart was cut into finger-sized slices. People in the crowd struggled to get a piece. The people were so numerous that I didn't even get a share. (Again, according to the file, Huang Paoci cut off a large chunk, took it home, and consumed it along with some hard liquor. Huang

PHOTO 1.10   Yi Wansheng showed no regrets for his cannibalism: "Didn't Chairman Mao say 'kill or be killed'?"

even shared some with the masses. Yi Wansheng got three two-inch slices of liver, which he consumed at home.[20])

What a courageous old hero. Even though he was nearly ninety years old, he still seemed quite strong. All of a sudden, heavy clouds appeared, and it started to rain cats and dogs. Drops of rain were dripping in through the skylight. I moved my bench and, sitting there silently, I found I couldn't ask any more questions. Looking around at the small, shabby hut, the old furniture, the aged stone grinder at the corner of the room, and the old man's patched shirt, somehow I couldn't generate any hatred. On the contrary, confronting this man, who ten years earlier had been a poor and lower-middle peasant, and now, in the prosperous 1980s, was still a poor and lower-middle peasant, I felt a sense of sympathy. As I recalled the cruel and ruthless scene of their killing and cannibalism, my mind was besieged with ten thousand different thoughts. These people had firmly engaged in class struggle and had cruelly participated in cannibalism, but where was the happy life promised to them by the Chinese Communist Party? What pathetic and hateful people! Although there is a saying that there's a reason for all mistreatment, and there's always someone to blame for debts, at this moment, I was at a complete loss to know what to make of the entire matter. My emotional pendulum inclined toward the Yi Wanshengs of this world. Of course, they had to be punished, but weren't they also victims? And whom could *they* sue? Yes, Mao Zedong and the Communist Party should be held accountable, but apart from that, was there some other more profound reason that might explain all of this? Perhaps it is the dark side of our national psyche and the hatred generated by class struggle that drove us to slaughter, to cannibalism, and that dragged the entire nation into a hell of mass killing.

In the darkness that accompanied the rain, I secretly snapped two pictures of the old man. I couldn't quite decide whether I took them out of sympathy for him, or merely out of sympathy for myself. My book would be a portrait of both myself and of my nation.

PICTURES OF HELL

June 9, 1986. Mengshan County.

In the morning I arrived at the county Party Reform Office to meet with Director Xiao, who had invited Lu Zurong and Zeng Chaozhang to join us. They had investigated leftover cases and therefore could provide a good deal of information.

The number of people killed in this small county during the Cultural Revolution was also quite astonishing. Total deaths numbered more than 850 people, that is, 6.6 people per 1,000 out of the entire population of

130,000; 603 people were lynched, 254 were persecuted to death, and 130 families were uprooted. The majority of the killings took place in mid-June 1968. Within a five-day period, 500 people were killed.

Before Spring Festival, the Chinese New Year, in 1968, the small county of Mengshan was an island of peace in the midst of the frenzied wave of the Cultural Revolution that was sweeping Guangxi and the entire country. Despite the red waves of big-character posters, Red Guards, large-scale criticism sessions, and acts of seizing power, Mengshan seemed to hold on to its honor of the belief that "gentlemen rely on words alone and avoid the physical." Incidents of large-scale criticisms and arrests had occurred, but there had been no killing. However, "the tree leaves might be quiet, but this does not mean the wind has subsided." The twelve-degree typhoon of class struggle would sweep through every corner of the county with nary an exception.

On the eve of the Chinese lunar year, a happy time of family reunion in traditional Chinese society, Jindong brigade declared an emergency, calling for imminent action by a purported anti-Communist national salvation gang! The following day, the first of the New Year, fifty people from Jindong were incarcerated in a detention camp. Wan so-and-so, then political commissar of the county Armed Police, traveled to the brigade to issue his personal instructions. Later, at a meeting of high-level cadres in the county, he praised their "revolutionary actions" in locking up the fifty people and sent a work team to the brigade to summarize their "advanced experiences." Since the Party and the political organs had long been paralyzed, all the power had been taken over by the military. Commissar Wan was thus in total control of Mengshan County. The county Public Security Bureau, nervous about offending Wan, immediately sent down a work team. However, the investigation by this team showed that it could not be concluded that an anti-Communist national salvation gang had sprung up there. In the midst of the atmosphere back then, such a verdict indicated that the witch-hunt had been a fabrication. The Public Security Bureau, however, did not dare to announce the results of the investigation to the masses. Commissar Wan, of course, ignored the report and continued to organize Mao Zedong Thought speaking groups to tour the county and to spread the advanced experience of Jindong brigade.

Very little time transpired in this area between the plowing of the fields and the harvesting of the grain. On March 20, Xinlian brigade uncovered a so-called popular party, which, it was claimed, had acted on the principle of killing the poor to protect the rich. Over night, three families, amounting to a total of sixteen people, including Zhou Jingtong (a former underground CCP member, a rightist, and teacher), and ranging in age from two to seventy-three years, were all killed. The next day, when this incident was reported to the county authorities, a meeting of army veterans and militiamen was suspended and all were instructed to go to Xinlian brigade to "visit and learn." And just to make sure the point was driven home, various capitalist roaders were also ordered to the site of the killing. Later, squad and platoon leaders, whose performances had been especially outstanding, were conferred awards at the meeting. Once again, the office of the armed police sent director Zhu so-and-so to go down to Xinlian brigade to affirm its great achievement in "seizing upon the new trend in class struggle" and to start a new wave of "whipping up a twelve-degree typhoon of class struggle."

On April 13, the Mengshan Revolutionary Committee was formally established.

On May 15, landlords, rich peasants, counterrevolutionaries, social dregs, and rightists, along with capitalist roaders from both neighboring communes, were paraded through the streets. It was market day in Mengshan. At the most crowded spot, three victims were stabbed to death in public with a spear. Now the red terror began to spread from the center of the county to the outlying villages.

On June 12, three groups, totaling nearly thirty people from Gupai brigade, were killed. Eight of them were buried alive together. The most well-known victim was Chen Xianlin—the grandnephew of Chen Manyuan, the former Party secretary of the Guangxi Autonomous Region, who is now a member of the Chinese People's Political Consultative Conference.* Chen Xianlin was only a little over twenty years old. While plowing in the fields, he was ordered to return home, where he was arrested, summarily pushed into a pit, and buried alive. At this point, Mengshan's generally slow-acting population was finally affected by the constant exhortations and went into action in a bloody frenzy. At the meeting, two groups of victims were killed with clubs and stones. Wenping brigade was also involved in the killing. Now the entire county was involved.

According to Lu Zurong and Zeng Chaozhang, Wenping brigade, located in the center of the county, was the most heavily involved in the killing. Less than 1 li [one-half kilometer] separated the main village from the local Armed Police Office, close enough that Commissar Wan would have heard the sorrowful yelling of the victims, along with the wailings of the chickens and dogs. Not far from Wan's direct jurisdiction, four groups totaling fifty-two people were killed between the hours of 10 P.M. June 10 and 8 A.M. the next day. Pathetically, Wan was then attending a meeting of security directors, where he publicly announced something

---

*A largely powerless "consultative" body to the CCP set up in 1949.

about stopping the killing. He also issued three declarations prohibiting indiscriminate killing. But behind closed doors, Wan noted with a profoundly authoritative air, "Once the meeting is over, the killing must be stopped." Yet the real message to his subordinates was that as long as the meeting remained in session, they should take advantage of the opportunity and kill off as many people as possible. This Wan so-and-so certainly can be labeled a second Wang Jianxun. On the one hand, Wan held meetings to issue prohibitions against indiscriminate killings, but, on the other, he declared at the very same meetings that fully thirty-eight brigades had yet to lift the lid on class struggle. Why the number thirty-eight? Everyone understood that these thirty-eight brigades had not yet become involved in the killing. Wan's real purpose was to convert a meeting devoted to prohibiting killing into a meeting to mobilize killing. Subject to Wan so-and-so's high-pressure tactics, all of the villages followed suit and joined in the slaughter.

In the aftermath of the "twelve-degree typhoon," the achievements were glorious. Sixty-two out of sixty-four brigades in the county joined in the killing. Their victims included 257 commune members, nineteen urban residents, sixty-nine students, 136 former four elements types, 115 offspring of the four elements types, fifty-two state cadres and workers, and nine others. (According to statistics gathered after the Cultural Revolution, twenty-six people were arrested for committing this crime.)[21]

The wind of indiscriminate killing was "prohibited," but it never really terminated until early 1970. According to documents, the last victim died in January of that year.

It is said that there were very few cases of cannibalism in Mengshan County, although specific records were not really kept. But the case of "consuming the beauty's heart" was quite renowned in the area.

Mo so-and-so, a teacher at the Gantang Brigade Elementary School of Mengshan, heard that consuming a "beauty's heart" could cure disease. He then labeled a beautiful 13- or 14-year-old student of his as a "target of dictatorship" and singled her out for killing. After the little girl was done in, the murderers fled the site, and Mo so-and-so remained behind for his provender. Under the cover of darkness, he cut open the girl's chest with a duck-beak-shaped tool, dug out her heart, and took it home to enjoy. All of this is recorded in a 1982 file. A year later, when the movement to handle leftover cases was in full swing, news of this case of "consuming the beauty's heart" spread over the entire district, leading both officials and the masses to demand that the murderer be executed. (One member of the leftover cases group confirmed that Mo had already been executed and was one of ten capital punishment cases in the entire district.) But in 1983, the case was reviewed, and Mo was exonerated. I, myself, read the document from the second trial, in which it was recorded that at the time of her murder, the young female student was carrying her baby brother in a sling strung across the front of her chest. The bands across her chest made it very hard to cut her open, and so, after the militiamen had departed, Mo became so frightened in the dark that he then took off without cutting out the heart. I asked comrades in Mengshan to search for the 1982 file, and I also went over to the archive to search for it myself. All was in vain. The 1982 materials had mysteriously disappeared. (According to regulations, "black materials" used to persecute people during the Cultural Revolution are supposed to be preserved to this day [1986], which of course has added to the psychological pressure on the persecuted.)

I took a walk over to Wenping brigade, the place where indiscriminate killing had most widely taken place. Pressed for time before dinner, I could only take a cursory look and snap some "emotional pictures" at the site of the killing—underneath the big banyan tree (Photo 1.11) and by the side of the pond. Standing there in silence, I wished peace for the souls of the dead.

That evening, I requested some information from Yu Zhiqiang, Party secretary of the brigade. Yu had recorded every violent act in his journal, which had been used as significant evidence during the movement to handle leftover cases (Photo 1.12). Moreover, as an act of sympathy, Yu had married one of the family members who had been persecuted. I assumed that Yu was a courageous and kindhearted person. He came in and sat down on the wooden couch and placed his rough hands on its handle and sat there for quite a while in complete silence. He was forty-five years old. He was wearing the kind of plastic sandals that urbanites generally disdain. His had been repeatedly mended with colorful plastic tape. After his initial shyness, Yu started talking.

He said he had not been courageous, and he had never suspected that his journal would someday be used as evidence. He had merely been angry about the ruthless measures. Were the landlords and rich peasants class enemies? In his mind, they were honest people, pathetically honest. They would head east if you didn't direct them west. Twice every month, they provided nearly 100 jin of wood to local militiamen so they could make fires in the winter. During the Cultural Revolution, Yu had been a production team leader, and he had attended the meeting when the killing plan was devised. The public security director ordered that no one reveal the decision, and whoever did so would himself be killed. The designated target was a rich peasant named Qiu Ming, hardworking and honest. Qiu was also Yu's neighbor, and Yu felt sorry for him. After the meeting, as he was returning home, Yu bumped into Qiu and tried somehow to inform him of the decision. Out of fear, Yu merely hinted. "Bad weather! Beware," he said ominously. Qiu, looking at the sky, replied, "It looks fine to me!" Yu dared say nothing more. He continued on his way,

PHOTO 1.11   Under this banyan tree in Wenping brigade, Mengshan County, children of opposition factions were killed in an effort to "uproot the roots to kill the grass."

PHOTO 1.12   Yu Zhiqiang (left), cultural secretary of Wenping brigade,
Mengshan County, who recorded the cruelty of the slaughter in a secret diary.

grinding his teeth. The designated murderers were mostly militiamen.
When the director of public security asked Party secretary Yu to reveal his
attitude about the entire matter, the secretary indicated that he did not
agree with the decision to kill so many people. The director pretended to
change his mind, and he announced instead that they would parade the
criminals on the streets for criticism. Here the secretary had no choice but
to agree. In reality, however, the militiamen had already set everything
up. During the meeting, the battalion commander had made an exit, returning ten minutes later to announce that the killing had already been
initiated in the county. The Party secretary was once again forced to express his opinion.

After the killing, Yu did not go to the site, for he felt that it was too
bloody. Brains and blood oozed over everything, and smashed dead bodies were scattered about the landscape. Later, the property of the deceased was publicly displayed and divided up, just as the property of
landlords had been parceled out during the Land Reform campaign.
Some of the items were sold off on the spot as though it were an auction.
The militiamen squandered the money in the manner of bandits.

In the middle of Yu's talk, I discovered that Yu's wife was, in fact, Qiu
Ming's widow. Realizing this, I carefully inquired about her condition. At

first Yu didn't respond. Then he started to talk again with an absolutely expressionless face. After the militiamen had killed the father (Qiu Ming), they went in search of the kids. Qiu's wife begged them to spare her youngest child, who was less than a year old, but her entreaties were spurned. Their entire house was confiscated, with only the quilts and cooking utensils left behind. This was the militiamen's idea of how to show her consideration.

Since I had already read the files on this case, I realized that Yu's simple description had left out a lot of the ruthless details. The following is the official version.

> When they had finished with Qiu Ming and Qiu Wu, the militiamen pro-ceeded to kill the three kids. Qiu's wife, Wu Jianzhen, cried out, "Please leave me one!" The militiamen replied, "Don't be afraid. We won't touch you." (They grabbed the children by their necks, pulling them off their beds. [Comment by Zheng Yi.]) Two men pulled at one child. The older child was not yet in school, and the younger one was still at the breast-feeding stage. As the kids were being dragged down the road, they were followed by a trail of dust all the way to Dongpingding. Two people held the rope while others threw the children down into a pit. Then we stoned them to death, the report concluded.[22]

Qiu's widow was spared because she came from a poor class back-ground. Yet, in a flash, her entire family had been destroyed. The death of her three young children was especially painful. Yu tried his best to help console her. At one point, she resolved to leave the cursed Wenping brigade forever, but she had no place to go. She had fled to Guangxi from Guangdong Province during the War of Resistance. At that time she was so young that later she couldn't even remember her hometown. So now she had no alternative but to continue to suffer on the land soaked with her family's blood. Yu and Qiu's widow were married in 1969 and now have two sons, ages seventeen and fifteen. The bitterness from the past is not easily forgotten, however. During the movement to handle leftover cases, the murderers one after another went to her house to beg forgive-ness. She locked them all out. Later, after a few sessions of "persuasion and education" by the local leadership, she agreed to forget past hatreds. The murderers showed up again, bringing gifts this time of pork, chicken, and pancakes, and kneeling down, asked her forgiveness. In this way, the widow's deep hatred was supposed to be expunged; as she poured her "guests" tea, the poor woman had to hold back her tears.

Yu continued his description of the past, off and on and with increasing pain. My heart began to tighten to the point where I could no longer ask any of the questions I had prepared in advance. I felt that I had no right to inquire into the details of their great sorrow. I merely asked Yu to recount anything else that might have left a deep and lasting impression on him.

The deepest impression: terror. When the militiamen were about to kill a child, they would not say a word, but simply put a rope around its neck and then yank the rope. Unaware of impending death, the child would suddenly become scared and say, "Seventh uncle, you are kidding, aren't you? Don't hurt me too much." The child was familiar with the militiamen, for they often came by to play cards. During those days, if it was decided that you should die, you would die. There was no hint or anything. Everyone was scared, as birds are frightened by the shooting arrow. Only the children were devoid of any sense of the danger of the situation. One evening, a group of militiamen on patrol grew tired and decided to take a rest at Yao Guang-xiang's house. On opening the gate, Yao was so frightened he started to yell, "It's all over. It's my turn. My turn." Yao then fled back into his house where he started to hang himself. After the militiamen entered the courtyard, to-gether with Yao's crying family members, they peered into the house and tried to reassure Yao. "We won't kill you," they called to him. "We're just passing by. Come on down!" Yao refused to listen and kicked away the chair, but fortunately the militiamen managed to push open the door and rescue him. (Yao Guangxiang, the offspring of a rich peasant, is now a pro-duction team leader.) The indiscriminate killing frightened everyone. No one dared to talk too loudly. Even the murderers were scared: They all con-spired and discussed their plans in a low voice. In that village of terror, the intangible terror penetrated every window like a cold draft and pierced di-rectly into everyone's hearts.

Cases of indiscriminate killing of the four elements and their offspring and the elimination of entire families were very common in Guangxi. During my second visit to Guangxi, a few of my literary friends there had discussed these cases with me in great detail. In one incident, a mother held back her tears as she dressed her child in new clothes, explaining to her son that his "uncles" were coming to take him to his grandma's. The innocent babe had no idea that these were the last moments of his life and that these were the last new clothes he would ever wear. So he set off in the company of the "uncles" with great joy. Killing the offspring to elimi-nate a family is a great national treasure of our Chinese nation. The most humane part of this act is the gender discrimination that precedes the killing: The woman is spared and the man is killed. In Lingshan County, for instance, where, "according to rough estimates, 520 families were eliminated," one member of the Huang family was lucky enough to be spared.[23]

She was only two or three when her landlord family was killed. At the site, someone said she was female and proposed that she be spared. The first murderer checked out her sexual organs. But the second murderer refused to buy it. After the second murderer checked out her sex, the third murderer wouldn't buy it. After all of the murderers had checked her out and con-firmed that she was female, the child was finally released.[24]

Then there's the famous "widow's lane" in Rongan County, northern Guangxi. All of the male adults and male infants were killed, so that only the women were left. And that's how Longchao Lane became known as the famous "widow's lane."[25]

Recording these cases made me think about a tragic scene mentioned to me by an old classmate, the writer Shi Tiesheng.

TIME: "Red August," 1966.

PLACE: Beijing Railway Station.

SCENE: The offspring of "five black elements" are about to follow their parents as they are expelled from Beijing. At the last "gate of hell," in the Beijing railway station, the children are ordered to kneel down on the floor. A Red Guard, wearing a yellow and green army outfit, holds a tea kettle above them and slowly pours hot water over their heads. The children are so scared that none of them dares resist or escape. The entire hall is full of sorrowful mourning. Onlookers are also scared and scatter about. A frightened youth pushes open a door and begins to scream, scaring people even more. Already there are a few people in the room trying to flee, while outside, Red Guards are cursing and beating people. When a belt is struck against the door, all inside the room feel their hearts stop. Although the door is never opened, everyone feels afterward as if they have already died once.

A picture of hell!

Such an act is beyond human description. To label it as "violence" does not adequately convey the sense of terror that invades the bodies and souls of the victims. Can it be called "maltreatment"? This too fails to depict the frenzy in their hearts. To label this act as "beastly" slanders all innocent species of beasts. We can do nothing but gaze emotionless upon it, astonished and frustrated by all the pain and terror. Has mulling it over for the past twenty years provided any real explanation for this scarlet memorial?

With mixed feelings, I departed from Mengshan County and continued my journey. As I left the guest house, there appeared before me a bright, everyday world.

*   *   *

Journal: The children were playing and swimming in the river. Most of them were girls, wearing shorts and shirts, not swimming suits (Photo 1.13). Their colorful, small, plastic sandal shoes were lined up in careful order along the post of the bridge. The acacia rachii trees covered the

PHOTO 1.13   Children enjoying the river near the fields where the locals used to work naked. The Communist Party brought the villagers pairs of shorts and cruel struggle.

ground with their light yellow flowers, and the magnolias exuded their fragrance into the atmosphere all about.

The children were so lovely!
Life was appealing!
Love was so tantalizing!

NOTES

1. *Binyang County Gazette (Binyang xianzhi)*, vol. 1, p. 458. [The reader should note that Zheng Yi does not always provide full citations for his sources.]

2. Wang Jianxun (deputy division commander of the local garrison), Wang Guizeng (deputy political commissar of the county people's armed police), Huang Zhiyuan (political instructor, local garrison), and Ling Wenhua (political commissar, artillery unit of the local garrison).

3. *Chronology of the "Cultural Revolution" in Binyang County (Binyang xian "wen-hua da geming" dashiji)* (Bingyang County Party Reform Office Publication Bureau, April 1987), p. 14. This document originated with the Binyang County Archives, 1982–1985, "Leftover Cases" file.

4. Ibid., p. 20.

5. *Facts Relating to the Case of the Numerous Killings Planned and Directed by Wang Jianxun (Guanyu Wang Jianxun cehua, zhihui daliang sharen de fanzui shiji)*, Appendix no. 2, Binyang County Party Committee, September 15, 1984.

6. Lai Zengjie organized the massacre of fifty-four people and was sentenced to eight years in prison. "Binyang County People's Court File" *(Bingyang xian renmin fayuan juanzong)*.

7. "Files of Binyang County People's Court Criminal Proceedings" *(Binyangxian renmin fayuan xingshi yifan susong juanzong)*, p. 61 (file no. 84, catalogue no. 143).

8. Recorded Interview, May 21, 1986. "Notes of a Talk with Li Zengming." Also, see *Facts Relating to the Case of the Numerous Killings Planned and Directed by Wang Jianxun*.

9. *Facts Relating to the Case of the Numerous Killings Planned and Directed by Wang Jianxun*, Appendix no. 2.

10. Chinese Communist Party, Shanglin County Party Committee Report, no. 24, 1984, *Investigative Report on the Handling of the Case of the Ruthless Killing by Lan Denggang during the "Cultural Revolution" (Guanyu Lan Denggang zai "wenge" zhong sharen shouduan canren de diaocha baogao ji chuli yijian de baogao)* and "File on the Lan Denggang Case During the Cultural Revolution" *(Lan Denggang wenge wenti dang'an)*, pp. 9–183.

11. CCP Shanglin County Party Committee Report, no. 11, 1984, *Investigative Report on the Planned Killings by Wu Futian, Mo Rongguang, and Pan Shengcai on "August 16" in Sanli District (Guanyu dui "wenge" zhong sanli qu "ba yiliu" shijian Wu Futian, Mo Rongguang, Pan Shengcai cehua zhihui chengpi sharen de diaocha baogao)*.

12. Zhongshan County, *Criminal Records (Weiji anjuan)*, pp. 85–420, "Materials on the Case of Pan Hongzhi" *(Pan Hongzhi wenti cailiao)*.

13. Notes from my Inquiry of Pan Xiangfu *(Xunwen Pan Xiangfu bilu)*. Also, see Zhongshan County, *Criminal Records (Weiji anjuan)* nos. 83–97: "The Case of Zou Qinghua and Pan Huixing, Mother and Son, Being Buried Alive and Ancillary Materials on the Case of Pan Huoxing" *(Zou Qinghua, Pan Huixing muzi bei huomai yi'an sheji Pan Huoxing wenti pangzheng cailiao)*, pp. 7–8.

14. Zhongshan County, *Criminal Records (Weiji anjuan)*, nos. 81–150, and "Letter by the CCP Zhongshan County Leadership Group on 'Handling Leftover Cases' Submitted to Superior Authorities for Approval of Arrests and Detentions" *(Zhonggong Zhongshan xianwei "chuyi" lingdao xiaozu tiqing pizhun daibushu)*, no. 83.

15. Ibid.

16. Ibid.

17. Ibid.

18. Party Reform Office, Qinzhou Prefecture Party Committee Publication Bureau, *Annals of the "Cultural Revolution" in Qinzhou Prefecture (Qinzhou diqu "Wenge" dashijian)*, July 10, 1987, p. 41.

19. Zhongshan County, Public Security Bureau, Preliminary Case Files, "The Murder Case of Yi Wansheng (Deng Jifang Victim)," *Investigative Report on the Disembowelment of Deng Jifang (Guanyu Deng Jifang de podu diaocha baogao)*, p. 4.

20. Ibid., pp. 6–7.

21. *Joint Report on One Year's Work of "Handling Leftover Cases" (Yinian lai de "chuyi" gongzuo qingkuang zonghe baogao).*

22. Mengshan County, *Criminal Records (Weiji anjuan).*

23. *Annals of the "Cultural Revolution" in Qinzhou Prefecture,* p. 41.

24. Ibid.

25. Recorded Interview, May 19, 1986, and Notes of a Conversation with Yu Yaqin, Member of the Leading Group of the Guangxi Autonomous Region Party Reform Office for Handling and Verifying Leftover Cases.

2

Some Leftover Cases

THE SLAUGHTER AT WUXUAN

Once I had conducted interviews in the four counties around Nanning and Wuzhou prefecture, I felt that I had an overall picture of the forest. Now it was time to look at some trees. I put all my energy into learning about the battle that had occurred in Wuxuan County.

On June 10, I arrived at Liuzhou city. I first contacted the Party Reform Office of the Liuzhou Prefecture Committee, which is the prescribed approach. Long Huang, deputy chief of the CCP Organization Department, provided me with some information on the issue of Party reform. He also recommended me to Deputy Director Men Qijun, who was more familiar with local affairs than he was.

Six thousand people had died in this prefecture during the Cultural Revolution, whereas the fatalities in Rongan County totaled over 1,000, and those in Wuxuan, over 500. (Punishment: Only nineteen people were arrested in Rongan, thirty people in Wuxuan; none were executed, and not even the relatively light sentence of suspended capital punishment was meted out.)

As for incidents of cannibalism: These occurred in some counties, the most outstanding being those in Wuxuan. Whenever victims were forced to parade through the streets while being subjected to criticism, the old women would turn out holding their vegetable baskets. Immediately after a victim was killed, the crowd would rush forward. Those at the forefront would get the good pieces of flesh. Those who came later divided up the bones among themselves. Quite a few cadres had engaged in cannibalism. For instance, Wang Wenliu (female), who had been promoted to the position of vice chairman of the Wuxuan Revolutionary Committee after engaging in several revolutionary actions, became something of a specialist in consuming male reproductive organs. When this particular perversion was reported to the CCP Central Committee by a Central Committee work team, the elite Party bureaucrats were flabbergasted. During May and

June 1983, the Central Committee telephoned the county on several occasions to inquire why this murderer had not been purged from the Party. Subsequent investigation revealed that her cannibalism had been limited to the flesh and the liver, so she was allowed to remain in the Party, with a reduction in rank from cadre to common staff worker *(yiban zhigong)*.

The practice of cutting out a person's organs and frying them in oil while the victim was still alive was surely the cruelest cannibalistic offense of all. Deputy Director Men told me that during the movement to handle leftover cases, a document had been issued by the Guangxi Autonomous Region that ordered those who had engaged in cannibalism be purged from the Party. All such documents were withdrawn, however, out of fear that such evidence, if leaked to Hong Kong journalists, would reveal just how widespread cannibalism had been in Guangxi. (It had been so severe that the autonomous region had to make special regulations to deal with such cases.) Of course, the orders in the documents to purge those involved in cannibalism were carried out nonetheless.

Up to this point, thanks to the cooperation I had received from various local Party organizations, my interviews had gone smoothly. Now, however, beginning with the Political and Legal Committee of Liuzhou Prefecture, officials started to shut doors in my face. On the morning of June 12, following an appointment with Lan so-and-so of the Political and Legal Committee, I went to have a look in the local archives. Another cadre, a certain Li, came out and, after examining my letter of introduction, refused me entry, even as he promised to provide all the detailed information I would need. All I got, though, was a bunch of irrelevant material, without any elaboration beyond the basics, on the cases I had inquired about. Lan so-and-so sat in on our discussion, nervously recording what we said and projecting a frightening appearance. I got the message. The admonition was clear, if unspoken: I would be held accountable for every word I wrote. By recording our conversation on paper they were also covering themselves. I came up with a vicious little form of retaliation. I intentionally interrupted Li during the course of his descriptions, thus breaking his sentences into fragments; then, when it was my turn to ask questions, I refused to pause during any of my sentences, producing a nonstop stream of words. Not surprisingly, Mr. Lan found it nearly impossible to record our dialogue. At times, he simply put down his pen and stared blankly in front of him. I realized then that the game of obstruction had begun. Go ahead, I thought to myself. You will never block me. Coldly, but politely, I interrupted Li's mumbling and said goodbye. The time had come to end the charade, since both sides by now were quite worn out.

The obstruction that I had all along expected, but which had not yet shown its ugly head, now began in earnest. Yet these attempts only ex-

cited and energized me further. Strolling along the streets, I glanced aim-
lessly at the store windows, at the signs of various work units, at the colorful skirts of the girls, and at the stands where bananas and oranges
were being sold. When confronting official obstruction, turn to the locals—that was my plan. But in Liuzhou, how could I ever hope to find
any willing local personnel? Just go ahead and take a chance, I told myself. There must be a way! I beat a path to the *Willow Catkin (Liuxu)*, a literary journal put out under the aegis of the Liuzhou Literary Association.
I sat down with the editor-in-chief and chatted over cigarettes for quite a
spell. To my surprise, I learned that *Willow Catkin* was a very popular
journal, with a circulation of 1.5 million and revenue per issue of 20,000
yuan ($4,500). Only after listening to the editor in chief boast about all his
moneymaking schemes did I discover that I had turned to the wrong person, and so I left. Next, I sought help from two other journals, *One Hundred Flowers (Baihua)* and *Harp and Sword (Qinjian)*, both of which were
put out by the prefecture cultural bureau. As soon as I entered the
premises and introduced myself, my fellow writers quickly invited me to
sit down and offered me a drink. It turned out that they were very familiar with my works and were extremely interested in the Shanxi writers'
group, of which I was a part. At last I have found the right place, I told
myself. After describing the purpose of my trip and the bureaucratic obstruction I was confronting, I asked my newfound friends for help. This
time my celebrity, which generally I find boring, worked on my behalf.
My new acquaintances tried their best to provide me with what they
knew and, what was even more useful, they introduced me to two important people who were familiar with the cases.

Wang Zujian was a former Party secretary of the Chinese Language Department of Nanning Teachers' College and is now retired. Once he had
served in the underground Party organization in Beijing. After the liberation of southern China in 1950, he had been sent to Guangxi, where he
had once served as Party secretary of Laibin County. Later, he was accused of being a rightist and was sent down to a labor camp in Wuxuan.
During the Cultural Revolution, he risked life and limb in order to convey
to the Central Committee considerable information regarding the cannibalism in Guangxi. Indeed, when it came to revealing the cannibalism of
Wuxuan, he was one of the heroes.*

Yu Guangmei was a veteran guerrilla fighter. He originally came from a
big landlord's family in Tongling, Wuxuan. After stealing guns from his
home, he betrayed his family and joined the revolution. He spent his
whole life in Wuxuan and was well-versed in the history of the county.

---

*Wang Zujian's heroic role in revealing cannibalism in Wuxuan County is described in fur-
ther detail later.

Knowledgeable and possessed of a good memory, he was another hero who ended up reporting on the cannibalism in Wuxuan. He also submitted many petitions to the central authorities on behalf of family members of victims. He now works at the office of the county historical annals.

With these courageous heroes, unafraid as they were of death, I could forget my worries about obtaining sufficient information. Nonetheless, I still anticipated possible difficulties in my adventurous sojourn ahead. I had learned from many sources that there had been numerous ups and downs in the handling of leftover cases. Some killers had threatened to take revenge; fearful of such a possibility, people were generally afraid to speak up. Thanks to a variety of personal and psychological factors, cadres at various levels were deeply suspicious and quite hesitant to handle these matters. Consequently, many of the killers were given light punishments, to say the least. My new friends also warned me: Be careful in Wuxuan. Wuxuan, Wuxuan, dire, but mysterious! Before even setting foot in the place, I had detected its frightening atmosphere. Yet, if one refuses to enter the cave, how can one ever hope to capture the tiger? Upon my departure, my friends warned me again: The Wuxuan cannibals particularly enjoy munching on the fat out-of-towners! I replied, please come and collect my body if I get in trouble. Everyone laughed.

I boarded a bus at 2:45 on June 13 and arrived at Wuxuan town at 5:00 that afternoon (Photo 2.1).

PHOTO 2.1   The center of Wuxuan town where the frenzy of cannibalism occurred in 1968.

Heeding my friends' warning and making use of my letter of introduction, I first went to settle in at the county guest house (Photo 2.2). In the evening, an acquaintance brought over Yu Guangmei. Short hair, barefoot, dressed in shorts and a shirt, Yu appeared to be full of energy. His face radiated a red glow. Not unexpectedly, he looked just like a veteran guerrilla fighter, rather than a senile person fearing the approach of death. Not only had his outspoken behavior prevented him from moving up the ranks, it had also made him the frequent target of one political movement after another. He had not married until he reached the age of fifty. Yet life at the lowest levels during the previous decade or so must have provided him with his easy-going personality and taut muscles, for he certainly did not look his age. We hit it off as soon as we started talking. In that one evening, Yu described the major cases from the Cultural Revolution in

PHOTO 2.2   The author, Zheng Yi, standing on the balcony of the Wuxuan County guest house in 1986.

Wuxuan, along with the political complexities of the local cadre situation. Yu told me that he had heard that I was coming: The announcements over the telephone to the autonomous region and the prefectures had made people quite apprehensive, and the atmosphere was tense. The "locals" had already put their heads together and decided how to confabulate the recent past. They had been fighting against the "cannibals" for years, but had yet to uncover their identities. And so, of course, the organizers and participants in the cannibal frenzy had yet to be punished. Thus, it seemed that despite my formal position as a certified journalist, nevertheless I would have to engage in some "underground activities" in order to get at the truth. I was quite moved by the just struggles of Wang Zujian and Yu Guangmei. That evening I made the following entry in my journal: "I should follow in the footsteps of these heroes and march forth to fulfill my responsibility! If I remain silent and withhold information, I will then be committing the same shameless crimes as those criminals!"

The next morning, I stopped in at the county Party Reform Office to see its deputy director, a certain Liu. I submitted my letter of introduction to the clerk, but got no response. All I could do was read the newspapers in his office. Later, I was informed that Liu had gone out to do "preparatory work." The plan was in force, and Liu never showed his face; instead, he sent word that he wanted me to talk to four people—Messrs. Li, Yang, Zhou, and He—who had been involved in handling leftover cases. Our talk was just as arduous as my discussion with the Political and Legal Committee at Liuzhou. Because they had been directed to talk to me, they had no choice. Talk they must. But they were hesitant indeed and mumbled about this and that, all the while exuding great anxiety. Before they said anything, they would look at each other in a sort of "After you, Alphonse" dumb show. It seemed as though they had fully worked out in advance how to handle me. Meanwhile, I tried to pass along hints to prompt them about information that I had already obtained. It was like working a millet grinder, which only moves if you push it. Eventually they did provide some information about several important cases. But in the end, when I asked for details, they said they had no idea of the whereabouts of the relevant files, and then they suggested that perhaps the materials could be found at the local public security organs, since after all public security personnel were the ones who had first embarked on the investigation of these cases.

Fortunately, I had done a little investigating on my own first and knew that the files were surely in this group's hands, and not somewhere else. They were cornered, and merely mumbled something like, "Can't find, can't find." Essaying such a base lie made it impossible for them to look me straight in the eyes. They looked down at the floor, glanced at newspapers, scribbled notes on some pieces of paper, or lit up cigarettes. During this embarrassing interlude, I just sat there, smoking one cigarette after another, while waiting to see how this situation was going to play itself out. Eventually, Deputy Director Liu emerged from his inner sanctum. I asked him where the relevant files were, but he tried to manipulate the situation his way. "Let's just *talk* about it. There's no need to *read* the materials." Indeed, Wuxuan was not easy to handle. I rose and made my way to the door. Liu stuck to my side like flypaper. First he tried to explain that the materials had already been sealed. Then, when that approach fell flat, he suggested that they were nowhere to be found. Later, he told me the materials were not that detailed and that I should rely on discussions for my information. At that point, I got angry and pointed out where the files could probably be found. When he realized that there was no more room for prevarication, Deputy Director Liu simply snorted, "Just forget about reading the files."

Why? What were they afraid of? Were they personally related to any of the criminals? What were they trying to cover up?

I bumped into Yu Guangmei at the gate of the guest house at lunchtime and briefly described my experience to him. Yu smiled and said that had been exactly how the locals expected an official visitor to behave. Yu also said that the locals had done considerable work in anticipation of my visit. This advance preparation included arrangements made for my personal safety with the cooperation of the local Public Security Bureau. I was very moved. Surely whoever dared to come to this place could not be a coward. Wuxuan, I will not leave without getting what I want!

I then started to employ local channels. I went to Wuxuan Teachers' College (formerly Wuxuan Middle School) and took some pictures there of the site where the victims' hearts and livers had been cut out (Photo 2.3). The person who let me in was extremely nervous and warned me repeatedly to keep it a secret and not to involve him in the matter, for the revenge by the local officials could be very vicious. That evening, Yu Guangmei came over and asked me whether that afternoon I had gone to Wuxuan Teachers' College and thence to the mouth of the river. He proceeded at that point to describe all the details of my trip. I was followed? This made me very nervous. But my anxiety was soon relieved. A person who had been persecuted at the college had seen me in the vicinity and had recognized my non-Guangxi dialect. He had immediately reported it to Yu Guangmei and suggested that Yu let people know that the central authorities had sent down someone to investigate. It seems that the situation between the two sides was quite tense, a veritable fuse dangling next to the front burner of a stove. Yu therefore warned me to be extremely careful and not to reveal my identity. To be sure, the murderers would not welcome me, but the masses, who were waiting impatiently to petition the higher-ups, would surround me and put me in an indefensible situation.

PHOTO 2.3   The campus of Wuxuan Middle School where human flesh was
cooked on makeshift barbecue pits.

In terms of punishing the murderers, I had neither the power nor the
authority.

Blocked as I was from examining the dead materials, I decided to seek
out the live people. I was told that many of the comrades who had been
stymied in handling leftover cases had been stopped in their investigation by local resistance forces. I decided to talk to these comrades, so I
went to the county Political and Legal Affairs Office and asked Director
Liu Yejin and Secretary in Chief Liao Huaiqiang to give me permission to
talk to four people. That's how my interviews of those small potatoes got
an official stamp of approval.

Du Tiansheng was a former director of the local Public Security Bureau
and director of the Party office charged with handling leftover cases.
Owing to the directness of his work style and his steadfast opposition to
people who had committed serious crimes during the Cultural Revolution, Du had always been unpopular. He was eventually invited to step
down and left with the empty rank of Party secretary of the bureau. He
suffered from heart disease, but the bureau refused to reimburse him for
his medical expenses. "Even the criminals were provided with medical
care and medicine," he fumed. He was full of anger. But he had to remain
levelheaded, for he knew that the very thing his rivals wanted was for
him to die of anger. This was a man with an extremely clear mind. In line
with my request, he provided an overall picture of developments in Wu-

xuan during the Cultural Revolution. Thanks to his cooperation, combined with materials from other sources, I obtained the following.

During the Cultural Revolution, there were eight communes, one township, 107 brigades, and six residential districts in the county. (Ninety brigades had been involved in beating people to death.) Among the population of 221,786, 524 people were either beaten or persecuted to death.

In terms of carrying out the Cultural Revolution, Wuxuan was one step, or half a year, behind the rest of the country. On January 13, 1967, the executive director of the county declared over the local loudspeaker system the formal inauguration of the Cultural Revolution in Wuxuan. Immediately thereafter, the director of the procuracy and the director of the grain bureau were paraded through the streets and subjected to mass criticism. Many capitalist roaders were also subject to criticism. But there were no cases at that time of people being beaten up or traumatized. On January 26, the Rebel Faction (*zaofanpai*)* declared their victory in seizing political power. Up to that point, Wuxuan had been basically in lockstep with the national progression of the Cultural Revolution.

In June 1967, however, a great change took place: a split between supporters and opponents of Wei Guoqing, the top leader in the Guangxi Autonomous Region. The masses were now divided into two "confrontational" opposition groups that were constantly engaged in mutual assaults. By September 1967, local production came to a halt and all local transportation was paralyzed.

In January 1968, the two factions fought it out with guns. On January 8, the Big Faction launched an attack on the base of the Small Faction—but without success. On February 1, the Small Faction launched a counterattack against the Big Faction—also without success.

Then, on February 28, 1968, the slaughter began. Dozens of middle-school students who belonged to the Small Faction went to the county office of the armed police, where they requested that the authorities address the problem of food and safety. That act, the Big Faction claimed, was really an attempt to seize guns. (Du Tiansheng, the former county Party secretary and former director of the committee for handling leftover cases, explained that this argument followed a certain line of logic. "Once the factions were set up, naturally the conflict was aggravated. Lacking material things, they both then started demanding supplies. When such requests were not fulfilled, they started stealing, looting, and arresting each other.")[1] Later, some militiamen were ordered to go to the school, where they surrounded the students and attempted to blow them up with

---

*The most radical of the nationally organized Red Guard groups heavily composed of children of the five black elements.

dynamite. But that was stopped by the local armed police. Then the militiamen started shooting and ordered the students to surrender. When the students came out, two people, Li Guowei and Zhang Jun, were promptly killed. The armed police did not investigate the matter. That was the first case of killing.

On March 5, 1968, the Small Faction arrested a certain Mr. Tan, director of the war office of the Big Faction. The Big Faction then mobilized its militia to surround the base of the Small Faction. Under such great military pressure, the Small Faction had no choice but to release their prisoner.

On April 15, 1968, the county Revolutionary Committee was formally established. But, soon thereafter, Wuxuan entered the bloodiest and most chaotic stage of its civil strife. Two representatives from each faction served on the Revolutionary Committee, but the leading cadre was from the Big Faction. Not surprisingly, the Small Faction pinned the committee with the somewhat roundabout label of "factional," and the Big Faction members made it their aim to eliminate the Small Faction altogether in order to "protect the newborn red power." The conflict was swiftly aggravated.[2] A large-scale armed conflict that would mark the turning point of the Cultural Revolution in Wuxuan was finally ready to explode.

On May 4, 1968, the Small Faction arrested Liang so-and-so and others, all of whom were minor leaders in the Big Faction. In addition to arresting these people, the Small Faction also seized some money, about 120 yuan. Citing this act, the Big Faction mobilized its militia in great numbers, entered the town, and encircled all of the bases of the Small Faction. On May 10, a certain Liao, who was a minor leader of the Big Faction from Dong Township, was shot to death by some stray bullets during an inspection of the battlefield. The Big Faction immediately launched a large-scale attack, employing the method of combining big sticks of dynamite with small ones (a tactic adopted from the Vietnam War said to be more vicious than the use of artillery). With the high ground of the Small Faction under severe attack, the armed conflict reached its climax.

In the midst of all of this (1 P.M. on May 10), the county Revolutionary Committee held an emergency meeting where they discussed how to handle the situation. Wen Longjun, director of the county Armed Police Office and director of the Revolutionary Committee, asserted, "Based on the current situation, our method to gain control is either to launch an attack or to try to use persuasion." Backed up by the "red regime," the situation became more and more serious.[3]

On May 11, the Big Faction issued an order to launch a general assault. In all of the battle districts (five of which belonged to the Big Faction) attacks were launched against various targets. The Big Faction adopted the strategy of blowing open each avenue and street to tighten the encirclement.

On May 12, the militia from Liuzhou in the north and from Gui County in the south came to the support of the Big Faction, thereby tightening the encirclement from both these directions. The Small Faction, isolated and lacking arms and food, was destined for defeat. That night, bombs were falling everywhere. Unable to hold on, the Small Faction decided to break out of the encirclement. Crossing the Qian River, the Small Faction was attacked in the dark. The survivors discarded their boats and escaped. The Big Faction deployed a tugboat with large search lights to look for survivors. By the next morning, the battle was over and it was time to sweep the battlefield clean. At a site known as "Shirenping," thirty people were arrested. Altogether ninety-seven people were killed (most of those killed had first been taken captive). This was the highest death toll in any armed battle in Guangxi, except for the one in Nanning city.

The general commander of the Small Faction, Zhou Weian, had himself broken through the encirclement on the morning of May 13 but he was arrested at Darong in Xinlu District and killed on the spot. When Pan Maolan, deputy commander of the Big Faction, received this information, he traveled to Darong to get Zhou's head and feet, which he hung on a tree as a way to "mourn the two martyrs," Mr. Qin and Mr. Huang, who had died during the battles.

Mourning with the head and feet of the enemy sounds cruel, but compared with what happened thereafter at the "mass funeral gathering," it was nothing. Just before that gathering took place, a frenzied crowd had grabbed two students, Qin Shouzhen and Wei Guorong, who were attempting to escape as their live sacrifice. The students were bound together under two big trees next to the road in front of the Luxin Grain Bureau Office and were "cut open alive as a live sacrifice. The custodian of the Luxin Central School cut open the victims with a knife used to slaughter pigs and then, holding the knife in his right hand, he cut out their hearts and livers. It was said that later the human flesh was taken back to the county seat, boiled, and shared among everyone, together with some pork."[4]

As a symbol of the defeat of the Small Faction and of the victory of the Big Faction, Zhou Weian's head, legs, and feet were to be fully utilized. The next evening, at the mass funeral gathering, Chen so-and-so of the Big Faction brought Zhou's head and one leg back to the county seat. Entering Zhou's house, Chen threw Zhou's head and leg at his widow, Wei Shulan, and mocking her said, "Are these Zhou Weian's head and leg?" "Yes." "Then, why don't you sleep with him holding his head and leg?" The next day, Zhou's head and leg were hung in public at the street market[5] (Photo 2.4). Throughout the day, thousands upon thousands of Wuxuan people witnessed the following scene:

PHOTO 2.4   The village center where the head and leg of Zhou Weian, commander in chief of the "April 22 faction," were displayed.

Zhou Weian's head was hung from a tree along with a bone from his leg. The eyes were still open on his face, and the flesh on the bottom of his feet had not yet been cut off. Zhou's widow, along with another woman, Liu Yuhong, were brought to the site and forced to kneel down. "Is this your husband?" "Yes." "Is he evil?" "Yes." "Is this bone your husband's?" "Yes." The two women were then ordered to take off their blouses in front of the large crowd, but they refused to do so. Someone then tore their blouses off them from behind and, poking both of them with a knife, commented, "Too thin. Not worth eating." The women ground their teeth to ease their pain. Their bodies were drenched in sweat. Both women were related to members of the Small Faction. At the time, Zhou Weian's widow was seven or eight months pregnant.[6]

Before the Zhou family tragedy came to an end, the ruthless attacks continued. This time, it was Zhou's four brothers' turn. They had indeed committed previous "crimes." In 1960, the year of great hunger following the disastrous Great Leap Forward, Zhou Shian had stolen a sack of rice, for which he had been sentenced to seven years in prison. Returning home from a labor camp in the middle of the Cultural Revolution, he was designated a member of the twenty-three categories. Along with the fact that his younger brother, Zhou Weian, headed the Small Faction, it would serve him right to be killed. The local barber, by the name of Liao Huoshou, pulled Zhou Shian from his home and pushed him into the street, yelling, "This is Zhou Weian's elder brother. He wants to take revenge for his brother!" Then he pushed Zhou to the ground, and the masses began beating him. When Zhou was all but beaten half to death, he was pushed into the local public sewage pit *(maotou)*.

> Wang Chunrong cut out his heart and liver with a five-inch knife. Once his chest was cut open, and Wang had one foot firmly planted on his body, the heart and the liver could be cut right out. Others followed suit. In no time, the body was completely stripped of flesh. The bones were dumped in the middle of the river. It was said that when Wang Chunrong was doing his cutting, Zhou was still alive and had let out a bloodcurdling scream[7] (Photo 2.5).

The succinctly prepared documents and evidence were merely an abstraction, accurately depicting the criminal acts but ignoring the tragic atmosphere and the people's emotions (Photo 2.6). I am not a judge. I wanted to search for the fervor and cold tears that transcended the words and had been ruthlessly washed away by time. After walking down a paved road, I came to a gravel street where I found the eldest brother of the Zhou family, Zhou Jiean, a man with a pair of frightened eyes and a lifeless, swollen face. Once I presented him with my name card and the letter of introduction to verify my identity, Zhou's eyes lost their trace of fear and instead generated a pale glow. Apart from the frustration and lifelessness, there was nothing else on his swollen face. His discourse was also deadly gray, not even enhanced by the scant feelings that revealed themselves in the documents. Where was his brotherly love? Where was all the hardship and pain? Not even the trace of a tear appeared in the corner of his eyes, nor any trembling at the sides of his mouth. It seemed that all normal human feelings had vanished. I almost could have vouched that he would have followed along as silent as a lamb if he had been ordered to submit to "mass dictatorship." After depicting the death of his two brothers without emotion, he then described what happened after they died.

> During the period of handling leftover cases, in accordance with the regulations, I was given 220 yuan to cover the burial and other expenses for each brother. So, two brothers for a total of 440 yuan. Oddly, I was still given the burial money even though their flesh had been eaten and their bones had been lost. Zhou Weian's three daughters and the one son and one daughter

PHOTO 2.5   The site where Zhou Shian, elder brother of Zhou Weian, let out a bloodcurdling scream as his chest was cut open while still alive.

of Zhou Shian are now grown-up, but none have been allocated jobs. Neither of my brothers were state workers, but they had made a living by moving materials for the labor team organized by the township at that time. Right now, it is very hard for us to live. Many of the neighbors on the street have eaten our flesh, but they still resent us. We cannot even raise our heads. No one has ever come over to apologize. They still hate us. You came by today. If you were someone from Wuxuan, I would not dare to utter a word. Our house was also confiscated. It had been given to us during the Land Reform of 1952. But in 1968 we were chased into the countryside and the house was taken away. To this day, there has been no resolution. Since our house used to belong to a landlord, we were never given a lease. So now they are claiming that we were never allocated the house. In the old society before 1949,

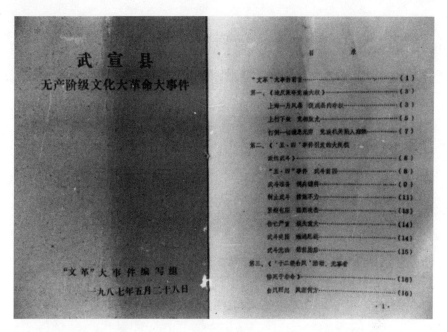

PHOTO 2.6 *Annals of the Cultural Revolution in Wuxuan,* which contains a special chapter devoted to recording the frenzy of cannibalism in the county.

our father was a worker and I became a worker at the age of fourteen or fifteen. During the Land Reform period, I was given the class label of poor and lower-middle peasant. Our hometown is in Guangdong Province but we came here years ago during the war to escape the Japanese.

Of course, 220 yuan was quite scanty, less than the cost of a pig. However, if 220 yuan had been given for every victim, the country's finances might have collapsed. Naturally, it sounds incredibly ruthless that people still resented those families whose members had been eaten. But if the leaders had not encouraged us to engage in cannibalism, would we not have had to carry this evil label?—Zhou Jiean's contagiousness reduced some of my anger as I gained some forgiveness and understanding. After getting his permission, I took his picture and then left, feeling rather embarrassed.

Traversing the narrow streets, I arrived at the old main avenue and immediately felt more at ease. It was not much of an avenue—two trucks could not drive along it at the same time—but there was a pleasant summer breeze. The small intersection between the two avenues was named Western Gate. The barber, who had never been punished, had dragged Zhou Shian to that intersection and had lynched him. The half-dead victim was then pulled to the dock area along the gravel street that now was right under my feet. The western street was not very long, so I quickly reached the end. Connected to the western street was a wide, stone flat area that led directly to the Qian River where a dozen or so boats were moored at the dock. That was perhaps the West Gate dock mentioned in the files that I had read. The long, wide stone stairs reminded me of one particular detail: Zhou Shian was pulled down to the dock. I could imagine the sound made by his head hitting the stone steps. Scattered traces of blood led to the riverbank.

As I looked down from above, the Qian River was dark green, reflecting the green mountains and trees in the background. The only difference was that as the river flowed the mountain and trees remained immobile. In the middle of the stream, there was a small island sitting quietly like a spear cavalierly thrown into the water. After inquiring of two passersby, I learned that this island was known as Shirenping (Photo 2.7). All of a sudden, I realized that it was the very place repeatedly mentioned in the files as the place where the captives had been killed. Yes! In the darkness, the general commander, Zhou Weian, had followed that road to escape. Retreating as they returned fire, his group had passed the wide, stone flat

PHOTO 2.7   The site known as Shirenping, where during large-scale factional fighting as many as thirty members of the Small Faction were captured and killed.

stairs and had withdrawn to the riverbank, thinking that once they crossed the Qian River, everything would be okay. They never expected that waiting on the other side were the militia. The river became a death trap . . . the machine guns . . . the search lights from the boats . . . the blood floating in the river. The next morning, forty middle-school Red Guards had been found hiding between the rocks on the island. With the exception of one student who was taken away, all were summarily killed on the spot.

How was it that both brothers had approached death by following the same path? Movers, manual laborers, workers in the lowest social stratum—both brothers had in their time shed unlimited sweat in their work of hauling boats. During the shameless hunger caused by human folly during the Great Leap Forward,* the elder brother had stolen a bag of rice from the state to express his right to live and to announce a vague spirit of resistance. Years later, the grown-up younger brother was respected as a youth leader who voiced discontent toward the existing order and resisted social inequalities with sword and fire. Perhaps the reason why this road had brought them both to death was because it had once also led them both to resistance.

I was walking along the road to the side of the river. I could not find any of the spent bullets from that time and I could not even be sure where on the riverbank Zhou Shian's blood had been shed. Suddenly, my eyes spotted something bright: It must be the sharp five-inch knife reflecting its fatal glint in the sunlight that resembled a long sigh and a mysterious embrace before the death of its victims. As I stood on the bank and let the soft river breeze bathe me, the ever-flowing river enlightened me with the crystal clarity of its water and its solemnity. The theft of a bag of rice led to a sentence of seven years in prison, and the victim was later killed and cannibalized, whereas the murderer Wang Chunrong, who had engaged in frenzied killing and feasted on human flesh while enjoying his liquor, was sentenced to only thirteen years in prison. I arrived at an insight. The former was an unsubmissive slave, whereas the latter, although also a slave, was one who had attempted to win his master's favor with the blood of one of his own kind. The master resented unsubmissive slaves, only enjoying the ruthless ones. The legal system in China was by no means a goddess, rather merely a second-class housekeeper. Following the change of color on the master's face and always abiding by the mas-

---

*A reference to projects promoted by Chairman Mao Zedong, such as the backyard steel furnaces and the close planting of rice seedlings, which led to massive economic disasters and famine in the early 1960s.

ter's expression, she dutifully convicted unsubmissive slaves who tried to destroy the master.

BLOW THE TYPHOON

The great battle was undoubtedly an important event in Wuxuan during the Cultural Revolution. It had led to the deaths of nearly one hundred people. Furthermore, along with the "meeting to blow the typhoon," it pushed creative cannibalism to its climax. The hearts, livers, and flesh of four victims had been devoured. The battle at Wuxuan, though, cannot be explained as the key to the outbreak of cannibalism or as its basic cause. In general, I thought I would agree with the view of the Wuxuan locals who believed that the spread of cannibalism was directly related to the cruelty in the battle and to the frenetic revenge mentality it aroused. However, after analyzing most of the cases of cannibalism, I realized that they had nothing to do with the battle or with its reverberations. Besides, many of the incidents of cannibalism cited later had occurred before, not after, the battle. On May 4, 1968, for instance, Qin Hejia and Qin Zhunzhuo were subjected to criticism at Guzuo brigade, Tongwan District. After being shot, the victims were cannibalized.[8] And on May 14, 1968, a passerby from a bordering county (Chen Guoyong from Lu village, Phoenix Township, Shilong District, Gui County) met his death at the hands of Wei Changmeng, Wei Changgan, Wei Binghuan, and eleven people from Huama town, Tongwan District. Chen was then cannibalized by his killers. "First, Wei Changmeng chopped the victim to death with a sword. Wei Changgan then cut out the victim's liver and brought it back to the village to serve as an evening snack. More than twenty people sitting at two tables joined in."[9] The case occurred at the same time as the Wuxuan battle, but was not related to it.

I personally think that the outbreak of cannibalism at Wuxuan originated from the movement to "blow a twelve-degree typhoon of class struggle" that was promoted by the local regime of the Party, government, and military. On March 19, 1968, the first death by lynching occurred in Wuxuan County. Far from being punished, the perpetrators were actually egged on. Thus, the killing quickly spread. At the end of May and in early June a meeting to blow the typhoon was called by the head of the Liuzhou Military Sub-District, with Wen Longjun, concurrently the chairman of the Revolutionary Committee and director of the local Armed Police, and Pan Zhenkuai, the chairman of the Sanli District Revolutionary Committee, in attendance. On June 14, the Wuxuan Revolutionary Committee held a conference of high-level cadres from the county, district, brigade, and production-team levels. At this gathering, the spirit of the meeting to blow the typhoon was passed on. At the meeting, Wen Longjun advocated that "a twelve-degree typhoon must be blown in the struggle against our enemies. The method employed should be: to mobilize adequately the masses, rely on the masses to carry out the dictatorship, and hand the policies to the masses. In engaging in class struggle, our hands must not be soft."[10] Thus, Wuxuan, which had been quiet for a month after the great battle, all of a sudden turned into a killing field and a hell of human-flesh consumption!

The killer barber who had cut open Zhou Shian while he was still alive and the injured veteran volunteer soldier, Wang Chunrong, had both been quiet for a full month. During the meeting to blow the typhoon, called by the county Revolutionary Committee, the barber was reborn. Picking up his five-inch knife, he resumed his special contributions to the great enterprise of the proletarian dictatorship. At a criticism rally held in Wuxuan, victim Tan Qiou was beaten to death and Huang Zhenji was beaten into a coma. When Huang Zhenji regained consciousness, he begged Wang Chunrong, "Comrade, forgive me!" Bearing the shiny five-inch knife, Wang Chunrong administered a twist of sarcasm. "We'll forgive you for five minutes," he said. Wang then ordered cadres to drag the victim ahead to the Zhongshan pavilion where, once again, Wang took out his five-inch knife and this time stepped on the victim's chest and cut out his heart and liver. The victim immediately died.[11]

The number of victims killed on that day was not recorded in the official documents that I examined. However, according to a list put together by Du Tiansheng and Chen Shaoquan from the office to handle leftover cases and the Public Security Bureau, "five victims were cannibalized on that day" and several people were killed by Wang Chunrong. This information, however, is not officially documented. But Chen Shaoquan and others from the Party Reform Office verified that when Wang "saw different colors on one liver"—"a spotted liver"—he threw it away and started to cut out the liver of the second victim.

Wang Chunrong was also the one who, on market day in Wuxuan—it was June 17—cut into the body of a temporary worker by the name of Tang Zhanhui (or maybe it was Tang Canwei) right in front of the local Xinhua (New China) bookstore during a street criticism parade *(youdou)*. "After Wang Chunrong extracted the liver with his five-inch knife, the crowd pushed forward to get at the flesh. Tang immediately died."[12] Full of excitement and pleasure, Wang Chunrong took the human liver to the pork counter of the food factory, added some spices, and boiled it together with some pork to serve as an appetizer with an aperitif.[13] At that time, it was indeed a situation in which a dry street flowed with men. The people were as numerous as the hills and the seas. It was a great revolutionary festival! In the sea of humanity that had gathered, a former director of the county court, who had already been purged from his position, protested to an army official standing beside him, "Such indiscriminate killing cannot go on. It's time you did something about it." The army officer was Yan Yulin, deputy director of the county Armed Police and deputy director of the county Revolutionary Committee. This patriarchical official, who now held almighty power, simply replied, "This is a matter for the masses. It is out of our control."[14] Naturally, he was not about to stand up and stop the killing and the cannibalism, since he had just come from the meeting to blow the typhoon, where he had occupied a seat on the podium. Now here he was in the crowd, present at the very kind of rally held at the site of the killing that the conference had championed. Hidden among the crowd, he was secretly overjoyed by the immediate results conjured up by the wizard.

In this way, under the general direction of the great helmsman, carried out by an army officer, and acted upon by a veteran soldier with great enthusiasm, an unprecedented and ruthless bloodbath in the history of human civilization came to a climax on the land of Wuxuan. From that point on, all "abstinence from cannibalism" ended. At every criticism rally, the victims were put to death. And each death was garnished with cannibalism. Compared with the big feast of cutting and eating live victims, earlier executions by lynching now seemed generous and merciful.

On the next day, June 18, at least three "feasts of human flesh" were held in three different places. What speedy action!

On June 18, 1968, a rally to criticize Chen Hanning, Chen Chengyun, Chen Chujian, and others was held at Taicun brigade in Sanli District. All the commune members were present as armed militiamen surrounded the site. An atmosphere of killing permeated the entire rally. Director of the Brigade Cultural Revolution Group, Chen Siting, led the rally. After "Chen Dangming, who was in charge of personnel dossiers, read out loud the so-called 'criminal evidence,' it was the masses' turn to give speeches. These lasted for about half an hour. Then Chen Siting called out, 'What should we do with these people?' The masses replied in one voice, 'Kill!' The militiamen immediately pushed the victims from the rally site. Chen Zhiming first chopped the victims to death with a large flat sword and then cut out their livers." Later, the villagers all shared in the boiled human flesh.[15]

On the same day, there was a criticism parade down Huangmao Street. The victim was Zhang Boxun, a man of poor and lower-middle peasant background, who held to Small Faction views, and who was a teacher at the Duzhai village elementary school, Shangwen brigade. Because he could tell that his death was fast approaching, Zhang rushed off in great fear, took the wrong road, and jumped into the river. "Militiaman Guo Lixiang pulled the victim to the riverbank and cut out his heart and liver with a five-inch knife. Guo shared the flesh with Wei Bingliang, who served it up in a casserole. In no time, the victim's skin and intestines were taken away. The consumption of the victims' flesh took place everywhere. The Huangmao Food and Supply Store was among the most prominent sites of cannibalism. A large pot, eight feet in diameter, was used to boil the victims, and then about ten people had a feast. The killers also forced others to eat from the pot. Two female workers, who had problems with their 'political standpoint,' were forced to join in. In those two units, 80 percent of the people participated in cannibalism. The masses referred to it as a 'feast of human flesh'."[16]

The ruthlessness of these acts was also recorded in official documents:

> After Zhang Boxun was beaten to death, his liver and flesh quickly disappeared, so that only his small and large intestines were left. The ruthless killer held up one end of Zhang's intestines while the other end dragged on the ground, and with manic glee he yelled, "take a look at Zhang Boxun's intestines! How fat they are!" Then, the killer took the intestines home to boil and eat.[17]

On the same day, "feasts of human flesh" were also held at Wuxuan Middle School. What follows is a simple record in an official document. "On June 18, 1968, after Wu Shufang of Wuxuan Middle School was beaten to death, his liver was baked for medicinal purposes. It is unfathomable that such a ruthless killing could have taken place in a school devoted to cultivating and educating people."[18]

It so happened that before I arrived at Wuxuan Middle School I was able to gain a good understanding of this case; otherwise, the ruthless actions that had occurred there would have remained buried in the simple descriptions in the official record.

In Liuzhou, pursuing a clue provided by Men Qijun, deputy director of the Party Reform Office, I located Wu Hongtai (Photo 2.8), supervisor of the prefecture Education Bureau. Wu was director of the group handling leftover cases, and he had once served as principal of Wuxuan Middle School; therefore, Wu had a lot to say regarding events in Wuxuan during the Cultural Revolution. I was warmly received by Wu, who originally came from Hubei Province and had been a student in the first graduating class of the Teachers' College of Zhongyuan University (now known as Zhongyuan Teachers' University). Wu had come to Guangxi in 1950 to work in support of the border regions, and thus he was among the first group of educated Communist Party cadres to serve there. Viewed in silhouette, he looked a bit like Zhang Chunqiao, leader of the radical faction

PHOTO 2.8   Former Wuxuan Middle School principal, Wu Hongtai (right), an
eyewitness to the killing of the teacher Wu Shufang.

in Shanghai.* Wu was an extremely kindhearted and straightforward person and a typical teacher. On the second day of my visit, he described some
of the major cases of cannibalism that had occurred in Wuxuan. On the
first day, he focused primarily on the outbreak of cannibalism at Wuxuan
Middle School. He had been a participant in the drama and was later designated to clear up the cases associated with these events, and so the memory of everything was still fresh in his mind.

Wuxuan Middle School was quite famous. It had been chosen in 1960
to participate in a national conference in Beijing. During the Cultural Revolution, Wu was its principal, and naturally he was branded as a capitalist roader. After he witnessed numerous ruthless killings, Wu felt his life
no longer had any meaning. So one day he quietly walked out of the
school and down to the river. He took off his shoes and neatly placed
them side by side on the riverbank. Just at the very moment he was about
to jump into the turbulent water, however, an old shepherd happened to

---

*Zhang Chunqiao, a member of the "Gang of Four" headed by Mao Zedong's wife, Jiang
Qing, was tried in 1980 for "crimes" during the Cultural Revolution and given a death sentence, which was later reduced to life imprisonment.

shuffle by with his flock of sheep. The old man's dim-sighted yet sage old eyes could perceive what was about to happen. So as the shepherd passed, Wu heard him mutter, "soon it will all be over." The old man's simple, yet wise, observation inspired Wu to abandon his idea of suicide. And so Wu put his shoes back on and returned to the evil world.

Although he had refused to commit suicide, Wu's heavy heart still was not relieved of its burdens. On the evening of June 18, 1968, a certain Wu Shufang, head of the school's Chinese Department and a teacher of geography, was beaten to death. At that time, this case was nothing out of the ordinary, because with the exception of five teachers of poor and lower-middle peasant background whose lives were spared, all of Wu's colleagues had been criticized. What happened next remains beyond belief, however, to this day. A group of armed students ordered Wu Hongtai and three other "old gang" teachers to drag the victim's body down to the riverbank. When they got it there, a few armed students stood behind them, while a larger number of students looked on from a distance:

Fu Bingkun, a sophomore, took a big knife and stabbed the side of the victim's body, saying, "Spy. Cut out his heart and liver to serve as an evening snack! Don't sever his intestines. If you do, I'll throw you into the river! We only want his heart and liver." The four of us squatted on the ground, and someone threw the knife over to me. I [Wu Hongtai] was trembling so much I was unable to do the cutting. Cursing, the students handed the knife to Qin Chineng. In the torchlight, Qin ground his teeth, forcing himself to complete the job. (Given the bloody atmosphere of that time, if Qin had not succeeded, the students would have done us all in.) After he had cut out the heart and liver, along with the flesh from the victim's thigh, the crowd took off. They carried some hunks of the flesh away in plastic bags, other hunks they simply slung on their rifles as the blood was still dripping down. They threw the victim's bones into the river (Photo 2.9).

Wu Shufang's flesh was cooked in three places: One was the school kitchen. Chef Zhang, a female, had let the group in. When the flesh was cooked, seven or eight students consumed it together. The second place was the dormitory room of Huang Yuanlou, deputy director of the school's Revolutionary Committee. There, the flesh was cooked in a casserole. Huang refused to join the dinner party, though four other students did partake of Wu Shufang's flesh. The third cookery was under the roof of the hallway, outside classrooms number 31 and 32.

As a result of subsequent investigations, the deputy director of the school Revolutionary Committee was expelled from the Party. His only comment was, "Cannibalism? It was the landlord's flesh! The spy's flesh!" He also said that he had offered some to the Party secretary, who now absolutely refuses to admit it. Yet at the time, they were proud of their cannibalism.

After I had arrived at Wuxuan, the first place I visited, in order to show my sympathy, was the middle school. Cannibalism is rare, but students

PHOTO 2.9   The site on the Qian River where the Wuxuan Middle School
teacher, Wu Shufang, was killed and his flesh consumed.

eating teachers is rarer still. I took some pictures of the large kitchen, its
big stove, and the hallway outside the number 31 and 32 classrooms
(Photo 2.10). I also took some pictures in a corner of the campus under
some lemon trees where the holy fire had been lit. Try to imagine the
scene. It's deep night. Thick smoke rises from the chimney into the sky.
Outside the classrooms, students cluster around the campus in groups of
three and four, perhaps even five, as light from the cooking fire glows on
their young faces. Is this a bonfire for some festival? It's a human-flesh
barbecue! Bubbling away in their big and small pots, big and small
casseroles, and in the "barbecue pot" sitting on top of two bricks and one
tile is their teachers' flesh! (Photo 2.11). Respect for teachers, teaching and
educating children, moral civilization? The twelve-degree typhoon of
class struggle has blown all that Confucian crap away! "Save our children," the great thinker Lu Xun called out at the beginning of the century.
For in this China with a "four-thousand-year history of cannibalism"
adults had joined in cannibalism, but never children. In its time, Lu Xun's
short story "Diary of a Madman," which depicted China's cannibalistic
culture, was merely a symbolic literary work, but unfortunately it had

PHOTO 2.10 Outside classrooms 31 and 32, teachers were killed and their flesh was barbecued.

been realized under the great and glorious banner of socialism.* In the midst of the most glorious idea of mankind, children have started to engage in cannibalism. Children are the hope and the future of the nation. When they are taught to consume their own species, surely the nation has lost all hope and its future.

If teachers could be cannibalized, then so could students. Three days later (June 21), a rally to criticize a Wuxuan Middle School student named Zhang Fuchen was held at Shangjin village in Dongxiang District. Not long after the rally began, a twelve-year-old child named Huang XX beat Zhang unconscious with a club.

> The killer then poked his chest with a five-inch knife. Zhang's body twisted in pain. Huang Peigang then picked up a stone and smashed his victim in the head and then stabbed his victim two or three times. Next, Zhang was cut open from his chest to his navel. His heart and liver were removed. Then,

*Lu Xun, *Diary of a Madman and Other Stories,* tran. William A. Lyell (Honolulu, HI: University of Hawaii Press, 1990).

PHOTO 2.11   The Wuxuan Middle School canteen where the flesh of victims was boiled and consumed.

> Liao Shuiguang cut off the victim's penis. The crowd rushed forward to cut at the flesh.[19]

The documents do not record whether the human flesh was consumed. But at least one point can be confirmed: Since the villagers usually possessed stoves, the cookery must have been handled in a more civilized fashion than that of the students, with their pots and barbecue pits.

Two days later, at Xiangsi village, an incident categorized as "ruthless" in the official documents occurred. It was a case of "wiping out an entire family," in which the husband was killed and his wife raped. According to Du Tiansheng, this act originated with a group of people headed by a production team leader who was implicated in the rape of the wife of a certain Mr. Li. Fearful that other members of the Li family might exact their revenge sometime in the future, the criminals declared that all of Mr. Li's uncles and nephews were four elements and that they had concealed guns in their houses. "If we don't kill them, they'll kill us," the criminals declared. They also decided to cross the Qian River and kill everyone on the other side who had the surname Li. The entire production team was armed with clubs and ordered into action. Those who refused to go would not receive any work points for their labor in the fields.

Around noon on June 23, 1968, the villagers from Xiangsi appeared in the center of the market.

> Li Binglong and others bound the feet of Li Mingqi, Li Zhongyuan, and Li Zhongjie (that way, the victims could only drag their feet). The victims were also bound around their necks and hands by a rope. Arriving at a vegetable stand, the three brothers of the Li family were ordered to kneel down. Li Binglong read off the so-called evil evidence, screaming: "Should they be killed?" The crowd replied, "Kill!" Li Binglong and others then immediately beat the three victims to death. Thereafter they dragged the dead bodies to the riverbank. Huang Qihuan and others cut open the Li brothers to get at their livers and their reproductive organs, and then they discarded their bodies by the riverside. (Huang Qihuan was a clerk at the county People's Bank. He took one liver back to the bank. Yu Yuerong baked and wrapped it in nice paper. Many people shared it as medicine.[20])

The murderers had achieved their victory and they returned to the village. That same night, the gang raped Li XX's widow, confiscated the furnishings of the entire house, and robbed it of everything else. They also slaughtered Li's pigs, cut down Li's vegetable patch, and feasted on these spoils to celebrate the great victory of the "masses' dictatorship." With all the males dead, and the widow subsequently remarried, there is no longer anyone from that village by the surname of Li (黎).[21]

It should be noted, of course, that the cases documented in this book are merely the most prominent examples of what occurred in Wuxuan. They by no means exhaust the list, nor are they even a major part of it. Considering the many incidents of cannibalism that followed within only ten days of the meeting to blow the typhoon of class struggle, the cannibalism at Wuxuan had reached the extremities of terror and insanity. Human blood is not water; therefore, no matter what convincing theories were used to justify these cruel acts, the murderers undoubtedly suffered psychologically when they confronted their own ruthlessness and cruelty. Finally, the murderers themselves could take it no longer. On June 26, the county Revolutionary Committee conducted a study of the ongoing class struggle. After the directors of the various district revolutionary committees and armed police offices had reported their progress (120 dead), they demanded an end to "street criticism parades." In the face of such weakness, Sun Ruizhang, political commissar of the county Armed Police Office and the first deputy director of the county Revolutionary Committee, expressed his discontent. "Don't be so chickenhearted! What is there to be afraid of? Without such an effort we cannot defeat the class enemies and inspire the willpower of the people. Fear not. We must press on."[22] Following this meeting, cannibalism in Wuxuan reached its climax.

The following is a typical case of how a victim was carved up while still alive.

In July 1968, Gan Kexing of the seventh production team of Dawei brigade, Tongwan District, organized a rally to criticize Gan Dazuo. They pulled their victim to the side of the field and ordered him to kneel down. Gan Yewei struck the victim on the head with a stick, but he did not die. Gan Zuyang then tore off the victim's pants to cut off his penis. "Let me die first, then you can cut it," the victim implored. Gan Zuyang showed little concern and continued to cut. The victim struggled and screamed his lungs out. Gan Weixing and his group then cut off the flesh from his thigh. Gan Deliu cut out the liver. The rest of the crowd pushed forward and stripped the body of its flesh.[23]

The following is a typical feast of human flesh.

On July 10, 1968, a criticism rally was held in front of the Shangjiang town hall, Sanli District. During the ensuing chaos, Liao Tianlong, Liao Jinfu, Zhong Zhenquan, and Zhong Shaoting were beaten to death. Their bodies were stripped of flesh, which was taken back to the front of the brigade office to be boiled in two big pots. Twenty or thirty people participated in the cannibalism. Right out in the open, they boiled human flesh in front of the local government offices. The impact of this was extremely deleterious.[24]

That day was also a day of bustling crowds rushing to strip the victims of their flesh. Someone saw an old gray-haired woman struggle to grab a piece of a human liver. How gleeful she was. On her way back home it began to drizzle. The raindrops, together with the blood from the liver, stained the road she was walking along.[25]

I also heard about another bizarre case involving escape. Chen Jinwu, a rightist and a teacher at the Sanli Middle School, was locked in an empty room on campus so that the next day he could be killed. But he was dramatically saved by the wife of the school chef, Yang Guanghuai (also a rightist). In great fear, Chen hurried to escape. Unfortunately, a "cross" had been shaved on top of his head to mark him as a rightist. Thus imprisoned within the proletarian net, he had no way out. Indeed, as he tried to leave Wuxuan, Chen was arrested by the militiamen. The director of the commune armed police, Xie Kainian, a veteran army officer who had fought in the Korean War, originally from Liling, Hunan Province, interrogated the prisoner. Chen had heard that Xie was from Hunan, and claiming that he, too, was from Hunan, he kneeled down and begged Xie to let him go. This aroused Xie's sympathy, and he came up with an idea: They would falsely claim that Chen was a "parachute spy" and put him in the county military prison. This was a brainstorm because by the time this case of a parachute spy was cleared in the courts, the wave of cannibalism had subsided. Chen was thus saved.[26] Surely Chen would forever remember his rescue by Xie with special gratitude, especially since it was rare indeed that a victim escaped being cannibalized during those times.

Perhaps the reader still can recall the woman Party member Wang Wenliu [p. 63], who was famous for purportedly consuming male organs, and whose case had aroused great indignation all the way up to the very top of the Party hierarchy. In the official documents I discovered the following information.

During the frenetic wave of indiscriminate killing and cannibalism, three social dregs with the surname Diao from Dongxiang Township, who held fast to Small Faction views, managed to escape up Hema Mountain. On July 10, 1968, Qin Zhonglan, director of the district armed police, ordered three squads of militiamen from his own district and another squad from nearby Jinggang Township to go up to the mountain to "defeat the bandits" and to arrest the renegades. Diao Qishan managed to escape, but Diao Qiyao fell into a cave and died. Diao Qitang was shot to death. "Luo Xianquan cut out Diao Qitang's heart and liver. He then loaded the remains of the body in a basket. When Luo Xianquan returned to the canteen of the district office, Diao Qitang's flesh was boiled and eaten. Squad member Wang Wenliu also brought two pieces of flesh back home to her mother.[27] Once Wang had achieved renown for consuming human flesh, she got one promotion after another. Eventually, she became the vice director of the Wuxuan Revolutionary Committee.

When contemporary liberal intellectuals in China dispute the vicious means by which military men get promoted, they generally use the phrase "painting the crown with human blood." However, that phrase cannot be used to describe Wang Wenliu and her ilk, for they earned their promotions not only by helping to kill people, but also by eating them.

Messrs. Li, Yang, Zhou, and He from the county Party Reform Office once tried to defend Wang. They argued that "while there were incidents in which people consumed reproductive organs, Wang could not have taken part in them because she was only eighteen years old at the time and unmarried. It is true that she consumed human flesh and for that reason she has been removed from the Party and has lost her position as a cadre. She is now a worker at the county reservoir." Should I believe the words of these officials, who refused me access to the official documents? Or should I believe the rumors? Emotionally, I cannot force myself to believe the officials. To conclude merely that it sounds impossible that Wang could have dined on reproductive organs is indefensible.

Various cases of cannibalism have been confirmed only after thorough investigations. The very few unconfirmed rumors are indicative of the absurdity and cruelty of cannibalism. For instance, when I first arrived in Guangxi, I heard one rumor that fat out-of-towners are drugged with a special medicine, cut open alive, and shown the entire procedure with a mirror. Initially, it seemed like a rumor, but, later, I unintentionally discovered that this "rumor" consisted of figurative language that actually informed the prototype for the brutal cases of cannibalism that were taking place. *Drugging the victim with a special medicine* was simply an exaggerated way of describing how a victim was knocked unconscious with a stick or a stone. The word *fat* simply indicated someone who wasn't appallingly lean, as most victims were, beset by poverty. (In a certain school, a decision had to be made about whether the Party secretary or the principal should be selected for execution. After some discussion, it was decided to kill the fat one—the principal. Thus, the Party secretary survived.[28] However, if a blow the typhoon campaign breaks out in China again sometime in the future, the "thin ones" will be victimized first, because all the fat people have already been done in.) *Out-of-towners* refers to the innocent. (Case in point: Wei Changmeng and others from Huama village killed a passerby named Chen Guoyong for no reason whatsoever and served him up as a "midnight snack.") *Cut open alive* simply implied fierce and brutal acts, of which there were numerous cases. Finally, *show the victim the entire procedure with a mirror* also refers to the ruthless and cruel torture. (For instance, forcing Zhou Weian's widow to kiss her dead husband's face and caress his decapitated head.)

We know that in ancient times rumors supplied a basis for comparing, symbolizing, and exaggerating the existing reality. Modern rumors are no different, especially in modern totalitarian countries where the masses can only spread important news via rumors and the social grapevine. Legends, stories, and rumors are a form of special rights enjoyed by the masses who are deprived of the rights of news, publication, speech, assembly, association, and so on. Not only can rumors not be suppressed, they can be spread extremely rapidly, poisoning the entire province and the entire country. This itself shows that rumors are believable. Not only do the masses believe in and spread the rumors, they also perfect and exaggerate them so that they reach a state of qualitative abstraction. Isn't the aforementioned seemingly absurd rumor the most representative generalization of the killing and cannibalism that took place in Guangxi? I myself think so. In a country where rumors and lies permeate official broadcasts, newspapers, movies, television, conferences, advertisements, official communiqués, university podiums, courts, economic reports, "internal reference materials restricted to top leaders," and bids for projects, only two things are believable: the date of publication and the rumors reported in the newspapers. Up to this point, I had not believed the "rumored account" of Wang Wenliu's consumption of the male organ, especially when I realized that she was only eighteen years of age, a time of life when I myself had been full of fascist frenzy. I also realized that she was being singled out for blame through the rumor mill because she was a woman. I even hesitated to describe her case in this book. But the pen in my hands was very heavy. I was deeply aware—I will be held accountable in both the legal and the moral realms for every word added or deleted in this book. Thus, I have only one choice, and that is to write down verbatim everything I have learned. I can only hope that in reading the rest of this book, the reader will develop some sort of understanding or sympathy toward people like Wang Wenliu, and others.

CHILDREN OF THE HOLOCAUST

The interviews in Guangxi overloaded me both physically and psychologically. I suffered from a kind of unprecedented fatigue, and I had reason to suspect that this had helped to bring on a recurrence of hepatitis. Before heading to Liuzhou, I'd had a physical checkup in the local hospital. Fortunately, everything seemed to be all right. Nonetheless, as the days passed by, my fatigue increased. Whenever I was out interviewing, I had to drag myself around, sometimes in a state of dizziness. As soon as I returned to my room, I fell into bed and only began to feel restored after smoking four or five cigarettes. Once, while walking a distance of only 2 li [1 kilometer], I had to stop several times to rest. One morning, after working only until 10 A.M., I had to stop. I returned to my room and took to my bed. I had no choice except to check into the hospital. So I made my way to the local Chinese traditional county hospital. When I realized that only one young doctor was on call, I returned home and waited until later when I could find an older doctor. But the young doctor had decided to follow me, and I felt obliged to let him examine me. As he took my pulse, he asked me if I was a journalist. That made me suspicious, and I asked him why he wanted to know. He replied that in the past few days he had observed me wandering back and forth in the county, looking for people. That's the kind of small town it was. The young doctor's diagnosis indicated that I was overly nervous and intense, and that I was suffering from a fever. In addition to some liquid herbal medicine, he prescribed his own personal "allocation" of Chinese ginseng. I still felt weak after taking the medicine, but I kept exhorting myself: There are only a few times in life when you have a chance to struggle to win a major victory. One of those times is now! During one interview with the Party secretary of the county public health bureau, I found it difficult even to hold my pen and I had to ask him to show me around the hospital instead. When my blood pressure was checked, it was very low. And I was sure that it had been even lower before I began to take the medicine. Even the ginseng didn't help much. But I could not slow down the tempo. My time at Wuxuan was worth more than gold!

Just then I received news through an unofficial channel that the decision that had prevented me from reading official documents had not come from Wuxuan County. Even before my arrival, Wuxuan had received on

June 12 a telephone instruction from a certain level with the warning, "Do not allow Zheng Yi to read the documents." What had happened? Once again I became tense. Where had the telephone call come from? The unofficial channel said that it was unclear. The telephone instruction had also advised that I be kept in the dark about the contents of the documents. What was going on here? Everything seemed so damned mysterious. I mulled things over and concluded that the powers that be had issued this warning against revealing the contents to me because they feared that I would use the material against them. Therefore, I reasoned, if they were afraid of me, why should I be afraid of them? I told a friend in Nanning to search for the source of the telephone instruction and, at the same time, I accelerated my interview schedule.

I visited the county court to examine its documents. The last time I had paid it a visit, I had been informed that the comrade in charge of the files was out of town. At the time, I had taken their word for it. Now, a few days later, they gave me the same excuse. However, now that I knew about the telephone instruction on the twelfth, I realized that the court had also slammed its gates in my face. It was just that their refusal happened to be more indirect. I thereupon changed tactics, deciding to interview people at the county Party Reform Office instead and to ask for a vehicle to drive into the village so that I could interview the children of the school principal, Huang Youmian, and to visit Tongling Middle School, where the victim had been cannibalized. At the office, I was kept waiting for the entire morning. At nearly 10 A.M., Deputy Director Liu came out to apologize. He explained that all the vehicles were being used. I realized, as I observed his disingenuous expression, that he was trying to deceive me. With great wrath, I stood up and left without turning back. From that point on, I had no further contact with the Wuxuan County officials.

Over and over, one line kept repeating in my head: You cannot hide it from me! By preventing me from reading the documents and then refusing to provide a vehicle, the Wuxuan regime was certainly doing its damndest to obstruct my research. My personal inclination would have been to hike up the mountains to the village immediately, but I was simply too weak to do that. However, the cannibalization of principal Huang was a big case not only in the district, but also throughout the entire county. I needed to collect as much material as possible on that case, and the only way to do that was to interview Huang's surviving children. Fortunately, they were still in Wuxuan.

I had learned that Huang's daughter was now a shop assistant at the county department store. That afternoon, I went there and pretended that I was doing some shopping. I happened to glance at one of the many graceful and quiet girls and was inspired to ask a middle-aged shop attendant with a kindhearted face, "Is Huang Qiling here?" She pointed to the same girl who had attracted my interest and I approached the counter where she stood. I nodded at a tape-recorder battery and beckoned her to come over. Then, as she was getting the battery, I showed her my press credentials and told her in a low voice that I had come to interview her about her father's case. This brought a sparkle to her eye, but it immediately disappeared. I asked her to come and see me and to bring along her elder brother. She cast her eyes downward without saying a word. As I left the store, I thought to myself, Does everybody here know the drill for underground activities?

That evening the brother and sister came to my quarters. What lovely children they were. When they sat down, they wouldn't touch the drinks or cigarettes I offered them. They just stared at me out of crystal clear eyes that betrayed a polite, but undoubtedly slightly suspicious, cast of mind. Once again, I produced my credentials and I asked the brother, Huang Qiwen, to verify them. Then I explained the purpose of my interview in great detail. The brother and sister gradually began to comprehend and slowly unburdened themselves of the cruelest nightmare of their young lives.

At the time of the slaughter, Huang Qiwen was ten years old and Qiling was five. After their father had been subjected to criticism, the whole family had been rusticated to the Huang's home village of Lizhi. In keeping with the methods of the national model (Dazhai agricultural brigade in Shanxi Province) of allocating work points—politics first!—their mother only received half a point for her labors. They lacked both food and clothing and were deprived of shelter. The entire family ended up living in their uncle's cow pen. Their father was also returned to the village and imprisoned there for more than a month. Every day, Huang Qiwen delivered food to his father. As far as his son could tell, the elder Huang was never really free of injury. When an old injury healed, he would suffer a new one. One time he had been beaten so badly that he could not even walk. With the tension in the area mounting, the father feared that he could no longer escape death, and so he asked his wife to turn for help to an old friend from the underground Party who resided in a neighboring village and who was also a member of the Revolutionary Committee. The father had intended to ask the friend to come and rescue him. Yet when his wife returned, all she could do was look down without saying a word. Even the children now felt the approach of an unrestrained terror. Soon the father was taken back to Tongling School. Then the news arrived: Their father had been beaten to death and cannibalized. The children well understood their mother's tears. They also learned to understand the cruelty of this world. The brigade would not allow the son, Qiwen, to attend school, and so he became a cowherd for four years.

But he was never able to enjoy the usual pleasures of a cowherd. Instead, he felt that he was being constantly pursued by the shadow of death.

The beating of children by other children is equally cruel. One day, a group of children ordered Qiwen to wash some old slogans off a wall. A cadre's child led the group of thirty or forty children who beat Qiwen up with a cattle whip. His mother rushed over, frantically breaking up the crowd and rescuing Qiwen, whose entire body was covered with blood. If his mother had not arrived, Qiwen surely would have been beaten to death. His uncle now realized that the family was in constant danger, so Qiwen was spirited off to Hainan Island off China's southeastern coast, where he became an all-purpose manual worker. He was fourteen when he arrived in Hainan and he did not return to Wuxuan until ten years later, when his father was posthumously rehabilitated.

Qiling also quietly recalled her childhood. She was only five when she first experienced the terrors of life. At that age, she herself was beaten. In school, whenever other children saw her, they would yell, "Traitor's daughter! Traitor's daughter!" Then the other children would chase after her and beat her, taking away her school bag, tearing up her books, and breaking her pencils. The fear of having no place to hide caused young Qiling's heart to beat uncontrollably. Each time Qiling cried, begging her mother not to send her to school, her mother sent her anyway crying. In those days, students had to engage in manual work. Qiling's heart couldn't take it. Every time she asked for leave, the teacher would scold her for faking illness. When in tears, she held the heavy tools, her heart would pump wildly.

At particularly sorrowful points in her account, the young woman would look down in silence. Her brother kept trying secretly to wipe away his tears. The experience of ten years of manual labor in exile had given the brother a rugged look. His elevated eye bones, the powerful jaw, and the muscular body, all suggested a youthfulness that could never perish. But his tears filled me with sorrow. Although my heart had become numb, I nevertheless somewhat cruelly continued to question the two young and anguished souls.

Qiling mentioned that many of her father's students who had taken part in cannibalizing him had since risen to positions of power. But they still deeply resented both her and her brother. At first, I thought I had heard Qiling incorrectly, due to the unfamiliarity of her local accent. When the brother translated her version into Mandarin and verified what I had heard, I was utterly astonished. According to the laws of common human feeling, murderers should feel guilty. Perhaps the soil of Wuxuan only generated hatred. Why was there such deep hatred in this land? How was it that even the act of devouring a victim's flesh did not remove the hatred?

8 P.M., July 1, 1968: Huang Jiaping (vice principal of the school) was subjected to criticism in the assembly hall of Tongling Middle School. Xie Dong, deputy director of the school's Revolutionary Preparatory Committee, chaired the meeting and gave a speech. After the criticism meeting had gone on for about an hour, Xie adjourned the meeting. Student Qin Tingduo and four other students brandishing rods escorted the victim out of the building. When they arrived in front of the post office, Qin gave the order, "Beat him." He then struck the first blow, and the other students quickly followed, beating the victim to death.

At a place to educate and cultivate people, veteran cadre Huang Jiaping's flesh was stripped away, so that only the bones were left. That very thought was scary.

Comrade Huang had joined the Communist revolution before 1949 and he had once served as a political commissar in the first company of the first battalion of the 121st division and commander of the 18th battalion of the central Guangxi division of the People's Liberation Army.

After Guangxi was liberated, he had become the deputy director of Cangwu County, and vice principal of Tongling Middle School. It was a great pity that he was ruthlessly killed during the Cultural Revolution.[29]

Wu Hongtai, the former director of the Liuzhou group for handling leftover cases, and a former principal of Wuxuan Middle School, provided me with a detailed description of the case.

Huang Jiaping was from a big landlord background. He joined the guerrillas in 1947 and was appointed to his position in Cangwu County soon after liberation. During the 1945 Guangxi underground Party rectification, he was accused of traitorous tendencies, purged from the Party, and demoted to the level of a common cadre. After a year-long investigation, just prior to the Cultural Revolution, he was finally rehabilitated and his Party membership and cadre rank were restored. He also became vice principal of Tongling Middle School. During the Cultural Revolution, however, he was once again accused of being a traitor and he was cruelly criticized. Prior to the criticism meeting held on July 1, 1968, the leaders of the local Red Guard faction decided to get rid of him. On his way back to prison, he was beaten to death. At 8 A.M. the next day, his body was publicly displayed in the school playground. After reading aloud Mao Zedong's "most sublime instruction," the crowd dispersed.

It was soon after this that the spontaneous stripping of flesh became very popular on campus. Who was the first one to do the cutting? A variety of accusations have been put forth. Most people accused the female student Qin Liufang, who was in love with the elder son of the victim. According to this version, in order to make it quite clear where she stood in relation to the Huang family, she took the lead with the first slice. But in her own account, Qin Liufang accused another student, named Huang Peinong, of launching the butchery.

Huang was the first one to get the liver. A female student named Chen Xiangjiao claimed that human flesh could help cure her mother's illness. I [Qin Liufang] then helped her slice off some flesh. Later, I helped an old man and another female student make cuts. I thought that Huang was a traitor and deserved to be cut up. I and Gan Piaoying and others saw Huang Peinong grab the liver, wash it in the pond, and then take it into the kitchen. Many other students also returned to the canteen carrying their own fair share of flesh.[30]

Qin Liufang was not the only eyewitness to see Huang Peinong washing the liver in the pond. Another witness, Qin Shixin, said, "I saw Huang Peinong carve the character for *person (ren;* 人 *)* on the stomach of vice principal Huang. Then he stepped on his chest and cut out the liver. He brought it back, boiled it, and ate it."[31]

Unfortunately, none of these accounts could prove that Qin Liufang was not the first one to do the cutting. It should be pointed out here that Qin Liufang was her former name. She changed it to Zhang Jifeng (which means "to inherit the legacy of Lei Feng"). Perhaps she respected the Communist soldier Lei Feng so much that she even made her name reflect his special revolutionary spirit.* It would not be hard to imagine that a person who was good at following the trends to serve her personal needs was more than willing to gain personal fame by cutting her own future father-in-law's flesh.

However, what defies the imagination is that even some of the teachers actively engaged in cannibalism. Huang Dahuang from the General Affairs Office of Tongling Middle School recounted the following:

On July 2 at noon I saw Xie Xiongbiao (a biology teacher) boiling human flesh in his room. Xie himself did the cutting and boiling. When it was done, Shi Zhende (a Chinese-language teacher) reached in and grabbed a piece out of the pot with his bare hand. The flesh had been boiled, together with some pork. Other people also joined in, while sipping white liquor. Liang Kaixu also cooked some human flesh on a tiled stove.[32]

But teacher Xie turned it right around and later accused one of his own students of coercing him to join the feast. "There was a student named Qin Songyu," he claimed, "who held up a piece of dried human flesh the size of a finger and said to me: 'You have chronic stomach problems. This is good for you!' Thus, I also ate the flesh."[33]

Couldn't the teachers have come up with better reasons? The biology teacher certainly could have argued that the experience offered a chance to prove that human flesh does not qualitatively differ from other mam-

---

*Adopting such "patriotic" names was a very common practice in China during the 1950s and 1960s.

mals. The Chinese-language teacher might have claimed it to be an experiment in revolutionary romanticism! But knowledge cannot be used to excuse cruelty. There are numerous cases of Chinese intellectual martyrs who sacrificed their lives for the emperor, but rare are those who were willing to devote their lives to humanism. Perhaps history can forgive the stupid and the timid, but it will never forgive the intellectual accomplices who joined the feasts of human flesh.

On that day, Tongling Middle School was preoccupied with cooking: Human flesh was boiled in the canteen, in the teachers' dorm, in the female students' dorm; human flesh was barbecued on campus under the roof of the classrooms. Two bricks with a tile overlay—"homemade barbecue stoves"—were seen everywhere. Even the always-restrained official documents did not understate this case. "Around the canteen, under the roof of the dorms, scenes of barbecuing human flesh could be seen everywhere on July 2 at Tongling Middle School," they reported. "Blood stains were all about. Even the air was thick with the smell of blood. The odor of burning flesh was everywhere. It was indeed scary and astonishing."[34]

The four "black gang" teachers who were unfit to eat the flesh of a class enemy and could only collect the bodies carefully placed principal Huang's bones in a bamboo basket and then "buried his bones just like the bones of an ox." Zhou Shurong, one of the four and a teacher of Chinese literature, recorded the following.

> At 5 P.M. on July 2, the four of us were ordered to bury the body, which had been left next to the public toilet outside the playground. Two bamboo baskets were used to hold the bones. The victim's head was beaten black, the flesh on the thighs, legs, and hands had all been cut off, and so had the heart, reproductive organs, and liver. The chest was empty and the intestines had spilled out onto the ground. Holding back our tears, but fearful of what might happen, the four of us put the body into the basket.[35]

The information provided by Wu Hongtai and by official and unofficial sources in Wuxuan gave me a general idea about Huang's tragic death. Nevertheless, I wanted to learn more about it, especially what unforgivable act this veteran guerrilla fighter had committed to deserve the accusation of being a traitor. I also wanted to know what kind of person he had been.

During a second visit to Guangxi, Bei Ming and I paid a special visit to Huang's second son, Huang Qizhou, who was then working at the Guangxi People's Education Publishing House. The son took us to his home, offered us a seat, and poured us tea, all in silence. I began by describing my first trip to Wuxuan two years before, when I had visited his brother and sister. In that way, I hoped to gain his trust and assistance. As I spoke, the son seemed to be engrossed in eating sunflower seeds and carefully piling up the shells. Sunflower seeds are small and hard, so are not easy to eat. But Huang Qizhou was very attentive and appeared to be rather skillful. Obviously, he was cool-headed and composed. After he had maintained his silence for some time, he offered to come to our hotel later that evening to talk. We figured his painstaking caution reflected a reluctance to talk about the tragedy at home in front of his poor mother, who would be reminded of her deep sorrow. Moreover, as a professional editor who knew about the shameless status of literature and journalism in China, he probably did not believe that talking about the case would be of any significance.

That evening, he arrived punctually on his motor bike and immediately questioned the value of talking about his father. Every year since 1972, he told us, he had written to the CCP Central Committee requesting a thorough investigation of his father's case. His petitions were like heavy stones. They sank into the abyss of the ocean without causing even a ripple on the surface. But in response to further entreaties by Bei Ming and me, he decided to open up about his father and himself.

My father was a man full of idealism. At the beginning of the Anti-Japanese War in 1938–1939, he was involved in the CCP-led reduction-of-rent-and-interest campaign aimed at winning support among the peasantry. Out of sympathy for the poor peasants, my father very actively engaged in the struggle in his hometown against the landlords in reducing rent and interest. In 1945, along with two other people, my father established a "masses bookstore" in his hometown of Tongwanxu. The bookstore was affiliated with the *New China Daily* in Chongqing, Sichuan, and was openly revolutionary. Since he was the oldest, he was chosen as the head of the bookstore. One of the other two people, Gan Desong, was an underground Party member. Besides propagandizing revolution, my father also organized the locals to attack stranded Japanese soldiers. In 1947, during the Civil War with the Nationalists, Liao Lianyuan returned from Yan'an and organized the "Mid-Autumn Uprising" in Gui County. My father led a contingent from Tongwanxu to join in the uprising. Wei Huaye was the head, my father was the deputy head, and the underground Party member from the bookstore served as the commander. They called themselves the "Dakai platoon."

At this time, the ratio of our forces to the enemy's in Guangxi favored the latter. After a few months, the Dakai platoon was separated, and my father led a small contingent to hide out in a large cave not far from his home village of Lizhi, where dozens of local people with large quantities of grain were hiding along with their pigs and cattle. There were two separate entrances to the cave that were used to blunt an attack from Kuomintang forces. After two days of assault, the KMT soldiers used dynamite to blow up the entrance. My father was in the cave protecting the locals. He had killed one enemy soldier. In the ensuing attack, the KMT employed pepper gas and nearly blinded my father. Most of the guerrillas managed to escape into the surrounding woods through the back entrance. However, seventy or eighty locals were left behind, all of whom were captured by the KMT, along with my father who, with the other guerrillas, had stayed behind and was forced to surrender his rifle.

In his autobiography, my father wrote that to have saved the lives of those people was something worth dying for. The locals had also implored him: "Just give them the guns. We can provide 20 percent of our grain to the guerrillas in exchange for the guns and prepare a counterattack. The vice commander, along with many others, has already given up his gun, so why don't you?"[36]

As we listened to this account, I asked, "Was the so-called traitor issue related to the surrendering of guns?" "Yes," he replied. "Alas! Now we understand it," I told him. "That means your father should have ignored the masses and fought to the bitter end at the price of having all the locals killed!" Originally, I'd thought for sure that Huang Jiaping must have engaged in some slightly traitorous acts. Otherwise, he would not have been persecuted all his life. To my great surprise, the truth was just the opposite of the accusation. Huang had been a man with adamant revolutionary beliefs and humanism. Out of love, he had protected the masses. But twenty years later, he was ruthlessly persecuted to death by the offspring of those people whom he had protected. Had this been a historical misunderstanding? That is the logic of violent revolution. Of course, had Huang ignored the lives of the locals and fought to the bitter end, he would have then become a hero and a revolutionary martyr. The Party would have been proud of him and the masses would have forgotten their sacrifice. Every April 5, the offspring of those innocent people would have gone to his tomb with flowers to show respect and to chant a song of remembrance. My heart was deeply agitated. Huang Jiaping was not only a victim of a false accusation, he had also sacrificed himself in the name of humanism. Whether or not he understood this from a theoretical point of view, this can be the only historical judgment.

Huang Qizhou silently waited for my angry outburst to end and then, in a calm and deliberate way, he continued with his account.

After my father surrendered, he did not sell out any of his comrades, nor did he do any harm to the organization. He immediately went into hiding in Laibin County. Two or three months later, he organized another small force in Shilong Township. Then, together with another comrade, he tracked down Liao Lianyuan, and they resumed the struggle under the leadership of the Party. My father's house was an underground hideout. The grain and other supplies had been burned in the cave, so they led a hard life. Once, my father led a contingent back to the village, where they had to sell his mother's embroidered wedding shoes in exchange for grain.

In January 1949, Liao Lianyuan reestablished ties with the Southern China Bureau of the CCP, and his contingent became known as the Central Guangxi Detachment. My father was appointed commander of the special detachment, which was a rank equivalent to that of battalion commander. Around August or September 1949, the authorities sent down a person who, at a meeting in my father's house, passed along the essence of a Central Committee decision that everyone should prepare for another two years of fighting (perhaps they did not quite understand that by then the KMT had virtually collapsed). Eastern Guangxi lacked cadres, and so Liao sent a contingent that included my father and his special detachment. Soon came liberation, but the authorities in eastern Guangxi would not allow my father to return. Later, he was appointed as the first deputy head of Cangwu County and concurrently the political commissar of the county militia.

In 1954, the Central Committee ordered a rectification of the former underground Party in Guangxi and Guangdong Provinces that aimed at enhancing the power of the center. Due to his "surrender," my father was purged, and he did not regain his CCP membership until 1966, when the Organization Department of the district Party Committee called for his rehabilitation. After he regained Party membership, he was appointed vice principal of the school. Soon thereafter, the Cultural Revolution began. For matters during that era, you perhaps have more materials than I and so I need not elaborate.[37]

Like his siblings, Qiwen and Qiling, Huang Qizhou avoided talking about the most tragic aspect of his father's life. But he did describe his own experiences in straightforward and simple terms.

At the beginning of the Cultural Revolution, I joined the Red Guards. I was a member of the Small Faction known as "April 22." After the "July 20" incident in Wuhan in 1967,* I realized that the Cultural Revolution was merely a struggle among the top leaders. The more I saw, the more I felt that we had been used. I suggested to father that he go into hiding. He found a hiding place from his old guerrilla fighting days, but he returned, believing, as a cadre and Party member, that he should not flee the mass campaign. Besides, while in hiding he was cut off from his salary, which made it very hard for him to make ends meet. I myself dropped out of the campaign, returned home, and worked at making bricks. I figured that near the later stage of the campaign, my father would surely be returned to his hometown. I planned to make as many bricks as possible during the time he was in hiding, so that when he was forced to come home, we would be able to build a house to shelter the family.

Later, the situation became worse and worse. "April 22" faction members were being killed everywhere. I hid out with my older brother in Nanning for a month. After the Revolutionary Committee was set up, my father wrote to

---

*An incident in which local military and political authorities in the central China city of Wuhan openly revolted against the central government over the carrying out of the Cultural Revolution, which brought China to the brink of civil war. The Wuhan incident led to Mao's call in late July 1967 to "arm leftists," a decision that dramatically increased the factional fighting and the involvement of the army in the Cultural Revolution.

tell me to return to school to participate in the "struggle, criticism, and re-form" movement. He also said that since the establishment of the Revolution-ary Committee, the situation had improved. If I continued to stay outside, he warned, I would be considered a bad element. Since the revolutionary com-mittees at various levels also guaranteed my safety, I returned home. Later I learned that some people from the village, when they heard about my im-pending return, hid along the road for a full day, waiting to ambush me and my family. Fortunately, I stayed overnight at a relative's house on my way home, so their plot was foiled. Two days after I returned home, I felt that something was terribly amiss—people were spreading propaganda about in-discriminate killing. I immediately took off from the village and hiked to Laibin County. Because I had nowhere else to go, I went to Liuzhou, where the Small Faction had yet to be defeated by the Big Faction. I calmed down there, and started to think through the Cultural Revolution, while making a living chopping firewood. I was also given food by people from my faction. I wrote to my father and warned him not to trust the revolutionary commit-tees. Wherever such committees were set up, I wrote, the killing would begin. I also advised him no matter what to try to escape. Later, after my father was arrested, my mother went to visit him. "It seems that our second son was more thoughtful," he said.

At the time my father was beaten to death, I was still in Liuzhou. After the Small Faction in Liuzhou was defeated, I was captured and sent back to school. I was then declared a counterrevolutionary and kicked out of school, imprisoned, and forced to do hard labor.[38]

Huang Qizhou had revealed only what he felt like telling us. He stood up in silence and was ready to depart when I suddenly asked him to ver-ify something for me.

Two years earlier, at the end of my interview with Qiwen and Qiling, I had asked the same question. Where, I wanted to know, are your father's remains? To my great surprise, my inquiry at that time had elicited a sen-timental story recounted by Qiwen.

His bones were placed in an urn, which was placed on the top of a cliff, al-though I don't know the exact place. One day, soon after my father's death, my elder brother asked me to buy a flashlight, which he said he would be using that evening. In the middle of the night, he and my uncle secretly dug up my father's bones at the spot where, after cannibalizing him, the murder-ers had buried his remains. When they brought the bones back home, my grandfather placed them in an urn, which that very night he hid on some mountain, which was unknown to everyone except my grandfather, my uncle, and my elder brother. They were afraid that the place would be re-vealed. In June 1981, a special high-ranking delegation of former under-ground Party operatives was organized by the Guangxi Party Committee to offer condolences. It was headed by the man who was my father's superior during the guerrilla years. Arriving at Wuxuan, a correspondent, or some-one like that, was ordered to visit my grandfather, because the leader of the delegation was supposedly unable, due to traffic, to make it to the village. The correspondent wanted to know whether our family had experienced any difficulties. Before liberation, my grandfather's house had been used as an underground hideout for the Party, frequented by many Party members. Many important meetings were held there, and my grandfather used to provide food and shelter for CCP journalists. Greatly angered by the failure of the leader of the delegation to make an appearance, my grandfather grumbled, "When you were engaged in the guerrilla war, you never complained about traffic on the roads." As soon as they heard of my grandfather's reply, the delegation went to see him in person. The former commander in chief and deputy commander in chief, who had been my father's immediate superiors, wanted to take a look at his remains. But my grandfather refused to inform them of the place where his bones had been buried. "It's not that I don't trust you people," he told them. "My only fear is that once you go there, the place will be revealed. My son devoted his entire life to the CCP and I have no complaints. My only wish is to hang on to his bones and prevent them from being destroyed."

When he saw the shabby house, the tattered quilts, and the torn mosquito nets on the bed, the commander in chief became very sad. He gave my grandfather two or three yuan to fix up the place and to improve his living standards. Then he took off. Later, the county Civil Affairs Bureau gave my grandfather an additional sum of money in compensation for the salary we had not received over the past few years.

I read my interview notes to Huang Qizhou and asked him whether he had anything to add to his brother's story. He replied, "The two leaders of the delegation were Liao Lianyuan and Wei Zhilong, former commander in chief and deputy commander in chief of the Central Guangxi Detachment. My grandfather is in his nineties. He was born in the same year as Chairman Mao."[39]

I saw him down to the street where, starting up his motorcycle, he turned to wave good-bye. The red taillights of his motorcycle were twinkling. At that very last moment, he stopped to tell me that he regretted the comment he had made earlier in the evening about how dredging up the past was useless and that literature and journalism in China were shameless. Then he took off like the wind. Only the sound of his motorcycle engine and I were left to linger on the road that night. I said to myself, "It will be useful. Someday, someday."

UNSUNG HERO

Wang Zujian is a name that should not be forgotten in history. His ancestors were from Luoding County, Guangdong Province, although Wang was born in Beijing, on December 15, 1924. As a young man, Wang fervently pursued the revolution. He secretly joined the underground Party organization on December 1, 1947. When the CCP swept across the face of mainland China, Wang followed the troops to the south, to Guangxi Province. During the "agricultural cooperativization movement" of 1956, under pressure from higher authorities, Wang forced the peasants in Laibin County to turn over large quantities of grain to the state. That movement led to the death of great numbers of peasants. Wang was stricken by the enormity of this tragedy. He felt a tremendous sense of guilt and concern and ordered that the entire county participate in an effort to save the starving. But it was too late. Almost 2,000 peasants died from the famine in the county. Although Wang was not held accountable, the tragedy greatly disturbed his conscience. The next year, 1957, during a meeting held to rectify work styles and oppose rightists, Wang labeled himself as a criminal who had escaped punishment. Unfortunately, he also made a superfluous comment that would cause him suffering for the rest of his life. "The Party's policy of unified purchase and sale of grain was correct," he declared. "However, the peasants should have been provided with one jin [one-half kilogram] of grain per day so as to avoid famine."[40] This elliptical criticism proved disastrous for Wang. He was accused of being a bourgeois rightist element, was purged from the Party, had his cadre rank reduced five levels, and was sent to a labor camp where he was forced to undergo thought reform. In 1960, after four years in the labor camp, Wang and his wife finally had their rightist labels removed. Wang was then assigned to be director of the Cultural Office in Wuxuan County. Six years later, Chairman Mao initiated the Cultural Revolution. Two years after that, following its own logic, the Cultural Revolution quickly turned into civil war. No longer having the leisure to struggle against "the dead tigers," Wang was fortunate enough to be left alone.

In mid-summer 1968, the "mass cannibalism movement" went into full gear in Wuxuan. Every morning on his way to the Cultural Office, Wang passed the town center. Disturbing and ruthless scenes of despotic mobs rushing to cut open live victims on grounds littered with dead bodies disgusted Wang daily. When the mass cannibalism movement reached its climax in Wuxuan, Wang Zujian, who had been expelled from the CCP and had only just been rehabilitated, couldn't bear it anymore. In great anger, he decided to send a message to the Central Committee proclaiming, "Emergency in Wuxuan!" A close friend named Zheng Junlü was taken aback by Wang's plan. "Old Wang, you must not write this letter," he warned his friend. "Never! Now that the situation has degenerated into such uncontrollable conditions, it will be very hard to protect your own life. It will also be useless to submit a petition. The post office blocks petition letters from ever getting out of the county. You'd be lucky to survive." Wang tore the letter to pieces to put his friend at ease. When he got home, he didn't dare discuss the matter with his wife. But he couldn't sleep. He stayed awake the entire night, disturbed in his troubled heart. To write or not to write a letter? He clearly knew that if he were to write the letter, the result would be very bad for him. He who revealed the murderers might himself be cannibalized by one of the murderers. He who revealed the cannibals might well be eaten by the despotic mobs. One after another, however, the skeletons of the dead appeared lucidly in front of his eyes. The ruthless scenes, the desperate screaming of the victims, and the deadly light that shone in the eyes of the despotic mob kept recurring. All of a sudden Wang's heart tightened. He could feel his blood pound against his chest. How lucky he had been to escape their destiny. However, any wrong move on his part could lead to his being cannibalized. Eating him would be the most legitimate thing for the cannibals to do given that he was an old rightist. Late at night, lying next to his wife, who was breathing smoothly and calmly, Wang's heart tightened in pain. If he alone were to suffer, or even die, for the sake of performing his obligations as a CCP member, Wang would have been at ease. But what about his wife, for whom he was a spiritual support, and his loving children? How would they be able to stand the suffering and the sorrow? Could they endure the pain of life without him? And what if he did not write the letter? Naturally, that would ensure the safety of his family.

One thing was certain. No matter how cruel and ruthless Wuxuan became, the mobs would never dare invade his workplace, for the group of cadres in power there were veterans who wisely avoided the struggles between the two factions. They had hung out a "neutral" sign, but whosoever dared to attack their workplace would suffer retaliation from them. Besides, since Wang was no longer a county official, he had no responsibilities or obligations to the local government. Nonetheless, what about the future? How would he confront his own conscience? For causing 2,000 people to die of hunger, he had been tormenting himself for over ten years. True, he should not have held himself personally accountable. He had even tried to resist the heavy pressure from the authorities. Even so, his conscience never left him alone. "Why did you fail to resist?" it kept nagging. "You are accountable, you are accountable." Late at night, Wang lay in bed, imagining his future as a walking corpse. To petition or not to petition? That was the question that tormented Wang Zujian.

Was there really a middle way? Yes. An anonymous letter. But he gave up that idea right away. An anonymous letter reporting such an important matter directly to the highest authority would be like no letter at all. Alas, Wang Zujian, you have no retreat, he thought to himself. You have to do it for the people's sake. Your own concerns for life and death must be ignored. He jumped out of bed and he started to write the letter. "To the Central Committee of the Communist Party: My name is Wang Zujian," he wrote. "I once was an underground Party member in Beijing and now I am a rehabilitated rightist." From the slaughtering at the Wuxuan battle to the frenzied wave of cannibalism, Wang continued, "School principals and teachers were killed and cannibalized. And the situation will only worsen if it is not stopped now. Cadres from military offices and Party county committees were onlookers. When will this cannibalism cease? Cannibalism should not be allowed during the Cultural Revolution, especially since the establishment of the revolutionary committees imposed controls over weapons. Why allow cannibalism?" After listing the names of some of the victims who had been cannibalized, Wang declared, "This frenzied wave of cannibalism has penetrated all of Wuxuan County. Emergency! The CCP should stop it immediately."[41]

This was how the cannibalism that had swept through Wuxuan and Guangxi came to be reported directly to "heaven" by a low-ranking cadre. But being brave does not mean that one must be blind and foolish. So the seasoned veteran of the underground Party employed one small trick to circumvent the censorship of the local independent kingdom. He sent out five letters at the same time, all addressed to his cousins, uncles, and sisters, who were instructed to forward the letters to Wang's old underground Party member friends in Beijing, who in turn would send his letters to the highest authority. In fact, Wang was successful and all five letters reached their destination. Premier Zhou Enlai was outraged! The commander in chief of the Guangxi Military Region—Ou Zhifu—immediately dispatched regular army troops to Wuxuan. It seemed that the uncontrollable cannibalism would soon be stopped.

Thus, one day in early July great anxiety befell Wuxuan, which was then at the height of the cannibalism frenzy. Rumors spread everywhere that a VIP was coming to make an inspection. A long line of vehicles indeed arrived shortly thereafter at the docks on the Qian River, and soldiers quickly took control of the high land in the area to ensure a safe river crossing for the VIP. Each boat carried three vehicles as the VIP, accompanied by guards and troops, slowly crossed the river and then headed toward the center of the town. The commander of the Guangxi Military Region, Ou Zhifu (a member of the eighth, ninth, and tenth Central Committees), saw for himself on the streets the blood stains and the skeletons, coated by swarming flies. Ou pointed right to the nose of Wen Longjun, the director of the county Revolutionary Committee and director of the county Militia Office, and bombarded him with curses and dressed him down. "How many people have been cannibalized? How come you haven't stopped it? And why didn't you report these incidents to the Central Committee? Somebody else from your county did," Ou shouted. "From tomorrow on, if one more person is cannibalized, I will blow your fucking head off!"[42] (The outrage expressed by Commander Ou was understandable. Wang Zujian's petition letter had shocked the

CCP leaders. Although Mao's totalitarian regime depended on military threats and street terror, it did not require cannibalism. It was said that Zhou Enlai ordered the commander of either the Guangxi Military District or the Guangzhou Military Region—which one is unclear—to stand up at a meeting so that he could publicly berate him.)

The situation which had never been under control was finally controlled. Wen Longjun's head was not blown off, but the cannibalism in Wuxuan was immediately stopped. However, the angry Wuxuan regime soon uncovered the "black hand" (*heishou*)* of Wang Zujian. Wang was criticized on numerous occasions as being the biggest black hand in the entire county, but cannibalism was never again mentioned and was buried along with the bodies of its victims.

FAREWELL, WUXUAN

The closer it came to the end of my interviews in Wuxuan, the more mysterious and tense the atmosphere became there. On the issue of the Cultural Revolution, especially on the issue of the killing and cannibalism, two political forces with different interests held opposing views, and the contradiction between them became more and more severe. Following my friends' admonition, I stayed home once it became dark, hiding in my room at the guest house. Before going outside, I would always inform the interviewees of the time and place of the interview. I dared not leave my interview notes, journal, or other materials in the room—they were with me all of the time, even when I ate, went to the bathroom, or washed. When walking on the roads, I anxiously observed people around me and never walked shoulder to shoulder with anyone, nor did I mingle with small crowds. I had to be very cautious even when eating. The cook at the guest house, who had learned the purpose of my trip, took special care of me. He always added meat to my bowl. But even this made me more cautious because I reasoned that if "some other sauce" was added to the bowl, the situation might become very unpleasant. Thus, I politely tried to turn down the cook's good intentions. I usually picked up some other bowl on the counter instead. Over time I was no longer a stranger in Wuxuan; in the courtyard of the county committee headquarters and on the roads, there were more and more unknown "acquaintances," some who gave me understandable smiles, some who gave me looks like daggers. But most scary was their careful observation of me. It was just like Lu Xun's description in his ingenious "Diary of a Madman": "When I

---

*A common political label for dissidents of all stripes in China.

made my way out the front gate this morning—ever so carefully—there was something funny about the way the Venerable Old Zhao looked at me: seemed as though he was afraid of me and yet, at the same time, looked as though he had it in for me. There were seven or eight other people who had their heads together whispering about me. They were afraid I'd see them too! All up and down the street people acted the same way. The meanest looking one of all spread his lips out wide and actually *smiled* at me! A shiver ran from the top of my head clear down to the tips of my toes, for I realized that meant they already had their henchmen well deployed and ready to strike."* Perhaps it was merely an illusion, or perhaps it was not. The main character in Lu Xun's story was a schizophrenic, whereas I was a normal person. "Diary of a Madman" was fictitious, whereas what had happened in Wuxuan was a bloody fact.

Let me summarize what I had learned in Wuxuan. An unprecedented frenzy of cannibalism in human history had occurred. Even uglier than the mere fact alone was that the frenzy was not caused by some uncontrollable defect in human nature. It was a violent act, caused directly by the very same class struggle advocated by Marxism-Leninism-Mao Zedong Thought, armed by the theory of proletarian dictatorship, silently agreed upon and directly organized by the power organizations of the Chinese Communist Party. After my intense interviewing in Wuxuan, I had put together a general picture of the cannibalism in Guangxi. Based on the characteristics of the people's emotions at that time, I categorized the process into three phases.

Phase one was the beginning, characterized by secretive and frightening actions. The numerous cases in Shanglin County were rather typical: In each case, the murderers made their way secretly to the killing fields late at night to secure the hearts and livers of victims shot some hours earlier. Out of fear, disorganization, and lack of experience, in almost all cases the murderers ended up puncturing a bowel or cutting open a lung by mistake. Once they discovered their error, despite their fear the murderers would return to the site to get what they wanted. After they had boiled the parts, dozens of people surrounding the fireplace would hasten to consume them in silence. The next morning, the murderers would call their pals and invite them over to share the leftovers. Afraid these associates would refuse their invitation, they pretended that the food consisted of the hearts and livers of cattle. Only after the pals had finished eating did the killers gleefully announce that they had just consumed so-and-so's liver.

---

*Lu Xun, *Diary of a Madman and Other Stories*, tran. William A. Lyell (Honolulu, HI: University of Hawaii Press, 1990), p. 30.

Phase two was the high tide. This was characterized by blatant expressions of enthusiasm. By this point, the act of cutting out hearts and livers while the victims were alive had evolved into a rather skilled technique. Based on the rich experience handed down by veteran guerrilla fighters who years earlier had engaged in cannibalism, the method was honed nearly to perfection. For instance, if you ever decide to cut a victim open while he's still alive, simply make a cut underneath the rib cage in the form of the Chinese character for *person* (*ren*; 人) with a sharp knife, then step on the stomach with one foot and immediately squeeze out the heart and liver. (If the victim happens to be tied up to a tree, push on the stomach with one knee.) The leaders assumed the privilege of cutting out the heart, liver, and genitals, and everyone else was free to scramble for all the other parts. Red flags fluttered and slogans were chanted. Altogether the scene had a certain disgusting magnificence about it. At some "get-together" parties in certain villages, a unique practice of boiling human flesh and pork together in a pot was indulged by the locals. When done, villagers would line up and take turns getting a single chunk.

After I had suffered the terrible shock of hearing these horrid scenes described in detail, I realized that it was an interesting psychological phenomenon. The collective frenzy that emerged from CCP labels and phrases such as "class hatred," "a firm political standpoint," and "drawing a line between enemy and comrade" had driven the people to cannibalism. The moral conscience, however, could not be completely suppressed and so a compromise had been worked out. People would join in the collective act of cannibalism, but each conscience was appeased by the random selection of a piece from the pot mixed with human flesh and pork.* This random selection reconciled two conflicting drives among the cannibals: on the one hand the drive to participate in the struggle against the victims and on the other the drive to shrink from the act of eating human flesh. Such was the supreme form of the swindling, and self-swindling, compromise that was stitched between a beastly mentality and human instinct, one which ensured some measure of psychological compatibility between collective frenzy and individual conscience. Naturally, this was not something invented by the folks in Guangxi. There had been similar cases during the Land Reform period (1948–1953), when the practice was devised of a collective act of killing that permitted each person to strike a blow with a knife or stone. Such scenes of "class struggle," along with the techniques of collective execution, sprouted forth from a

---

*Zheng Yi is suggesting here that in consuming a piece of human flesh, people would rationalize to themselves that what they had actually eaten was pork, not human flesh.

domineering psychological mentality no different from the collective cannibalism of Guangxi. The only nuance to the collective cannibalism was that it represented the zenith of such thinking. And it ended up generating rather dramatic styles of the technique.

Phase three could be summarized as the mass movement of cannibalism. In Wuxuan, for instance, the masses simply went berserk in their cannibalism, like a pack of hungry dogs who feed on the dead after an epidemic. Every so often, some victims would be singled out "to be criticized." Each criticism rally was followed by a beating, and each death ended in cannibalism. Once the victim fell to the ground—whether the victim had stopped breathing was irrelevant—the crowd rushed forward, pulled out their cutting knives and daggers, and started cutting at whatever piece of flesh was closest to them. After the flesh had been cut away, they targeted the large and small entrails, along with the broken bones. I was told that a certain elderly woman, who had heard that a diet of human eyes helped to restore eyesight, used to wander from criticism rally to criticism rally with a vegetable basket over her arm. She would hover about for the opportune moment to rush toward a victim. Once the victim had been beaten down onto the ground, she would quickly pull out her sharp, pointed knife and use it to dig out the victim's eyes. Mission accomplished, she would scurry away.

There were also a few elderly men who made a specialty of eating the human brain. Because it was hard to smash open the skull and get at the brain, they developed their own unique method of feeding on the brain. Each one procured a medium-sized steel pipe, with one end sharpened to a point. Once the crowd had finished cutting away the victim's flesh, they would then slowly advance toward the victim (at that point they had no competitors). After they had pierced the victim's skull with their steel pipes, they would kneel on the ground and suck the brain through the pipe, rather resembling a small group of people in the act of sharing a jar of yogurt with straws. At the scene, women with children on their backs rushed in to grab a piece of flesh to show off to their parents. Not only common people, but everyone, even innocent young boys and girls and teachers, joined in the delirious wave of cannibalism. The very last sense of sin and humanity was swept away by the mentality of following the crowd. The frenzied wave spread like an epidemic. Once victims had been subjected to criticism, they were cut open alive, and all their body parts—heart, liver, gallbladder, kidneys, elbows, feet, tendons, intestines—were boiled, barbecued, or stir-fried into a gourmet cuisine. On campuses, in hospitals, in the canteens of various governmental units at the brigade, township, district, and county levels, the smoke from the cooking pots could be seen in the air. Feasts of human flesh, at which people celebrated by drinking and gambling, were a common sight.

Gaze at this dire picture of hell. In any religious classic, has humankind ever witnessed such a frenzied and horrible picture of hell? The book that in my opinion best depicts the picture of hell is Dante's *Inferno*. However, after he had utilized his whole imagination in the endeavor, the great poet was still only able to come up with punishments like bitter labor, the bearing of heavy weights, being bitten by bumble bees, decapitation, the cutting of the tongue and hands, whipping, submersion in blood and waste, and other such unpleasant torments. In Eastern culture, depictions of hell include the ghost town of Fengdu, located along the Yangtze River, where victims are forced to climb mountains full of spears, are pushed into frying pans, have their hearts pierced by 10,000 arrows, have body parts sawed off and ground by stone. The worst fate was to be thrown together with beasts, so that in the next life victims would be transformed into cattle and horses. The cruelty and ruthlessness of the proletarian dictatorship outperformed humankind's imagination tens, hundreds of times. The most horrible punishment suffered by religious heretics during the religious inquisitions of the Middle Ages in Europe, the very idea of which scared the hell out of everyone, was nothing worse than being burned at the stake. There were no practices at that time to equal the grand feasts where human flesh was consumed in public. The reason people weren't burned at the stake in Guangxi had nothing to do with some failure of imagination or a creative lapse on the part of their executioners. The cannibals simply didn't want to miss the fleshiness of the flesh. In numerous instances, fire was used to singe the pubic hair of women. Fireworks were also inserted into the vaginas of female victims. Such cruelty and ruthlessness outperforms and would even embarrass those who merely torched people at the stake! Lu Xun's description was best. "The people under the rule of the despot are more vicious than the despot himself," he wrote.

All this in Wuxuan and Guangxi, do people believe it? When I was copying the materials from the archives and files, listening to the sorrowful accounts of the victims' relatives and the testimony of fearless and calm eyewitnesses, hearing the confessions of the murderers, some without remorse and others with a deep sense of guilt, being introduced to this by the case clerks, and even as I am recording and documenting this on paper today, there has always been a little din ringing in my ears. Can people believe this? I wondered. Can history believe it? Chen Shaoquan, secretary in chief of the Wuxuan County Party Committee for handling leftover cases, once told me, "Those who did not witness it refuse to believe. Even people like me who were assigned to investigate these cases took a skeptical attitude in the beginning. Could such ruthlessness really have occurred? We wondered. Later, after our investigations, in the course of which we obtained many eyewitness accounts and much material evidence, we started to believe it. Beforehand, most of us believed that these were just stories concocted by those who harbored resentment against the Cultural Revolution." If even some of the locals in Wuxuan refused to believe it, how could people around the world believe it? Will humankind believe it? Impossible. From Adam and Eve, from Fu Xi and Nu Wa,* from the ancient world, to the twentieth century with its creation of automobiles, computers, and spacecraft, has such ruthless and inhumane mass mania ever taken place? Humankind put on trial in Nuremburg the German fascists who had run the gas chambers. In West Germany, 80,000 to 90,000 Nazi suspects were tried in court, and the murderers who remained at large were eventually captured no matter where they had tried to escape. Even as gray-haired Nazis were dying, humankind spent costly sums and engaged in prolonged journeys to capture and imprison them. In dealing with Stalin's slaughter, Khrushchev delivered his shocking historic speech at the 1956 Twentieth Party Congress of the Soviet Union. A group of Soviet writers stood up and revealed the fascist cries in the concentration camps. Among them was the strong soldier of mankind, Aleksandr Solzhenitsyn, whose 150,000-word *Gulag Archipelago* has provided a seamless web of evidence of Stalin's crimes. Of course, even before these trials and revelations, the crimes committed by Hitler and Stalin were considered mere rumors or concoctions. So today the question must be asked: What should China and the world do about the holocaust that occurred in Guangxi? Reveal it, expose it mercilessly. If one legal suit is allowed, tens of thousands will follow. I firmly believe that someday, somehow, humankind will condemn this crime. Although under the present Communist dictatorship it is impossible to carry out a Nuremburg-style trial for the Guangxi incident, someday in China people will be able to carry out their settling of accounts in such a trial.

Evidence! I am very much aware that I must obtain more airtight evidence.

Eventually, I was able to get a list of victims' names from Du Tiansheng, the former director of the office for handling leftover cases, who is now Party secretary of the Wuxuan County Public Security Bureau.[43] Unfortunately, this list of victims has shrunk a great deal. Due to the unlimited generosity of the Communist Party's policy on handling leftover cases, many of the convicted who admitted their criminality at the beginning of the investigation later requested and had their rehabilitation approved. Also, there was a lack of hard evidence for the many cases of cannibalism that involved the cutting off of the flesh of the dead at night and the disposal of bodies in the Qian River. In addition, many of the organiz-

---

*Brother and sister consorts, they were the first legendary rulers of China.

ers of the cannibalism are still in power and have tried their best to obstruct these investigations. Thus, no one from the office for handling leftover cases could guarantee the completeness of the victims' list mentioned previously. The list only includes renowned cases that the murderers can do nothing to "negate."

As for the total number of victims who were cannibalized in Wuxuan, a correct figure has not been ascertained. There are conflicting claims from the locals and from the official sources. Wang Zujian's claim that there were more than 100 victims caused him considerable trouble. One day, Yang XX, a relative of one of the victims, informed Wang that a man named Zhao Maoxun, accompanied by more than twenty cadres from the district Party committee, had come to Wuxuan and stayed there for more than twenty days. In his report to the district Party committee, Zhao claimed that Wang Zujian had "concocted cases and slandered the county leaders of Wuxuan." It was also said that Zhao had insisted that Wang Zujian should be held accountable for his accusations. "Why did he report to the Central Committee in such a manner?" Zhao is alleged to have exclaimed. "Cannibalism did indeed take place, but only twenty-seven people were cannibalized, not one hundred." Zhao also stated that he would compile materials in response to the request of the Central Committee and the *People's Daily*. Zhao had also claimed that Wang's letter, which had been reprinted in the confidential "Internal Reference" section of the *People's Daily*, was "full of exaggerations and sensationalism." Zhao also emphasized that Wang was a rightist. When he informed Wang Zujian of this information, Yang XX also expressed some doubt. "Are you sure that over one hundred victims were cannibalized?" he asked. Wang became very angry. "There were eight in Tongling, twenty-one in Wuxuan. In the four communes I visited myself, I discovered more than seventy cases, and there were four other communes in the county that I did not even visit. How could the figure not exceed 100?" Later, when the Central Committee sought verification from Wang Zujian, he staked his own Party membership on this number. "If there was one case fewer, expel me from the Party," he told them. "If there was one case more, then Zhao Maoxun should be held accountable." Wang Zujian threw down his gloves like a gentleman.[44] However, no Party organization, or any other leader for that matter, dared to take up his challenge. Under the one-party rule in China, it should not be hard to verify the cases of cannibalism in Wuxuan; especially once Wei Guoqing, the Guangxi Autonomous Region leader, was removed from power and the movement for handling leftover cases from the Cultural Revolution was ended.* Even so,

---

*Zheng Yi is intimating here that since this "movement" never intended to ascertain the real facts, it should be replaced by a genuine investigation.

what benefit could possibly be derived from thoroughly investigating this incident? Another bloody line for the totalitarian criminal record? Hence, the total number of victims of the cannibalism in Wuxuan County will remain a mystery in history forever.

I should make one point clear to the reader. Cannibalism was by no means restricted to Wuxuan County. It occurred throughout all of Guangxi. Wuxuan was by no means the only county that went insane. During my investigations, many officials and cadres at various levels revealed to me the names of other counties where similar events had occurred. It was a pity that I was unable to do further investigation in those counties. But I did get ahold of another official document that mentions cannibalism. "According to some typical materials provided," this document states (though obviously not the result of a thorough investigation since they are only 'typical materials'), "there were twenty-two cases of cannibalism in Tanxu and Xinxu communes of Lingshan County; eighteen cases in Shikang commune, Hepu County; nineteen cases in Dinggeng brigade of Beitong commune, Pubei County; three cases at the Xiaodong Tea Farm in Qinzhou County."[45] In sum, the following can be said: Cannibalism was pervasive in Guangxi and in some places it was comparable in number to Wuxuan, or even surpassed Wuxuan. Wuxuan became so infamous only because Wang Zujian demonstrated such great courage in "reporting the incident to heaven." When people dare not challenge the darkness, then evil will get away with murder under the cover of darkness. When accounts of old crimes aren't settled, new crimes will certainly occur.

A thorough settling of accounts under Communist Party rule, however, is impossible. All totalitarian regimes are willing to punish disciples—disciples who in their excessive zeal have committed foolish acts—if only for the sake of warning everyone not to embarrass the master. But if a punishment is no more than a simple slap on the face, or a kick in the rear, without due process, then this is truly detrimental to the Party. But the truth of the matter is that the despot has to rely on vigilantism. The maintenance of a totalitarian regime calls for violence and terror; no despot is willing to put away his sword of violence. This is why out of all the murderers who beat or persecuted 524 victims to death (of whom more than 100 were cannibalized) in Wuxuan County, only thirty-four were punished. The longest prison sentence was fourteen years, and the shortest was two years. The average was seven to ten years. Most outrageous of all, no one was sentenced to death, or to life imprisonment. By a rough calculation, beating one victim to death brought less than half a year in prison. When added together, the prison sentences of the thirty-four murderers came to slightly over 200 years. According to the law in certain

Western countries, multiple criminal acts committed by one criminal alone can earn a sentence of over 200 years.

As for those who committed acts of cannibalism, none were punished. And the Wuxuan office for handling leftover cases compiled a list of over 400 people who had engaged in cannibalism. Of course, only the names of those involved in the most famous cases were on the list. The exact number of cannibals in Wuxuan remains a mystery. But we can still come up with a rough estimate: eighteen victims were completely cannibalized. If on average there was 50 jin [25 kilograms] of flesh per victim, and each cannibal consumed one-half jin [one-quarter kilogram] of flesh, at least 2,000 people must have joined in the cannibalism. And if the flesh was spread around, then perhaps 5,000 people might have participated. The other sixty victims, although their flesh was not completely consumed, would have provided food for 5,000 cannibals, who in the act of cannibalism experienced class vindication. According to this calculation, altogether over 10,000 people must have participated in the cannibalism. This obscene arithmetic is based on the officially recognized list of "seventy-six" victims. But if Wang Zujian's estimation of over 100 is correct, then 10,000–20,000 people from the county must have engaged in cannibalism. Thus, when I label what occurred in Wuxuan as a "mass cannibalism movement," I should not be questioned by any readers with sound judgment.

Of the 10,000 possible cannibals, none was punished under the law, however, about 130 people were subjected to internal Party discipline.[46] But such symbolic punishment could not even ease the anger of outsiders, let alone the victims' relatives.

In this vein, the following is a tragicomic scene that took place in Tongwan Township. Zang Liangxing, Party secretary of Wuxuan County, was on an inspection tour of local neighborhoods when he was surrounded by a crowd of victims' relatives. They demanded punishment for the murderers and financial compensation for their relatives. Secretary Zang ordered his subordinates to hold the crowd at bay, while he escaped along a deserted path. Although the relatives failed to "capture" the Party secretary, they held his car captive for eight days. Secretary Zang did not even have the guts to meet with relatives of the victims. The crowd therefore decided to petition the Nanning District Party committee. They attached a big-character poster to the front of Zang's car that read: "This car belongs to Secretary Zang from Wuxuan County. After he refused to meet with us, Zang made an escape, leaving his car behind. Our only choice is to push it to Nanning. We hope that policemen along the way will let us pass." This incident soon turned into something more than a bitter joke. A cadre from the Nanning district attempted to persuade the crowd not to push the car to Nanning city. He expressed his sympathy and pointed out that Nanning was over a hundred miles away and that pushing a vehicle on the road for such a long time was a traffic violation. The cadre also warned the crowd that pasting a big-character poster on the car was also a violation of the law. The relatives replied with great indignation, "This is not a big-character poster. This is our pass!"

Quite unexpectedly, I subsequently had the opportunity to meet with Secretary Zang in his capacity as the director of the office for handling leftover cases. When I met with him on the evening of June 15, 1986, I was initially somewhat prejudiced against him because of the story involving his car. But to my surprise, Secretary Zang was a rather modest person and he provided rich details about the armed struggles and cannibalism in Wuxuan during the Cultural Revolution. As a recently retired county Party secretary, he especially liked to talk about the difficulties and the complex situation during the period of handling leftover cases.

That particular movement began in 1982. In Wuxuan it did not have an auspicious beginning, because the director of the office for handling the cases was the deputy Party secretary of the county, Wei Riguang.* Wei had already cut his own throat. When he headed the Revolutionary Committee in Rongan (perhaps the same Rongan that was famous for the "widow's lane"), he "nodded" his approval to the killing of more than ten victims. Later, after 1982, he was removed from the Party and became a common state cadre. Sometime after that, Li Huankui, deputy Party secretary of the county and the county executive director, was made director of the office. But Li had also nodded his approval to the killing of two victims in 1962. When the masses focused on this historical issue, it became impossible for him to carry out his appointed duties for the leftover cases. So in April 1983 Zang Liangxing was appointed as the director, and it was he who began the first phase of the work. The more responsible cadres won the support of the masses. No chaos appeared and during his tenure, twenty-five people were convicted for killing.

According to Zang, the killing and cannibalism in Wuxuan had their own characteristics.

> Only twenty-eight victims were killed prior to the establishment of the Revolutionary Committee, but nearly 500 were murdered after the committee was set up. The Armed Police had considerable say during the period of handling leftover cases and they were able to control the situation. Things were not as chaotic as they were in Sichuan and Yunnan. Production resumed, and social order was restored. Thus, I proposed not to be too strict with the locals and not to pay attention solely to the culprits among the masses. But an order came down from the prefecture committee: If the organizers and commanders of the killing refuse to confess, then we as the work team han-

---

*Reliance on such "internal" investigations obviously led to cover-ups.

dling leftover cases must not come to any conclusions. There was no way to conclude anything. There were many complaints from the masses, who thought that those who were convicted were not the organizers, but merely were followers. Those who had organized or planned the killings went unpunished, nor were any of the district-level cadres punished. The masses protested that "those who confessed were severely punished, while those who refused to confess got away with murder" and that "the honest were punished severely while the stubborn received generosity."[47]

In April 1984, it was time to nail down the cases. Zang was county Party secretary and in charge of the overall work. Yet this veteran cadre, who himself had been wrongly accused for over thirty years, was kicked out of his chair before it was even warm. The reasons given were old age (he was fifty-four at the time) and lack of higher education (he had only completed middle school). So what about the new secretary and the new group for handling leftover cases? Those who had already been convicted were rehabilitated and those who were not yet convicted were given lighter treatment or even a chance to have their cases dropped. Some were convicted and removed from their positions, but after moving on to a new place, they were promoted again. "I was very angry that the work for handling leftover cases did not continue," Zang told me. "Those who are still involved in this work are angry at me now, for in the past I had encouraged them to carry out their responsibilities. Now, with the change in the leadership of the group for handling leftover cases, those comrades have been expelled or given less power. Some of them were even laid off from their work units. Right now, five types of people in Wuxuan criticize me. Relatives of the victims who think the accused were treated too leniently criticize me; those convicted who complain that the treatment was too strict hold it against me; I am in bad odor with those involved in the investigation of the cases who consider they have had bad luck; and the relatives of the convicted are at my throat along with fair-minded people who believe that 'those who confessed got severe punishment and those who refused to confess got away with murder' and 'big matters were made small, and small matters were turned into nothing—nothing, nothing, nothing!' Because of my history, I was initially warmly received in Wuxuan. Now that I have been involved in the investigation and treatment along strict lines, however, I have become isolated. Everywhere I go, I am greeted with angry looks."[48]

When I recalled the tragicomedy of his escape while discarding his car, I could not help accompanying his bitter smile with one of my own.

The top level of the CCP once issued rather severe instructions. Deng Xiaoping (or was it Hu Yaobang, I can't recall) sent down the order that "Those evil elements in Guangxi who committed cannibalism, if proven guilty, must be expelled from the Party. Do not let our offspring believe that the Guangxi CCP is a party of cannibals. Severe measures must be implemented." Liu Tianfu, director of the Guangxi Party Reform Liaison Organization of the CCP, issued the same orders at the start of the movement to handle leftover cases. Superficially, at least, the Party was really outraged at what had happened, but if one reads between the lines, it is not hard to see that whatever their apparent motives or means, the purpose was to wash the blood off their own hands. Pity the Guangxi folks; when they saw that asking for justice was impossible, they yielded and ended up merely demanding that those who committed cannibalism should not receive promotions. Yet even such a trivial request was ignored by the various governmental levels in Guangxi. It was said that Wei Guoqing, the biggest murderer and the former Party secretary of the Guangxi Autonomous Region (who was later appointed the head of the PLA General Political Department) once commented in a rather thuggish manner: "Why shouldn't those who committed cannibalism be promoted as cadres?"

The CCP regime's attempts to hide crimes and hold on to its power has degenerated to such a degree. Only then did I realize why they had tried their best not to allow me to carry out my investigation.

Deceived by the so-called "revolutionary humanism" (*geming rendaozhuyi*), while at the same time slaughtering our fellow countrymen, we surrendered our conscience and humanism to the devil. We attempted to bring about a beautiful society at the cost of our humanity. We thought that after treading through the quagmire of blood and dead bodies we would be able to face the most magnificent dawn in the history of humankind. But we ended up not having the magnificent dawn. Instead we consorted with the beasts and stepped into the darkness of hell. Chinese people, my blood brothers and sisters, please ponder this point: Is Guangxi only Guangxi? Do those cannibals only number a few thousand? No! Guangxi is not only Guangxi. Guangxi is China! The cannibals were not merely individual cannibals, they were and they are our entire nation! Moreover, in addition to cannibalizing others, we also cannibalized ourselves! This self-cannibalism not only refers to cannibalizing ourselves and our fathers, brothers, and sisters, but also to cannibalizing our very souls, cannibalizing the humanity upon which a nation depends for its existence and for establishing a joyful worldly home along with humankind. God forgive us!

It was time to retreat. My health had become worse and worse. My persistent low blood pressure was preventing me from continuing with my interviews. Besides, the materials I already had acquired were putting enormous psychological pressure on me. The murderers, I thought, will somehow find out that I did not have any high-level clearance from Beijing, that I was merely representing myself. If that were ever discovered, those invaluable materials could be lost.

Once I made the decision to leave, I immediately headed for the long-distance bus stop. I hurriedly departed Wuxuan. As the bus flew along the road, I felt as though I could see the smiling faces of the victims. All of a sudden, I realized that I had not said good-bye to them. I should have poured the best liquor into the Qian River, placed the best cigarettes onto the red soil, and kneeled down between heaven and earth to make a silent vow. But I had forgotten to do it. Will they forgive me? I think so, for they understand my heart and my soul.

The magnificence and beauty of Guangxi is just like a southern girl's smile at dawn. Guangxi is pure beauty, tranquility, and peace. This consoling beauty will make it impossible for anyone who has experienced Guangxi to believe the story I am unfolding. Yet although the facts are cruel, they are true.

In the past, whenever Guangxi was mentioned, people would think about the mysteriously beautiful landscape in Guilin; but from now on, when Guangxi is mentioned, people will say: There stands a forest of scarlet memorials, beyond all human understanding.

NOTES

1. Recorded Interview *(Fangwen riji)*, June 15, 1986. Notes of a Talk with Zang Liangxing *(Zang Liangxing tanhua jilu)*.

2. Ibid.

3. CCP Wuxuan County Party Committee, Leading Group of the Party Reform Office Publication Bureau, Compilation of Documents from the "Cultural Revolution," *Annals of the Great Proletarian Cultural Revolution in Wuxuan County* [Hereafter, *Annals, Wuxuan County.*] *(Wuxuanxian da wuchanjieji wenhua dageming dashijian)*, May 1987, p. 12.

4. Recorded Interview, June 15, 1986. Notes of a Talk with Du Tiansheng.

5. Recorded Interview, June 17, 1986. Notes of a Talk with Zhou Jiean. Also, see Recorded Interview, June 14, 1986. County Party Reform Office, Notes of a Talk with Messrs. Li, Yang, Zhou, and He.

6. Recorded Interview, June 17, 1986. Feng Shuji (Party secretary of the County Sanitation Bureau and director of the county hospital during the Cultural Revolution), Recorded Notes.

7. Recorded Interview, June 17, 1986. Notes of a Talk with Zhou Jiean.

8. Recorded Interview, June 15, 1986. Notes of a Talk with Du Tiansheng.

9. *Annals, Wuxuan County,* p. 26.

10. Ibid., p. 17.

11. Ibid., p. 20.

12. Ibid., p. 21.

13. Recorded Interview, June 15, 1986. Notes of a Talk with Du Tiansheng.

14. *Annals, Wuxuan County,* p. 21. Also see Recorded Interview, June 17, 1986. Notes of a Talk with Chen Shaoquan; and Recorded Interview, June 15, 1986. Notes of a Talk with Du Tiansheng.

15. *Annals, Wuxuan County*, p. 20.

16. Recorded Interview, June 13, 1986. Notes of a Talk with Wu Hongtai; and Recorded Interview, June 16, 1986, Notes of a Talk with Chen Shaoquan.

17. *Annals, Wuxuan County*, pp. 27, 28.

18. Ibid., p. 26.

19. Ibid., p. 22.

20. Ibid., pp. 22, 23, 26.

21. Ibid., p. 23.

22. Recorded Interview, June 15, 1986. Notes of a Talk with Zang Liangxing.

23. *Annals, Wuxuan County*, p. 21. Also, see Recorded Interview, June 13, 1986. Notes of a Talk with Wu Hongtai.

24. *Annals, Wuxuan County*, p. 27.

25. Recorded Interview, June 14, 1986. Notes of a Talk with Messrs. Li, Yang, Zhou, and He.

26. Letter from Wang Zujian to Author, June 18, 1988.

27. *Annals, Wuxuan County*, pp. 23, 27.

28. Recorded Interview, June 14, 1986. Notes of a Talk with Men Qijun.

29. *Annals, Wuxuan County*, pp. 18, 26–27.

30. Recorded Interview, June 13, 1986. Notes of a Talk with Wu Hongtai. (Wu also let me examine the notes he had taken during his own investigation.)

31. Ibid.

32. Ibid.

33. Ibid.

34. *Annals, Wuxuan County*, p. 27.

35. Recorded Interview, June 13, 1986. Notes of a Talk with Wu Hongtai.

36. Recorded Interview, Nanning City, April 1988.

37. Ibid.

38. Ibid.

39. Ibid.

40. The material in this section is based on descriptions provided to my wife, Bei Ming, by Wang Zujian and Wang Ding.

41. The lines quoted here are not from the original letter but are based on a reconstruction provided to me by Wang Zujian at his residence in Nanning City in April 1988.

42. Ibid.

43. A list of victims cannibalized in Wuxuan County (as determined on July 4, 1983, by the office for handling leftover cases) includes nine victims from Huang-mao commune: from Xinggui village: Huang Likang, Qin Weicheng, Huang Dean, Huang Dehui, Qin Naiguang, Huang Rongchang; from Dalang village: Qin Shiqing; from Shangwu village: Qin Huiwen; from Matian village: Qin Shouzhen; two victims from Ertang commune: from Sitong village: Qin Guoliang; from Lang village: Fang Hongnan; nine victims from Wuxuan commune: from Guanlu village: Wei Shangming, Tan Zhengqing, Huang Zhenji, Tan Qirong; from Ya village: Qin Rongsheng, Lu Hancai; from Dalu village: Chen Kuida; from Caochang village: Huang Zhihua, Guo Yiji; six victims from Wuxuan Township: from Wubei village: Qin Naiwu; from Beijie village: Zhou Shian, Zhou Weian; from Hebian village: Yang Guicai (?); from Xijie village: Tang Zhanhui, Liang Wen-

zhen; ten victims from Sanli commune: from Shangjiang village: Liao Jinfu, Zhong Zhenquan, Zhong Shaoting, Liao Tianlong; from Tai village: Chen Chengyun, Chen Hanning, Chen Xujian; from Wuxing village: Li Zhanlong, Li Jinliang; from Wufu village: Chen Tianchang; eight victims from Dongxiang commune: from Sanduo village: Lei Bingxu, Wu Huatang; from Jingang village: Diao Qitang, Liu Darui, Liu Maohuai; from Changlong village: Zhang Fuzhan; from Liyun village: Li Ruizi; from Ma village: Liu Yelong; two victims from Luxin commune: from Gulu village: Lin Xinzhong; from Shangkang village: Liang Daobang; three victims from Tongling commune: from Tongan village: Wei Guorong; from Datong village: Liao Nainan; from Xinlong village: Tan Shitan; eleven victims from Tongwan commune: from Huama village: Chen Guoyong; from Dachang village: Zhang Wenmei, Zhang Yongheng; from Datuan village: Gan Jiaji, Gan Dazuo; from Shangman village: Chen Guanghou, Zhang Mengtuan; from Jianglong village: Chen Bingxian; from Guzuo village: Qin Hejia, Qin Zhunzhuo; from An village: Chen Tianran; four victims who were state cadres: at Tongling Middle School: Huang Jiaping; at Wuxuan Middle School: Wu Shufang; at Huangmao Elementary School: Zhang Boxun; at Siling Infirmary: Wei Jinguang.

44. Interview conducted by Bei Ming, April 8, 1988. Notes of a Talk with Wang Zujian.

45. Party Reform Office of the Qinzhou Prefecture Party Committee Publication Bureau, *Annals of the "Cultural Revolution" in Qinzhou Prefecture (Qinzhou diqu "wenhua dageming" dashijian)*, October 1987, pp. 48–49.

46. The complete list is available in the original Chinese edition of *Scarlet Memorial*, p. 100.

47. Recorded Interview, June 17, 1986. Notes of a Talk with Zang Liangxing.

48. Ibid.

3

Wherein Lies the Blame?
A Defense of a Nation Known
for Its Benevolence

HAN FALLACY

Although *Maple Tree (Feng)*, my earliest literary work, was the first published effort on mainland China to directly expose the Cultural Revolution, I had never agreed to "thoroughly negate the Cultural Revolution." Later, in another article, I explicitly proposed a theory of "two Cultural Revolutions." When the wave of "thoroughly negating the Cultural Revolution" swept China in the late 1970s and early 1980s, I repeatedly examined my own overzealous behavior during that time. What caused the unthinking fervor that characterized the Cultural Revolution? The blind worship of Mao Zedong unquestionably led to a whole-hearted fanaticism that included even the sacrifice of one's own life. Worship—religious, irrational, and frenzied—does not adequately explain everything. Were there other historical factors? I felt a true sense of emancipation during the Cultural Revolution, and Mao Zedong was the banner of my emancipation. From the earliest age, I realized that I was situated on the lowest level of the new society created after 1949 and indeed had almost been deprived of any existence. My academic excellence and my passionate belief in Marx and Lenin were of little help. As the child of a national bourgeois family,* my destiny was predetermined. At the beginning of the Cultural Revolution, my mother, who had always been an active political member of the neighborhood, was criticized and sent off to the countryside. A work team at Qinghua High School accused me of being a "rightist student," which at

---

*Zheng Yi's class label.

the time seemed odd because I was close to the Party secretary of my academic department, who was labeled a "protector of the emperor" (*bao-huangpai*).* Qinghua High School, affiliated with Qinghua University, was the cradle of the Red Guards. Veteran Qinghua Red Guards called me an "SOB" and beat me up. I barely escaped death. Yet in a way their preeminent status restrained the Qinghua Red Guards, whereas those from other middle schools were less restrained. Those people were involved in all kinds of brutalities, lynchings, beatings, and such acts as forcing victims to kneel on sharp slabs of coal, slathering faces with paint, the airplane torture,† pounding heads, setting hair on fire, slashing buttocks with knives, and bathing people in boiling water. Their dungeons were ornamented by big-character posters, "Long Live the Red Terror!" written in human blood. (In the twenty-four Beijing universities alone, more than 10,000 students were accused of being rightist. Thousands of professors and lecturers were labeled counterrevolutionaries.[1])

But Mao Zedong's call to oppose the bourgeois counterrevolutionary line emancipated the previously persecuted and humbled elements in society like me. For the first time in many years, students and intellectuals were given the right to oppose and retaliate against the suppression orchestrated by the Party organizations in the schools and their privileged high-ranking offspring. I truly felt for the first time that I was human. Furthermore, this individual sense of emancipation was in harmony with the campaign to overthrow capitalist roaders in the Party and the ideal of liberating all of humankind. Such an identification with national ideals enabled people to experience a sense of overall freedom. Mao Zedong's Cultural Revolution line became a lifeline, which we were willing to defend with our lives.‡

When I left Beijing and joined the movement in other provinces, I strongly felt that the masses were undergoing a transformative emancipation. In Yibin, Sichuan Province, recalcitrant farmers surrounded us and condemned the "three bitter years" (1960–1963) as a period when they were only given 3.75 liang (about 5 ounces) of food per day. It was for this reason that they had now stood up to rebel. The "Red Flag Faction," which our "Congress of Red Guards in the Capital" had supported, pointed its collective finger even higher, at Li Jingquan, Party secretary of Sichuan, who was considered the source of the people's suffering. As

---

*A faction committed to protecting high-level cadres during the Cultural Revolution.

†Forcing a person to bend at the waist and spread eagle in the form of an airplane for several hours at a time.

‡The mobilization of students, such as Zheng Yi, from "bad" class backgrounds in the Cultural Revolution is analyzed in Hong Yung Lee, *The Politics of the Cultural Revolution: A Case Study* (Berkeley: University of California Press, 1978).

Qiao Xiaoguang, leader of the Guangxi Party Committee, once wrote, "The farmers in Guangxi ate lousy food, wore shabby clothes, and lived in dismal housing. Several families shared one house. Peasants in the western part of China had to share living space with cattle, pigs, chickens, and ducks. In terms of transportation, it was their two legs along with one shoulder pole. They could only afford to maintain consistent levels of production and were unable to leap forward"[2] (Photo 3.1).

According to the Shanglin County archives compiled during the leadership from 1981–1987 of the more open-minded chairman, then general secretary of the CCP, Hu Yaobang, Party cadres had been cruel to the peasants during the Great Leap Forward era.

> The problem of the "four styles" (coercion, blind instructions in agricultural production, privileged lifestyles, and exaggeration and concoction of production figures) was extremely serious. Among the nine former leading and deputy Party secretaries in Dafeng commune, five were involved in beating up the masses. Among the thirty-one commune cadres, eleven were involved in vicious beating of the masses. The chief Party secretary of the commune beat up twelve people. For instance, in requisitioning grain in Dali village, he coerced the peasants and ended up requisitioning 360 jin of grain

PHOTO 3.1   Impoverished peasants of Xilin County, Guangxi Province.

by beating them up. Afterward, he held a small-scale meeting that summarized and spread the "experience" of beating people up to requisition grain. In Yuncheng, he beat up commune member XXX and forced him to deliver 30 jin of grain. But the secretary was not satisfied and he continued to search up and down the house. In addition, he forced the entire village to kneel down as a form of punishment. The work team in Yuncheng totaled seven members, all of whom were involved in beatings. The total number of people beaten up by them was twenty-six. Cadres used their fists, feet, clubs, and torchlights to administer the beatings. XXX was beaten so badly that she was unable to comb her hair for seven days and could not work in the fields for half a month. Neither older people in their eighties nor young teenagers could escape the beatings. Some pregnant women ended up giving birth while being forced to work in the fields, and three pregnant women suffered miscarriages due to the beatings. The cadres not only beat up people themselves but they also forced the masses to beat up one another: fathers beat up sons, sons beat up fathers.

A vaudeville routine ensued from the ruthless exploitation and oppression suffered by the masses prior to the Cultural Revolution, which became popular all over China. The poor and lower-middle peasant was invited by Party officials to "recall the bitterness of the past and cherish the sweetness of the present." But this simple and innocent peasant invariably forgot the instructions he had been given and, with a slip of the tongue, discoursed instead about the bitterness brought on by the new. The peasant was then invited to step down. During the Cultural Revolution, discontented masses from all walks of life gathered under the banner of Mao Zedong's "rebellion" and thus obtained power to oppose the power structure.

The glorious seventeen years prior to the Cultural Revolution, 1949–1966, praised to the skies by "old aristocrats," were actually not all that glorious. In fact, the seventeen-year era was a political black hole that absorbed even the faintest light. Under the strict proletarian dictatorship, the slightest complaint would be immediately suppressed. The most trivial criticism of a local-level Party secretary or Party member was considered anti-Party and antisocialism. Then came the Cultural Revolution. People not only could criticize and protest, they could also attack and seize the power of the leaders from the local Party secretaries all the way up to Party secretaries at the provincial level, up to and including the vice chairmen of the Central Committee. The masses were also allowed to organize groups and factions and to protect that right with weapons. Anyone who has never lived under the proletarian dictatorship will never be able to understand this great sense of emancipation.

The complex and incomprehensible Cultural Revolution can in fact be categorized as two cultural revolutions. The first Cultural Revolution was Mao Zedong's struggle by which he used the mass movement to crack down on various organizations within the CCP in order to get rid of his political enemies and reclaim power that had slipped from his grasp. The second Cultural Revolution was a democratic struggle in which the people, using the emperor (though subconsciously), cracked down on corrupt cadres. From the perspective of the common people, the Cultural Revolution was by no means the chaotic large-scale frenzy depicted by the present-day contemporary power holders. All mass movements have profound social causes. As Carl Jung, the famous psychologist, once said, "In the beginning we are unaware of our actions. We only discover the motives for action after a long time. Moreover, we are always satisfied with the 'rationalization' for our actions until we discover, eventually, that these explanations are merely inappropriate alibis."[3] Although the slogans during the Cultural Revolution were many and the objectives varied, mass opposition to violent politics was the most fundamental driving force. The conventional explanation, that Mao used his charisma to mobilize a political storm that ended up involving one-quarter of mankind, simply does not fly. As early as the 1950s, totalitarian rule by the CCP had created enormous suffering for the people. In this country, with its complete ban on freedom of the press, people were unable to learn the scope and depth of the suffering, nor could they realize that the cause of the suffering was the totalitarian system, with Mao Zedong sitting on top of the pyramid. Thus, the common people could only focus their anger at middle and lower-level cadres of the CCP.

Mao Zedong and his colleagues were quite aware of the hatred and anger among the masses. A dialogue at a high-level meeting about the 1962–1965 Socialist Education Movement ("four cleans")* reveals this to be the case.

> Liu Shaoqi: There is a problem. What is the primary conflict in the rural areas? According to Tao Zhu [Guangdong Party secretary], a rich and privileged class has already formed in the countryside. According to Tao, the major conflict is that between the innumerable poor and lower-middle peasants and the rich and privileged class. But according to Li Jingquan [Sichuan Party secretary], the conflict is still between landlords, rich peasants, counterrevolutionaries, bad elements, and bad cadres opposed to the united force of the peasants. Is that so? (Li Jingquan said: Yes.)
>
> Chairman Mao: The landlords and the rich peasants are now in the background. The four unclean cadres are on the front stage; they are the power holders. If you only concentrate on struggling against the landlords and the rich peasants, the poor and lower-middle peasants will not be satisfied. The

---

*A mass movement designed to crack down on cadre corruption and abuses of power, especially in the countryside.

urgent task is to shake up the cadres. Since the landlords, rich peasants, and bad elements are not in power and were attacked previously, the poor and lower-middle peasants do not care much about them. Their real discontent is reserved for the bad cadres sitting on top of their heads. They are so poor, they can't tolerate it anymore. The landlords and rich peasants stink because they have undergone land reform. As for the power holders, they have never been criticized and do not stink.[4]

Mao and the VIPs in various provinces had no illusions about the sharp conflict that had developed between the people and the CCP. Mao had formulated a theory about this in his December 12, 1964, instructions, titled "Chairman Mao's Instructions on Socialist Education," in response to a report given by Chen Zhengren, who had gone down to the lower levels to feel the pulse of the locals.

> I myself agree with the notion that there is a sharp conflict between the bureaucratic class and the massive workers' class and the peasants. Management is also a kind of socialist teaching. If the managers do not go down to the workshops and small groups to eat, live, labor together with the masses, and to invite the veteran workers to be their teachers and to master some techniques, then they will forever be entangled in the sharp conflict with the working class and eventually they are bound to be attacked by the working class as the bourgeois class. . . .
>
> These leaders walking on the capitalist road have become or are becoming bourgeois elements sucking the blood from the working class. How can they be adequately clear about the necessity for socialism? These people are the objects of struggle and revolution and cannot be relied upon during the socialist education movement. We can only rely on those cadres who have no hatred against the workers and who possess revolutionary spirit.[5]

In the middle of the 1960s, when Mao felt that his power was slipping away, he made up his mind to use this conflict to get rid of his political enemies and to protect his power. In the beginning, he used the word "rebel" (*zaofan*), an aggressive term that evoked the guerrilla days of the CCP during the 1940s, to characterize his attacks on local Party organizations. The focus of the movement, he insisted, was to rectify capitalist roaders in the Party. The Chinese people who had suffered under the despotic system for 2,000 years had not originally dared to rebel. Suddenly, Mao's rallying cry gave the green light to all rebellions. If not now, when? The usually submissive common people responded. They shot forth a strong spray of hatred toward the cadres. Mao and the people simultaneously discovered a way to "publicly, thoroughly, from the bottom to the top, mobilize the masses to expose the dark side in our society."[6]

At this point, however, a small conundrum should not be ignored. If the second Cultural Revolution (the people's Cultural Revolution) constituted the people's struggle against corrupt cadres, why did the most violent and cruel internal fights occur among the various factions? In my opinion, if one analyzes the process of the Cultural Revolution, the answer is not hard to find. Everyone aimed at rebelling against the "seventeen years" and the CCP. Due to political immaturity, however, the people were easily divided into warring camps. At the beginning of the Cultural Revolution, for example, both in Beijing and in other provinces, there was a powerful faction, known as "protect the emperor," which had nothing but good things to say about the "seventeen years' rule." There were also various branches of this faction, such as the "veteran red guards," "red guard detachment," "industrial army," "the workers' patrol team," and so on. Soon after the masses were organized, however, the faction to protect the emperor was quickly defeated by the "rebel faction" *(zaofanpai)*, which thoroughly rejected the seventeen years. The angry wave that condemned the seventeen years quickly overwhelmed the efforts of the protect the emperor faction. In no time, the rebel faction expanded, gaining power in important Party, political, financial, and cultural circles. This very process exposed the original nature of the Cultural Revolution as an internal Party struggle. Unfortunately, on the matter of filling vacant positions of power and redistributing power, the masses, who thought they had gained power, were thwarted by Mao Zedong, who continually undermined the people's Cultural Revolution by creating new divisions within it. After the red guard detachment *(chiweidui)* and the industrial army *(chanyejun)* were destroyed, the once unified rebel faction in Sichuan split into two opposing groups: "August 26" and "fighting to the end" on one side, and "Red Guard Chengdu detachment" and "August 15" on the other. In Guizhou Province, after uniting to defeat the protect the emperor faction, the masses split into two factions: "April 11" and "support the Red Guards." In Beijing, the same process unfolded as the student rebels split into two: the "heaven" and the "earth" factions. (These two factions were the most complex because, since they were located in the capital, various political forces spread their influence within them.) Due to perpetual divisions, instigated by Mao, the popular struggle against the privileged class never reached a theoretical level. Mao and his followers skillfully employed all kinds of political devices at the time to achieve their ulterior ends. For instance, they would support one faction at one time on one issue and then support another faction at a different time on another. This is how they successfully split the masses and maneuvered them to engage in internal fights, instead of uniting together. Meanwhile, Mao and his followers' conspiratorial methods made it impossible for the factions to form a true threat to the CCP one-party rule, and so ensured that dominant power lay safely on Mao's side. In my opinion, the violence and cruelty of struggle during the Cultural Revolution erupted from the CCP's suppression and exploitation of the common people. The deeper the exploitation, the more violent the rebellion. I personally think that cruelty during the Cultural Revolution (including cruelty among the masses) was an expression of rebellion and wrath in response to the violent politics of the seventeen years.

The situation in Guangxi was much simpler. The Guangxi regime attempted to protect itself by directing the struggle against such old-style class enemies as landlords, rich peasants, and bad elements. It did not criticize capitalist roaders in the Party until 1967. Factions emerged only in April 1967, with the appearance of the "United Headquarters of the Proletarian Revolutionaries" *(lianzhi)* (the conservative faction) and the "April 22" (the rebel faction). The mobilization of the "April 22" faction to overthrow Wei Guoqing expressed the strong resistance of the various ethnic groups in Guangxi to the violent politics of the CCP. The *"lianzhi* faction"* consisted of people who had been deceived by Wei Guoqing. They were told that the source of all suffering was to be found in the anti-CCP and restorationist activities of the class enemies. It can be said that the Cultural Revolution in Guangxi was a struggle to smash the rebel faction with machine guns and cannons, by using the conservatives and the military forces. It was not an internal struggle among factions. It was a struggle between armed groups aimed at attacking counterrevolutionaries and counterattacking against counterrevolutionaries. Its cruelty was beyond description. How did such cruelty develop into such massive slaughter and cannibalism?

During my first trip to Guangxi, I spent days in the local archives and libraries attempting to trace the origins of these events. Numerous materials prove that throughout history the minorities in Guangxi had a tradition of cannibalism. The earliest written record of this comes from Qu Yuan's poem "Summons to the Soul" in *The Elegies of Chu:*

> O soul, come back! In the south you cannot stay.
> There the people have tattooed faces and blackened teeth;
> They sacrifice flesh of men and pound their bones for meat paste.*

Fan Ye from the Song dynasty (960–1279 A.D.) provided this description in his *Records of the Later Han:* "In the west lies a kingdom of cannibalism where the firstborn son is consumed, a practice known there as 'discharging duties toward the younger brother.' . . . The flesh is passed to the gen-

---

*The *Elegies of Chu (Chuzi)* is a second century A.D. anthology of poems by southern poets, including Qu Yuan (a fourth century B.C. official during the Warring States period in the Chu kingdom and one of China's greatest poets—who was forced to commit suicide after political schemers in the imperial court impugned his integrity and loyalty). *The Songs of the South: An Anthology of Ancient Chinese Poems by Qu Yuan and Other Poets,* tran. David Hawkes (New York: Penguin Books, 1985), p. 224.

tleman who enjoys his father's flesh. . . . South of Canton, human hands
and feet are consumed as delicacies. The old folks are also cannibalized."[7]
Although the traditions of Guangxi's minorities provide the most conve-
nient explanation for the massive slaughter and cannibalism during the
Cultural Revolution, I cannot agree, however, with such an analysis.
Deep down, I resent these attempts to gain an understanding of cultural
history from a perspective that is nothing but Han chauvinism. I have
concluded from my contacts with the Zhuang people that they are modest and kindhearted. Numerous classical works demonstrate the existence of a tradition of cannibalism in Guangxi, yet I am strongly inclined
to trust the Zhuang. Nevertheless, I find myself in a theoretical dilemma.
Intuition is intuition, but it does not possess the convincing power of
logic. I decided, therefore, to search for a theoretical explanation for the
inhumane activities that had occurred in Guangxi. I knew that the answer
to this mystery was hidden in the cultural history of the Zhuang. Analyzing the Zhuang people from the perspective of cultural anthropology became the purpose of my second trip [1988] to Guangxi.

After our interview with Wang Zujian, Bei Ming and I interviewed various Zhuang experts and scholars specializing in the cultural history of
the Zhuang people. At the end of each discussion, we usually asked the
question: Why did cannibalism occur during the Cultural Revolution in
Guangxi? None of the people we talked to had ever considered this question. Most simply pointed out that cannibalism was a tradition in the area,
although they were somewhat helpful in allowing us to piece together an
overall explanation. Among the scholars and experts, Lan Hongen, a
specialist in Zhuang historical legends and folk literature, helped us the
most. During our first interview, Lan directed us to the Zhuang history
of legends and epics. The story of the hero Dong Lin, who was transformed from a primitive being into a civilized man, was especially
thought-provoking.

April 18 is the Zhuang people's "March 3 Lunar Calendar Song Festival." On that day, the literary association of Guangxi joined the activities
in Baning County. The Baning County seat is located in Puchao Township, a place with a history dating back 257 years to the ninth year in the
reign of the Yongzheng, emperor during the Qing dynasty (1644–1911).
Activities held to commemorate the county's history combine with a song
festival, making it an especially clamorous occasion. Dancing lions,
dragon teams, horseback riding, stilt-walking, and parading ghosts are all
part of the jubilee (Photo 3.2). The only pity is that the local regime sets
up a "guest stage" so that every team passing by has to bow in front of
the "leaders" and guests from afar.

"March 3" is a festival for lovers. According to one legend, once upon a
time there was a young lad and a young girl who grew up loving each

PHOTO 3.2   March 3 Song Festival: In the eyes of the Zhuang people, the
ghostly world is the world of humankind, a beautiful world full of wonders.

other and they often expressed their love by singing to each other. Later,
the girl was forced to marry an old man. But she escaped to meet her
lover. Her parents and in-laws threatened to punish the young lad, so the
devoted couple ended up dying together under a scarlet silk cotton tree.
In yet another legend, a young unmarried girl, in order to flee her oppres-
sive parents, scaled a local mountain, climbed a big maple tree, and began
to cry. Her tears reddened the maple leaves and the fragrant grass be-
neath the tree. She was not discovered until the third day in March.[8] To
mourn both the devoted couple and the young crying girl, on every
March 3, people eat glutinous rice dyed red like the maple leaves and the
fragrant grass and sing romantic songs to their lovers. The tradition has
been maintained from generation to generation and has gradually developed into the "March 3 Song Festival." According to the historical
archives, the Zhuang people's tradition of song can be traced back a thousand years.

    After the festival, we visited a village famous for its benevolent witches,
and while there, we interviewed two young female field hands, ages fourteen and fifteen, who described their "tour through the netherworld."
These were two girls who, it is said, had, with the help of witches, "toured

the netherworld on several occasions." A local novelist named Cen Longye, who accompanied us to the village, has conducted extensive research into the witch phenomenon. According to Cen, the tour through the netherworld is an important component of Zhuang witchcraft. In the Zhuang language the term "netherworld" literally means "the trembling netherworld." People who tour the netherworld can visit villages, streets, houses, and can also talk to their dead relatives, friends, and neighbors. If the day they tour the netherworld happens to fall on a market day, they can also go shopping with the souls and ghosts of the netherworld. Touring the netherworld can be understood as a way of connecting this world with the next. The skills of the witches enable living people to meet the dead and thus to integrate the world of the living with the world of the dead. The girls we talked to were very innocent and timid and soon after they started to speak, their faces became flushed. They had to go back to their work in the fields and so they described their tour in only the simplest of terms.

Some locals arranged for my wife and I to observe an elderly witch perform. The two girls whom we had talked to earlier in the day would once again tour the netherworld. There was a huge incense table in the middle of the living room, which every local family used to worship "heaven and earth." On the wall were large posters of foreign movies with beautiful actresses and handsome actors along with foreign metropolitan scenery. Compared to the generally low living standards, these decorations seemed quite fancy. The witch sat in front of a small table next to the wall. On the table were three bowls full of rice, and on top of the rice were three incense joss sticks. After lighting the joss sticks, the witch murmured something and then started to pray, while burning two paper horses. At the same time, the two girls sat facing the wall with their heads buried in their two arms between their knees. The witch spat a mouthful of water at them. It seemed that the witch had completed what she needed to do. Three minutes later, the two girls started trembling. With eyes closed and heads down, they began to murmur. The witch placed two fans with bells in the hands of the girls and the two girls then started waving the fans nonstop. The fans symbolized the horses used to tour the netherworld, and the ringing bells symbolized the horses' movement. In the beginning, the girls described an ambiguous and poetic world: "Alas, why is it so cold? I am cold. I am chilled! What place is this? I cannot see anything— fog rolling in all over the sky! I can see nothing! Everywhere fog, everywhere fog. Chilly." In the fog, the two girls meet each other. Riding the horses, they probe their way forward. About five minutes later, they stopped trembling and started to cry, "At last, the sun! The sun has come out! I see the sun. What warm sunshine!" At that point, they returned to their normal state, riding forward full of glee.

Soon they arrived in front of a river. There was a beautiful bridge crossing the river. At the entrance, they were stopped by a muscular guard
who inquired about their destination, since it was not a market day. The
girls begged the guard to let them go, saying they would "just like to go
take a look." But the guard was persistent, fearing that the commoners
would be so attracted to the beauty of the netherworld that they would
never return to their world. But after the girls begged over and over, the
guard finally let them pass.

The two girls then started to describe in Zhuang songs what they had
seen in the netherworld. The crowd gathered around them in the room,
following their songs closely and imagining the scenes. The humorous
girls often described unexpected scenes and even cracked jokes that made
the crowd burst into laughter. There were nine streets in the netherworld.
The girls walked along each one, depicting the houses and the tranquility
of the streets (it not being a market day). They bumped into acquaintances by accident and started to chat. Some people told the girls to go
back home as soon as possible; otherwise, they said, it would be too late.
Since there was not much going on in the streets, the two girls started to
head home before they had toured all nine streets. The return trip evidently was as pleasant as the one going there, because the scenery was
equally soothing. The description of the naked village, where neither the
men nor the women wore any clothes, made the deepest impression on
me. Young lads watched over the cattle and plowed the fields. When they
beheld the two girls, they started to flirt with them by singing folk love
songs. Cen Longye and another local writer translated the songs for us,
but no matter how fast I tried to record them, I simply could not write
down all of the beautiful words. Sometimes when the two girls' horses
stopped, the witch would quickly open the fans in the girls' hands. Then
the horses would start up again. Obviously, the witch was "watching
over" every move made by the girls. When the girls decided to buy some
snacks on the street, the witch quickly burned some paper money. But
most of the time, the witch just sat there, smoking her huge water pipe.
The witch at times also held a baby on her knee, just as any loving and
kindhearted grandmother might. I quickly realized that the atmosphere
was not as mysterious as I had thought it would be. The people in the
crowd were enjoying the activity as if they were at a song festival.

The girls continued to walk, but a young lad fell in love with them and
begged them to stay by singing love songs. One girl seemed to be moved
by him and showed reluctance to leave. The other girl persuaded her to ignore the young lad. "If you continue to listen to him, you would . . . !"
That remark made the entire crowd, including the witch, burst into laughter. The translator stammered. It seemed that it was a rather coarse remark.
Intent on returning home, the girl ordered the young lad to go away in a

song: "If you do not go away, my mother will come out to drive you away, or my dog will come out and bite you." When the witch saw that the girls had finally returned home, she put down her water pipe, made a gesture, and flipped over a bowl. "Open the door, they have finally returned home," she commanded. When the bowl was once again flipped on its side, the girls collapsed. Seeing that someone was coming to help them, they then sat up and leaned against the wall. They were obviously fatigued. I could tell they were not faking. The next day, we went to the fields to thank them with gifts of candy and fruit, and we noticed that their faces were still very pale.

Whether or not they really "toured the netherworld" and crossed the bridge, we should heed the Taoist saying of Zhuangzi: "I have left behind the six points of direction and entered the region of nothingness, the wilderness of spacelessness."* Even if the netherworld did not exist, they had traversed the witch's scene. If they had not really entered an unusual world, at least they had been converted into a hypnotic state of mind. The "tour" took three hours and was described as a rather short one. The girls waved the fans and their feet throughout the tour, singing nonstop. (It is said that during the tour one has no reaction to outside stimuli such as being pinched.) After they woke up, they were unable to describe what they had seen in the netherworld, and thus they had to rely on others to describe their experience. During their tour, their consciences were relaxed, so that secrets they would not normally reveal and repressed feelings and aspects of their personality were disclosed. I thought they had attained a supra-self mentality. That evening I had truly experienced witchcraft and had come to a profound understanding that witchcraft was an integral part of Zhuang life. It was all very natural, real, pleasant, relaxed, and commonplace. The children watching all of this were themselves educated in witchcraft. They had learned early in life that they could form a worldview that allowed them to express their consciousness of religion, society, and morality through witchcraft. This would serve as a solid foundation for their lives. For witchcraft is a religion so benevolent that it knows no sin. It is a religion that is totally unprepared in the face of sin. A young and innocent religion ignorant of sin created young and innocent Zhuang people ignorant of sin.

In China's big family, the minorities in the south are relatively new. A myth of the Yao people describes this well. The lady creator of the world had three sons. At birth, the eldest carried a balance scale and went to a

---

*Zhuangzi, "Ruling an Empire," in Martin Buber, *Chinese Tales, Zhuangzi: Sayings and Parables and Chinese Ghosts and Love Stories,* tran. Alex Page (Atlantic Highlands, NJ: Humanities Press International, Inc., 1991), p. 35.

prosperous place to engage in business. He established a family of sons
and daughters and led a good life. This eldest son became the Han people. Soon afterward, the second eldest son left and went to plow the
fields. He also settled down and became the contemporary Zhuang. The
youngest son left last, when all the family's assets had already been taken
away by his brothers. He had no choice but to take a shabby tool, some
leftover rice, and a handful of buns and go into the mountains to plow the
nonarable land.[9]

Obviously this is not the original version of the myth, but it does
vividly depict the historical fact that at the dawn of Chinese civilization,
the minorities in the south were a just-awakening younger brother.

During our trip in northeast Guangxi to study folk customs, we heard a
great many stories depicting the custom among the Zhuang of "not cohabitating with the husband's family" *(buluo fujia)* immediately after marriage. According to this tradition, on the night of the wedding the bride
goes to bed with a female companion from her parents' side and ignores
her husband. The next morning, the bride gets up and immediately returns to her own parents. The union between husband and wife is merely
a formality. Zhuang friends accompanying us during our trip told us that
whenever the bride returns to her husband's village, she informs him
ahead of time; however, whenever villagers see the bride they have to inform the husband right away. The bride formally settles down with her
husband only after she becomes pregnant. The practice of "not cohabitating with the husband's family" can last at a minimum for two or
three years or for as long as seven or eight years. During busy times,
when the bride is away, the husband's mother or his elder sister goes to
pick up the bride and brings her back to the husband's house for a few
days. The bride eventually returns to her parents' home. During the period of "not cohabitating with the husband's family," the wife may still
participate in song festivals and may even go out with boyfriends. In addition, she also has some economic independence. In villages such as
Longlin, as soon as the girls are able to work in the fields (at the age of
twelve or thirteen), the parents designate a piece of land for them (if
arable land is unavailable, the girls plow the fields of their parents). The
girls work the land independently and save the income as their personal
money. By the time they get married and settle down with their husbands, their handsome savings serve as a basis of independent financial
support.

This independence undoubtedly grew out of a residual resistance by
women during the transition from a matriarchical to a patriarchical society. The CCP once condemned such customs as "backward" and attempted to eliminate them. For instance, during the Land Reform period,

regulations were issued that either deprived of land anyone who refused to cohabit with their husband, or granted the land exclusively to the husband. This was an attempt to rid the Zhuang of their customs at the outset of the liberation. Later, during the period of agricultural cooperativization in the early 1950s, when all land was returned to public ownership, the Zhuang practice of not cohabitating with the husband's family once again became popular. Consequently, new regulations were issued that barred women from being assigned work in the fields, or prohibited them from earning work points, if they refused to cohabit with their husbands. Thus, the custom was once again suppressed. However, some women still refused to conform and chose to plow their own fields in the mountains.[10]

In addition to the practice of not cohabitating with the husband's family, we discovered many other traditional family and marriage practices among the Zhuang. For instance, there is the "night wedding" *(yehun)*, which is a symbolic remnant of the old practice of selecting a bride in the dark. And then "the birth-giving man" *(chanweng)* (a practice now defunct), in which the husband holds onto the baby during the postnatal month of confinement. This was a means used by the husbands to obtain certain rights over their children. "The rights of maternal males" *(jiuquan)*, a custom in which the rights of the wife's brothers and maternal uncles override those of the male members on the husband's side of the family, was a legacy of the practices during the primitive matriarchical society. Marriage between the first nephews and nieces was also popular. (According to statistics from Mahai village of Longshenglongji Township, Guangxi Province, marriages among closely related nephews and cousins, which were socially acceptable, constituted 50 percent of all marriages.) Certainly, one can say that the Zhuang have retained prototypes of just about all the forms of marriage that have existed in human history.[11] From this we can see that the Zhuang are not only a younger sibling awakening to the call of civilization, but also a younger sibling whose development has been delayed.

In the great epic *Muliujia* of Zhuang literature, the original form of the universe was swirling air. As it swirled faster and faster, the universe consolidated into an "egg." A vermin pushed at this universe egg and caused it to rotate, while a corn earworm dug a hole in it. In this version of the big bang theory, when the hole was complete, the universe egg exploded into three parts. The top part was heaven, the bottom was water, and the one in the middle was earth. In between the top, bottom, and middle parts, there was emptiness and loneliness. However, at a great moment, a fresh flower grew out of the earth. In the blooming flower was born a goddess. She was pretty and wise, with long flowing hair, and she was naked. She was known as Muliujia, also referred to as "Miliujia." "Mi" in the Zhuang language refers to mother and "liujia" is a bird that the Zhuang use to symbolize wisdom. Thus, "Muliujia" refers to the mother of wisdom, the founding mother of mankind. After the universe exploded into three parts, the corn earworm flew to the heaven and the vermin remained on earth. One created heaven, the other earth. The vermin was very industrious and created vast lands. The corn earworm, however, was very lazy and only created a narrow sky. As a result, the earth and the heaven that they created did not match. Muliujia rumbled the earth in her palm to make it wrinkled and in so doing she matched heaven and earth. The wrinkled earth now had mountains, valleys, and rivers. Muliujia's interminable menstrual blood became the source of life of the Zhuang—the Red River.

The earth, covered though it was with mountains and rivers, nevertheless lacked vitality. Muliujia opened her legs and stood on the peaks of two adjacent mountains. All of a sudden, a wind rose and Muliujia could no longer hold back her urine. The lonely Muliujia picked up the urine-soaked dirt and out of it she molded many mud figurines in her own image, covering them with grass. When, after forty-nine days, Muliujia removed the grass, the mud figurines stood up. Muliujia gathered together a bunch of hot peppers and peaches from the forest and threw them to the crowd of figurines. Those who grabbed the hot peppers became male, and those who got the peaches became female.

In order to make the earth more vital, Muliujia also made a bunch of figurines out of mud and threw them up into the sky indiscriminately. Thereupon birds and beasts appeared. During a torrential rain, the people and the beasts lacked shelter and so Muliujia sat down with her legs wide apart. Her reproductive organ was transformed into a huge cave, which became the primeval home of safety for both humankind and animals.[12]

The creator of the world also created the sun and taught humankind how to fish and retain fire. Humankind was therefore healthy and led a prosperous life. However, as more and more people were born, food became scarcer. The Goddess of Thunder who came after Muliujia decided that senile people incapable of work should be eaten, along with the dead. In the words of Zhuang folk songs of years past, "A long long time ago, people were primitive. The sons ate the fathers, senile mothers were killed to celebrate the New Year. The senile people plowing the fields were slaughtered with knives to be served as a feast." Later came a boy named Teyi, a cowherd up in the mountains who noticed that his cows suffered while giving birth, rolling on the ground in pain. When he returned home, Teyi described the suffering of his cows to his mother and asked how it had been when he was born. Teyi's mother replied, "I gave birth to you and your two brothers. Each time I suffered so much that I almost died!" Teyi decided then and there that the consuming of the flesh of elderly people was too cruel. He talked the matter over with his brothers and decided that from then on they would refuse to eat the flesh of elderly people sent over to their home and instead they would dehydrate it for preservation.

Teyi's mother died. The villagers rushed to Teyi's house to get a share. Teyi refused to let the villagers cut into his mother's flesh. The villagers were outraged. "Unfair!" they cried. "How is it that you shared our parents' flesh and now refuse to let us do the same?" Teyi took out the dehydrated flesh and told the crowd, "I did not eat the flesh you sent over. Therefore, you cannot eat my mother's flesh either!"

The people would not leave. They demanded fresh flesh. Teyi and his brother then killed their family's cattle and shared the meat with everyone.

The Goddess of Thunder, upon hearing that Teyi had violated her regulations, decided to chop him to death. The Teyi brothers turned to Buluotuo, the God of Enlightenment, who said, "The Goddess of Thunder has an almighty power that relies on her copper drum. You must make a leather drum and beat it nonstop. Since you have more people, the Goddess of Thunder will be defeated."

When the Goddess of Thunder flew down to chop Teyi, Teyi and his brothers started to beat the leather drum to resist the copper drum. The Goddess of Thunder was startled and couldn't figure out what trick the Teyi brothers had up their collective sleeve. So she sent her daughter, the frog, to find out. The Teyi brothers captured the frog and questioned her about the shape of the copper drum and the frog revealed the secret. Because of the image of six frogs on the drum, she told them, the drum makes a loud sound when struck. The Teyi brothers fashioned a similar drum out of copper, with the same image of six frogs. It was so loud that it shook the mountains and valleys, causing the white clouds in the sky to tremble. The Goddess of Thunder dared not compete with the Teyi brothers and, seeing that the people had flesh to eat, she finally gave up.[13]

Fortunately, there was no paragon of virtue like Confucius in Zhuang history. So the descriptions of cannibalism in the epics have been retained to this day. According to Friedrich Engels, "During the period when food was scarce it is conceivable that cannibalism occurred. Such practices persisted for a long time."[14] In primitive societies where food was scarce, cannibalism was necessary and cannot be judged according to modern-day standards. If one insists on making such judgments, then one can say that this form of cannibalism, a product of need, was based on a kind of primitive morality. If one views the cannibalism of primitive tribal societies from the perspective of modern times, however, then such cannibalism can only be considered a mortal sin.

HAN GUILT

The Han people who recorded the cannibalism of the primitive Zhuang tribes in derogatory terms were the same ones who judged this primitive practice in modern terms.

New forms of morality could only emerge among the Zhuang as production progressed, making cannibalism no longer necessary for survival. What the Teyi legend described was a great historical progression of the new morality defeating the old. Teyi was a hero who should remain in the historical memory of human civilization. Ancient humans who had just lost their animal hair, who were still at the fishing and hunting stage, who were not distant from the activities of the beasts could not yet recognize the highly esteemed position that only humankind possesses. With the emergence of animal husbandry, certain wise individuals recognized the importance of a fundamental respect for humankind. Such a self-conscious realization of the esteem and respect for humankind finally distinguished humankind from beasts. Such a realization also strengthened the internal cohesion among humankind and enabled a primitive sociability to be developed into a pursuit of morals. From then on, people finally became human beings and established their own home of joy in the primitive world. The struggle between the Teyi brothers and the Goddess of Thunder was the epochal war among the Zhuang's ancestors. The tribes representing the new morality and the new forms of production—a more advanced lifestyle—defeated the leading tribes who held to the old morality. From then on, the natural law of cannibalism was eliminated.

Substituting beef for human flesh was a mutual compromise during the transitional period from the old morality to the new. The ceremony marking this natural transition was known as "slaughtering the cattle" *(kanniu)*. In the magnificent cattle-slaughtering ceremony, villagers sing, dance, and eat, consuming beef as a substitute for human flesh. The activity subsequently became an epic ceremony and a festival that is celebrated to this day. I am positive that this is the Zhuang's way of celebrating their progress from primitivism to civilization.

The slaughtering of cattle is the most formidable scene at funerals in the Zhuang and Yao cultures. Zhuang and Yao funerals can only be held from the end of autumn until the early spring, because this is the only time when there is no thunder (which hints at the historical defeat of the Goddess of Thunder). Those who pass away in the spring and the summer are initially buried in the living room, next to the stove, or in the front or at the back of their house. When the proper time arrives, the bodies are dug up to undergo a formal funeral ceremony. In general, funerals are grander than weddings. Ten days prior to the funeral, notices are sent out to family members, relatives, and friends. Five days before the funeral, copper drums are beaten.

The cattle-slaughtering ceremony is held one day before the funeral. Participants attend from villages both near and far with their copper drums. They also set up a wooden stand more than 10 meters in height upon which all the copper drums are hung in order. The Zhuang and Yao view copper drums as important musical instruments to be revered in specific holy places. They prohibit the beating of the drums in ordinary times. They are only used when it is time to communicate with the souls of the dead. The scene of the drum beating is also very magnificent, with at least six to ten or as many as seventy to eighty drums being beaten at the same time. No matter how many drums are involved, they all follow a huge cowhide drum (an allusion to Teyi's defeat of the Goddess of Thunder and to the fact that Teyi's victory was not just a victory of the drum, but a victory of all the tribes engaged in animal husbandry). The leather drum determines the tempo and the tune. When the time has arrived, the person beating the leather drum lights up three incense joss sticks and honors the drum by covering it with delicious food and liquor. The rest of the drummers take a drink of rice wine and spray it onto the drums. Then they lightly beat the surface of the drums with wheat stalks. Following the lead of the leather drummer, all the other drummers sing in honor of the drum:

Alas—
XXX has passed away.
The heartfelt crying shakes the mountains and rivers.
The river runs forward, weeping;
The mountain lowers its head sobbing in silence.
The God has heard no word of this.
The beat of the drum,
 Please pass on our sorrow to His Divinity.
Alas—
The beat of the drums travels swiftly
To inform His Divinity of our sorrow.

When the ceremony honoring the drum is over, the drummers, led by the leather drummer, start to perform all kind of songs. Behind each drum stands a person holding a wooden bucket that shakes and vibrates with the beating drums. The sound of the drums flows into the wooden bucket. This makes the drum beating more complex, beautiful, and far-reaching. The leather drummer dances while beating the drum, and the other drummers follow his lead, at times moving swiftly, at times at a slow tempo, at times heavy and at times light, at times high and at times low. The thick, deafening sound "Tong! Tong! Tong!" is heard throughout the sky. After fourteen rounds, the drum beating stops (the first seven rounds are in memory of the dead, the last seven are to bless the living). Then the cattle slaughter begins.

Three cannonballs are shot into the air, informing heaven to open the heavenly gates to receive the dead and to open the gate to the cattle yard. Soon after the cannon shooting is over, the maternal uncle (the rights of the uncles on the mother's side are still recognized by the Zhuang) appears. His head is wrapped in a white piece of cloth and he is wearing newly embroidered garments. Accompanied by an elderly man, the maternal uncle holds a three-foot long knife with both hands while humming an elegy. He slowly walks toward the coffin to bow and to honor the dead. Then he walks around the coffin once and heads toward the cattle slaughtering ground. Three or five strong hatchet men walk toward the maternal uncle and stand behind him. The other mourners, standing in two parallel lines, bow and lower their heads. Putting their left hands over their hearts while holding a stalk of wheat and a small bamboo stick, they walk slowly toward the slaughter ground and stand behind the maternal uncle. Then, the family of the deceased bring in one, or sometimes more than one, strong cow and tie it to wooden posts festooned with flowers. The village elder reads the elegies and hums an elegiac tune while throwing white rice at the animal. This is meant to send seeds to the netherworld so the soon-to-be-slaughtered cow will plow for the dead.

After the song, the maternal uncle toasts the sacrificial cow three times and then kisses its head while weeping. The crowd weeps along while singing an elegy. Children and relatives surround the animal, caressing it with great sorrow, kissing its face, feeding it with fresh green grass and wheat, and kneeling down before it to bid farewell. The weeping is so loud that it shakes the mountains, valleys, and the villages near and far.

Then, the maternal uncle takes out the sharp knife from under an umbrella, bows three times to the cow, and hands the knife over to the hackers. They in turn take the knife and bow to heaven and earth three times respectively while someone else whips the animal to move it quickly around the grinding stone. A hacker targets the head of the cow and chops at it suddenly. Blood shoots out and the injured animal prances around madly. The second hacker delivers another blow to the cow. One blow per person is allowed until the animal's head hangs loosely (the head cannot be completely severed). The crowd of people rush forward to skin the animal and consume the meat. This process may be repeated when there is more than one sacrificial cow. At this point, three cannonballs are shot into the sky to inform the heavenly gods and the ancestors. Usually by this point in the ceremony, darkness has fallen.

On the next day, at a scheduled time, the coffin is buried in the mountains. After the funeral, wooden posts with cattle horns nailed to them are erected in front of the tomb. The number of wooden posts matches the number of cattle slaughtered and the pairs of horns. The cooked beef is then distributed among the mourners along with rice wine until everyone is drunk. When darkness falls, the drunkards are seen lying all over the mountainside and the near-drunken ones stumble about.[15]

In watching the cattle-slaughtering ceremony, Han people hold different views from those of the Zhuang and the Yao. The Han consider it unbearably cruel and bloody, whereas the Zhuang and Yao consider it magnificent and holy. The Han also view the hackers as killers; however, the hackers consider the slaughter to be an act of heroism. In fact, whoever does the best job of hacking wins the love of the local girls. From the Han perspective, cattle slaughtering is backward and superstitious, destructive of productivity. The CCP once simplemindedly prohibited it from being performed. In reality, cattle slaughtering is a magnificent memorial symbolizing the Zhuang's (and Yao's) progression from primitive life to civilization.

*   *   *

The slave system of the Zhuang originated during the Warring States Period (475–221 B.C.) and flourished during the Six dynasties (222–589 A.D.) and the beginning of the Tang dynasty (618–907 A.D.). From the mid-Tang onward, however, it declined and it finally perished during the Northern Song dynasty (960–1127 A.D.). Although it lasted for at least 1,000 years, it had basically been stuck at the stage of patriarchical slavery *(jiazhang nulizhi)*. Throughout this stage of underdevelopment, many primitive remnants were retained. Among them, communal rural practices and primitive marriage practices have been retained to this day.

Perhaps we can finally answer some of the claims made over the years about the Zhuang.

The Zhuang's ancestors were militant.

True. But tribal wars were characteristic not only of the Zhuang but also of many others.

The Zhuang's ancestors maintained cannibalism as a custom.

True. The low productivity of the primitive society drove them to cannibalism. And in this the Zhuang were not alone.

The Zhuang's ancestors cannibalized their first son.

Also true. Here I can also describe a legend as a supplementary example.

A long, long time ago, the sun and the moon lived alongside humankind. They gave birth to many children—the stars. But the empty sky
could not feed that many children. The father sun began to worry and
eventually started to resent his children. He was determined to eliminate
them, so he captured them one by one and ate them. The mother moon
was very sad. But she could do nothing but go into hiding with her children. She only allowed the children to come out and play after sunset. But
some of the children were not careful and came out to play before sunset.
They ended up being captured and eaten. Thereafter, their blood painted
the sky red at dawn and at sunset.[16]

Due to the scarcity of food in primitive society, and to the practice of
not cohabitating with the husband's family, most Zhuang children were
brought up by their mothers and were considered wild children. Seen in
this light, the practice of eating the first son is not incomprehensible.

After combing the chaotic mess of history, folk culture, epics, myths,
legends, and witchcraft as well as additional historical research, my wife
and I continued to probe our way forward. Perhaps we have walked a
path leading us out of the jungle toward the light of rationality. Unfortunately, however, to this day we are still unable to answer the fundamental
question: Is Zhuang culture solely responsible for the cannibalism and
wholesale slaughter that occurred during the Cultural Revolution in
Guangxi?

I think not. In my opinion, the cause of such an appalling crime was
probably the interaction of Zhuang culture with Han culture. The Zhuang
are the most populous minority group in China. (According to the 1982
national census, among a total of 13 million Zhuang, 12 million live in
Guangxi, accounting for 50 percent of the total population in the Guangxi
Autonomous Region.) After the Zhou dynasty (1100 B.C.–221 B.C.), for
over 3,000 years the Zhuang maintained close contact with the Han people. In fact, some Zhuang in effect became Han. Present-day Zhuang are
perhaps the minority most assimilated into the Han. For this reason, it is
necessary for us to examine Han culture.

Please allow me to cite a few examples on the narrow topic of cannibalism committed by the Han.

In his *General History of China,* the famous historian, Fan Wenlan, described a case of cannibalism committed by soldiers in 883 A.D.: "According to historical records, during the famine in Henan Province, Huang
Chao, the leader of a peasant uprising, ordered that humans be consumed. According to one belief, the dead bodies were crushed into pieces
by grinding stones and were consumed along with powdered bone. According to another belief, live people were thrown under the grinding
stone. The 'food' distribution center was designated as 'the grinding village.' That historical record is nothing but a baseless slander. . . . The ex-

ploiting classes slandered Huang Chao by describing him as someone engaged in beastly acts. . . . In reality, neither Huang Chao nor the ruthless Qin Zongquan committed such an act."[17]

As a Marxist, Fan Wenlan was following Mao Zedong's comment that "peasant uprisings were an important driving force of historical development" and so, putting his own imagination to use, in one line he effectively deleted a case of cannibalism committed by Huang Chao. Fortunately, other historical works were not written by Fan Wenlan. During my period of exile since 1989 I have read widely and, in one source, I found the following quote from the "Huang Chao" segment of *Records of the Late Tang (Jiu Tang shu):* "In May of the third year in Zhonghe, Huang Chao defeated Chenzhou. The thief had numerous grinding villages where live people were ground into pieces and consumed along with powdered bone."[18]

Si Maguang also described the following: In 891 A.D., the soldiers of Qin Zongquan "captured the elderly and the young and sold them on the market. The captives were slaughtered like sheep and the entire market was covered with blood."[19]

Yet another example comes from the period at the height of feudal society, when the rich competed in wealth, a sport that included competition over cannibalism.

> At the end of the Sui dynasty (581–618 A.D.), there was a wealthy man named Zhuge Ang who was open and high-spirited. . . . To prepare a big feast, ten chefs were put to work boiling pigs and sheep. Dozens of meter-long pancakes were also baked. . . . Hundreds of guests attended . . . with singing and lion performances staged throughout the evening. A pair of teenage twin brothers were also boiled. When their heads, hands, and feet were presented, everyone vomited. . . . A few days later, Ang ordered his concubine to serve some liquor. The concubine giggled, which irritated Ang. He ordered her to put on makeup and dress in silk garments. Then he made her sit on a silver plate. Once she was thus prepared, he carved a piece of flesh out of her thigh, which frightened everyone. Ang then proceeded to cut away a piece from her breast, which he consumed with gusto. The concubine was so embarrassed that she fled in the night.[20]

Further documentation comes from *Notes on Coarse Musings (Yuewei caotang biji).*

> A long time ago at the end of the era of the Chongzhen emperor, a severe drought broke out in Henan and Shandong Provinces. After they had devoured all the grass roots and tree bark, human beings cannibalized each other out of a need for food. The situation was so dire that the government could do nothing about it. Women and babies were arrayed in the market as human food and were sold by the slaughterers just like mutton and pork. One day, an old man returning from business stopped by the butcher some

time during the afternoon. "The meat has all been sold out," the butcher said. "Please wait for a moment." The old man watched with dismay as two women were dragged into the kitchen. "The customer has been waiting for a long time. Let him have the first piece!" the butcher yelled. When he heard that, the old man rushed in to save the women. He arrived just in time to hear a long scream and to see that the girl's arm had been cut off and had fallen onto the floor.... The girl begged for a quick death.... The old man was moved ... and stabbed the girl in the heart.

Given that so many techniques have been used in the act of cannibalism, unique skills must have been developed in slaughtering people.

Back to Huang Chao. As the leader of the peasant uprising, apart from killing Chinese, he also slaughtered foreigners.

According to documentary records compiled by the Arabs, in Canton Huang Chao killed Muslims, Jews, and Christians, altogether 120,000 to 200,000.... Huang Chao also killed merchants and religious believers for his own reasons. [What reasons? According to Fan Wenlan's estimation: "Perhaps Huang Chao viewed himself as a Confucian and therefore considered all others to be heretics. In addition, most of the religious disciples were merchants who were exploiters of every stripe." Note this rationale for killing by Huang Chao as provided by the most authoritative "general history" text in contemporary China—comment by Zheng Yi.] However, it is not possible that there were so many foreigners in Canton.[21]

The primitive era of cannibalism is history from the remote past. Since then the Han have advanced into civilization. At the subconscious level, the concept of "cannibalism out of need" that existed in the primitive era was eliminated long ago from the minds of the Han so that cannibalism has long been condemned as a pure evil. However, the Chinese nation, known for its high level of morality, somehow lacks the spirit of forgiveness that is revered by both Eastern and Western religions. On the contrary, China rewards revenge and advocates a policy of an eye for an eye. The morality of this nation never opposes abstract evil just as the CCP refuses to acknowledge abstract humanism. No matter how cruel the means, as long as it is an act of revenge against an evil or against an enemy, the cruel act is then queerly transformed into morality. If writers are considered the conscience of the nation and the engineers of the human soul, then let us look at how Chinese writers have depicted the soul and conscience of this nation!

Numerous descriptions of mass slaughter and cannibalism that exemplify the taking of revenge and the eye-for-an-eye "morality" are evident in the Chinese classical works *Romance of the Three Kingdoms* and *Outlaws of the Marsh*.

In *Romance of the Three Kingdoms*, for instance, after Guan Yu is murdered, Liu Bei sets up a mourning dais for Master Guan.* Liu himself reveres the master by holding the severed head of his enemy, Ma Zhong, in front of the mourning stand. Liu then orders that two of Guan Yu's subordinates—Mi Fang and Fu Shiren—be killed. He strips them and orders them to kneel down in front of the mourning stand where Liu cuts off their heads in honor of the master.

Prior to becoming emperor, Liu Bei had engaged in cannibalism himself. After he is defeated at Xuzhou, "one day, he seeks shelter. The young son of the family comes out, bows, and introduces himself as hunter Liu An. When Liu An discovers that there is no meat to serve, he kills his wife. Liu Bei asks, 'What kind of meat is this?' Liu An replies, 'Wolf meat.' Liu Bei eats heartily and then falls asleep. The next morning when he is fetching his horse to leave, he notices that in the kitchen are the remains of a woman without any flesh left on her arms. To his surprise, Liu Bei realizes that the previous night he had consumed the flesh of Liu An's wife." Later, Liu An is bestowed with rewards by the emperor as his devoted servant.

Now let us examine some of the pages of *Outlaws of the Marsh*, particularly the story of Lin Chong's revenge.

> Lin Chong . . . ripped open Lu Qian's clothes, stabbed the blade into his heart and twisted. Blood spurted everywhere. Lin tore out his heart and liver and held them in his hand.[†]
>
> The little soldiers had tied Gao Xiannei onto the four legs of a horse. After he had stared at Xiannei, Lin Chong felt like chewing him up whole and spitting him out. Suddenly, Lin had a brainstorm. "Go fetch Xiannei's chef," he ordered his subordinates. In no time, the chef came. "What is your master's favorite cuisine of lamb and pork?" Lin asked him. The chef replied, "Pig's ears rolled up into dumplings, sheep's eyes fried in oil, dehydrated mutton, barbecued pork." "Great," Lin replied. He then ordered Xiannei to be cleaned up and brought to him. Song Jiang ordered that the feast table be removed and a mourning stand be set up for Lin Chong's mother. Lin Chong expressed his gratitude. After the subordinates had washed Xiannei, Song ordered, "Get three cups of blood wine first to toast the mother." Three holes were cut into Xiannei's body. The cups were offered up to the departed spirit of Lin's mother. Once again, Lin expressed his gratitude.
>
> The mourning of Lin's mother having been completed, the feast was resumed. . . . Lin Chong ordered that pork, mutton, beef, and horse meat be

---

*Luo Guanzhong (1330–1400), *Romance of the Three Kingdoms (Sanguo Yanyi)*, tran. C. H. Brewitt-Taylor (Rutland, VT: C. E. Tuttle, 1949).

[†]Shi Nai'an and Luo Guanzhong, *Outlaws of the Marsh (Shuihu zhuan)*, vol. 1, tran. Sidney Shapiro (Beijing: Foreign Languages Press, 1981), p. 167.

served. At about 3:00 A.M., Lin Chong ordered the chefs to follow the recipe for fried sheep's eyes. To prepare Xiannei's own eyes, a soldier poked a sharp knife into Xiannei's eyes. His face was covered with blood. Then Lin ordered him to get the ears. The ears were surprisingly easy to pull off. The soldier didn't have to use a knife. "These ears are fake," the soldier reported. "How can you be so sure?" Lin replied. "Perhaps somebody took a few slices earlier." Everyone laughed like crazy. The poor Xiannei was scared into a wretched pile.

Then there is the story of Wu Song, who took revenge against the nefarious Golden Lotus for the murder of his brother: "Wu Song yanked her over backwards by the head, planted a foot on each arm, and tore open her bodice. Quicker than it takes to tell, he plunged the knife into her breast and cut. Then, clenching the knife in his teeth, he ripped her chest open with both hands, pulled out her heart, liver, and entrails, and placed them on his brother's memorial tablet."*

And, finally, there was the Black Whirlwind, Li Kui, who randomly slaughtered the common folk.

> Li Kui . . . continued consuming lives with his big axes like a blazing inferno. . . . By now the bodies of soldiers and civilians were sprawled all over the crossroads, and blood flowed in rivulets. . . . Li Kui slaughtered down to the stream's edge, his whole body spattered with blood. He went on killing along the bank.
>
> Halberd in hand, Chao Gai shouted, "Don't hurt the ordinary people. This has nothing to do with them!" But the big man wouldn't listen. He cut down victims one after another.[†]

If someday a scholar were to compile a complete version of the Chinese Civil Punishment (*Zhongguo xingfa kao*), we would surely discover that China's methods have been the most sophisticated and cruel in the world. They have included applying hot irons, quartering the body with five horses, severing it at the waist, and others. Each and every method has its own special Han characteristics, and punishments reserved for women have been especially cruel. For instance, there was the method known as "riding the wooden donkey." Women who were accused of committing adultery were forced to ride on the wooden donkey (a punishment device). The woman was tied to the back of the donkey where there was a wooden stick. The donkey was then rocked so that the stick would be thrust into her vagina. And as the donkey swirled about, the stick would swirl as well, causing the woman great pain. Men were subjected to cas-

---

*Ibid., p. 425.

[†]Ibid., p. 642.

tration. Recently, it has been demonstrated that a woman can be punished with a technique whereby a sudden blow to the lower stomach causes the womb to descend in such way that her vagina is permanently blocked. Lai Junchen, an official infamous for his cruel punishments, created the method of "hanging the woman upside down and wrapping her lower body with bamboo, whereupon a man then strikes her so hard that it causes enormous pain. Another method involves inserting several boiling hot eggs in her vagina, which also causes enormous pain."[22]

The Chinese have yet to understand the practice of humanism toward criminals used in the West. As for the abolition of capital punishment, this is nothing but a farce in China. Our cruel and ruthless tradition makes us Chinese incapable of even comprehending the spirit of Western legal philosophy, which in theory does not perceive the law as a vehicle for revenge, nor the criminal as a victim. In the West, the law is supposed to restore justice in the name of God.

Lu Xun stated in his first short story, "Diary of a Madman," that throughout China's history books, we read about nothing but cannibalism! Lu Xun did not intend this observation to be sensational. I for one believe it. In my opinion, the entire totalitarian Han culture is one of cannibalism. The most pitiful thing is that the inhumane characteristics of the culture of cannibalism have not been eliminated over time. Quite the contrary. Cannibalism was recently pushed to unprecedented extremes by the CCP theories of struggle and dictatorship.

I am deeply ashamed of my nation and of the communism in which I used to fervently believe.

NOTES

1. Gao Gao and Yan Jiaqi, *A Ten-Year History of the Cultural Revolution (Wenhua dageming shinian shi)* (Tianjin: Tianjin People's Publishing House, 1986), p. 13.

2. "The Ten Criminal Acts of the Revisionist Element Qiao Xiaoguang," in *Congress News (Dahui xiaoxi)*, no. 8, Guilin "Grand Alliance," Southern Naval Detachment Publication Outlet.

3. Carl Jung, *Recognition of the Psyche in Modern Man (Tansuo xinling aomide xiandairen)* (Beijing: Shehui kexue wenxian chubanshe, 1987), p. 170.

4. *Long Live Mao Zedong Thought (Mao Zedong sixiang wansui)* (1969), pp. 440–460.

5. Ibid., p. 417.

6. Mao Zedong, Talk on February 1, 1967. See Lin Biao's Report to the 1969 CCP Ninth Party Congress.

7. Fan Ye, *Records of the Later Han (Houhan shu)* (Beijing: Zhonghua Book Company, 1965), p. 2834.

8. Qin Jianping, *Records of Guangxi Minorities' Idle Diversions (Guangxi shaoshu minzu fengqing lu)*.

9. Ibid.

10. Lan Hongen, *Popular Samplings from Guangxi Literature (Guangxi minjian wenxue sanlun)*, pp. 104–105.

11. Zhou Zongxian, *Essays on Southern Minorities: Existing Forms of Primitive Matrimony in Zhuang Society (Nanfang minzu lungao: canzun zai Zhuangzu shehui zhong de yuanshi hunyin jiazu xingtai)*.

12. Lan Hongen, *Divine Arrows and Treasured Swords (Shengong baojian)*, Compilation of Guangxi People's Literature (Guangxi minjian wenxue congkan), vol. 2, pp. 1–2.

13. Ibid. Qin Jianping, *Records of Guangxi Minorities' Idle Diversions*.

14. *Marx-Engels Collected Works*, vol. 4, p. 87.

15. Meng Ainong, "A Brief Review of Yao Minority White Pants Weddings and Funerals in Nandan County" *(Nandanxian baiku Yaohun sangxisu jianshu) Journal of Guangxi Folk Literature*, vol. 14.

16. Lan Hongen, ed. *Selection of Old Folk Tales of the Zhuang (Zhuangzu minjian gushi xuan)* (Shanghai: Shanghai Literary Publishing House, 1984).

17. Fan Wenlan, *A General History of China (Zhongguo tongshi)* (Beijing: People's Publishing House, 1965), vol. 3, p. 442.

18. *Records of the Late Tang (Jiu Tang shu)* in *The Twenty-Five Histories (Ershiwu shijinghua)*, no. 3, p. 171.

19. *A Synopsis of History from the Zhou Dynasty Onward (Zizhi tongjian)*, vol. 257.

20. *Illustrious Stories of the Tang (Tangren shuohui)*, vol. 5.

21. Fan Wenlan, *A General History of China*, vol. 3, p. 415.

22. *The Twenty-Six Histories (Jingbian ershiliu shi)*, p. 335.

4
Scarlet Memorials All over China

After a long journey, we finally walked out of the jungle and were able to expose our attire with its rotten smell to the bright sun. However, our delight did not last long. Instantly, we found out that we were still in the jungle. In the thick jungle ahead, we found yet another grand scarlet memorial. Fighting through the bushes that hid all the lies and swindles, we finally approached this memorial. Covered though it was with human blood, we were still able to read a few Chinese characters carved into the memorial stone. Behind the moss of time was clearly written, *Prison of the Wrongly Accused.*

On each and every granite stone was carved the history of a violent case. It was frightening. We silently recalled recent history, but we felt nothing but a sense of alienation that aroused a long-forgotten nightmare. Indeed, we are in the process of forgetting everything. As Solzhenitsyn put it, what remains in our memory is not the events we experienced, not the genuine and reliable historical facts, but the self-swindling propaganda and lies. The crimes that caused us pain in our consciences have long been forgotten. What is in our memory is the loudspeaker, the red slogans, and everything that the officially organized rallies ordered us to remember. It is as though someone had installed an information filter in our minds with the instruction to carve in our memories only that which we are allowed to remember. Only that is history.

Violence and ruthlessness did not occur in Guangxi alone, but all over China.

THE CASE OF ZHANG ZHIXIN, SHENYANG CITY, LIAONING PROVINCE

Zhang Zhixin was a heroine who was ruthlessly tortured and then killed.

Violent acts of beating, smashing, looting, burning, and killing quickly spread all over China at the beginning of the Cultural Revolution. In the midst of this great chaos, Zhang Zhixin of the CCP Propaganda Department of Liaoning Province kept her cool and became increasingly distrustful of the "progressive" factions, including Jiang Qing, Lin Biao, and the Central Cultural Revolution Group. In conversations with her comrades and at public meetings, Zhang Zhixin courageously expressed her views.

> I have doubts about Jiang Qing. What's wrong with making critical remarks about her? Why shouldn't Jiang Qing's problems be revealed? We should even expose the Central Cultural Revolution Group!
>
> What's all this talk about a "zenith" (*dingfeng*)? And just what's this business about "one line is worth ten thousand lines"? And why should we go along with the notion that "even if you do not understand, you must obey"?* If this is allowed to continue, the situation will get out of control! This is all an effort to fortify Chairman Mao's reputation and that of Lin Biao. I personally have no trust in Lin Biao!

Here was a loyal CCP cadre who, in following her conscience and the Party's principles, made public some of her politically dissident opinions and for this she was handcuffed and thrown into prison. At a meeting to "clear out the poison," another courageous person stood up and protested, "I don't see anything wrong with Zhang Zhixin! Why should a CCP member who expresses her own opinions be accused of violating the law? Her opinions sound very reasonable!" That person too was summarily arrested soon thereafter and sentenced to eighteen years in prison.

Zhang Zhixin persisted with her learning while in prison. She saved up her meager monthly 2.00 yuan [$1.00] allowance and purchased dozens of works by Mao, Marx, and Lenin. Taking a stick and dipping it into ink, she recorded tens of thousands of study notes on toilet paper. Immediately after her imprisonment, Zhang was rather restrained with the guards. But when the guards confiscated her pen, she became outraged and condemned them for being "helpless in front of the truth," and she declared that "neither the murderers nor their accomplices will get away with murder! No way! I will reveal and condemn you to the Party and the people! You will be punished by history if not sooner, then later!" In order to take revenge on her, the prison authorities put two sets of leg irons on her feet and a harness on her back, incarcerating her in a small cell for as long as a year and a half. The prison authorities also ordered hooligans and thieves among the prison population to beat her up.[†] For their ruthless torture of Zhang Zhixin, their sentences were reduced.

---

*Phrases propagated by Jiang Qing, Lin Biao, and other radicals to bolster the personality cult of Mao Zedong during the Cultural Revolution.

[†]For a comprehensive look at China's prison system, see Hongda Harry Wu, *Laogai: The Chinese Gulag* (Boulder: Westview Press, 1992).

One day, the prison guards tied Zhang Zhixin up in ropes and pushed her into a prison vehicle. In order to prevent her from calling out any slogans, they stuck bubbled plastic in her mouth and sealed her lips with cellophane tape. A few prison vehicles headed toward the Niuguantun execution grounds located on the outskirts of the city. Zhang Zhixin realized that the last moments of her life were approaching. Nonetheless, she was cool, calm, and collected, and held her head up. On the execution ground, two male prisoners from Zhang's vehicle were executed by firing squad while Zhang still remained in the vehicle. Looking at the two bodies lying in two pools of blood, she realized that she had been brought there to witness death. A slight, cold smile quivered in the corner of her mouth.

Zhang Zhixin was a woman full of grace. Even in prison, she maintained her noble self-esteem. A simple rip in her sleeve made her very uneasy. When the prison authorities refused to provide her with a needle and thread, she used a grass stick, and thread from her clothes, to mend her sleeve. On holidays, she would make up her hair in an attractive style. She was well turned out for each interrogation. When asked to sit, she would remain standing; but when no offer was made to sit, she would then sit down. Each time, she would declare, "I am not a criminal. I did not commit any crime. You should not talk to me as if you are talking to a criminal." And if her interrogators still refused to change their tone of voice, Zhang would refuse to answer any of their questions.

Even after Zhang was illegally sentenced to life imprisonment, she refused to admit to any crime. Her job in the labor reform camp was to assemble shoes and her quota was 1,200 pairs per day. Soon after she finished her quota, she would turn off the machine. When the boss in the workshop questioned why she turned the machine off, Zhang would reply, "I am a Party member, not a criminal! I have assembled 1,200 pairs of shoes, which contributes to the wealth of the country. You claim that making more shoes will reduce my crime. But since I am not a criminal, I will not make one more shoe."

In order to destroy Zhang Zhixin's willpower, the CCP pressured her husband into seeking a divorce.* This came as a heavy blow to Zhang. After wiping away her tears, Zhang tore the divorce paper into pieces and declared, "There are twenty-one people from both families. It doesn't amount to a hill of beans if I give it up in order to pursue the truth—which is the only worthwhile thing to do. Life itself should not focus on the small family circle. I no longer have any burdens, which will enable me to fight to the end!"

---

*Such "political" divorces, which revealed the CCP's assault on the family, were commonplace during the Cultural Revolution.

At last, the prison authorities adopted the most ruthless means to torture her, which was insistent rape and group rape. The heroine with high self-esteem finally went berserk. However, her enemies were not victorious. Whenever she was conscious, she continued to fight. The Party secretary of Liaoning Province finally angrily concluded, "As long as she lives, Zhang Zhixin will adamantly fight against us. Just kill her!" He ordered the court to add this punishment to her sentence.

During her last trial, Zhang Zhixin gave a speech in which she insisted on maintaining her political views. The first judge quit, and the second judge had nothing to say in response. Finally, the trial ended in a great rush. The court asked her to sign her name to the court record. Zhang insisted that she be able to read the contents of the stenographic record but she was refused. She replied, "It is against the law not to show me the record. I refuse to sign!" The trial record without her signature became the basis of her capital punishment. According to the legal procedures provided by the CCP, a convicted criminal is given twelve days to appeal. These murderers were so anxious that they killed Zhang Zhixin the next morning.

During her six years of imprisonment, from 1969 to 1975, Zhang never once yielded. The murderers were afraid that Zhang would reveal their criminal acts on the execution grounds, and so they ruthlessly cut her throat to prevent her from yelling anything out.

On the morning of the execution, Zhang was pulled into an office where medical instruments including a scalpel and scissors had been arranged on a table. A bucket of water sat on the floor. In the middle of the room were some bricks. All of a sudden, Zhang was thrown to the floor face up like a pig and one brick was jammed under her neck. Her hands and feet were bound and another brick was placed on her head. It was hard for her to breathe or to move. Her last words went something like, "Party! My Party! Where do you want to take me?" The knife was raised, blood spurted out, and the pain was excruciating. A metal pipe was stuck into her throat.

At 10 A.M., at Shenyang's Donglingda execution grounds, Zhang Zhixin walked toward the autumn fields, cool, calm, and collected. She stopped in front of a small hut. The red flag was raised along with the gun. Zhang Zhixin fell into a pool of blood, silently. After that, the frightened murderers decapitated the martyr in order to destroy the evidence.

*   *   *

In the spring of 1979, Zhang Zhixin was officially rehabilitated. The story of her bravery spread to each and every corner of the country. The people were outraged. Letters and wires demanding that the murderers be pun-

ished flew into Beijing in a blizzard. The murderers were eventually protected, however. The most open-minded leader in the CCP, Hu Yaobang,
mediated. Just stop investigating this case, he advised. If the murderers
were to be punished, the consequences would be too great.

April 4, 1979, was the day designated as the memorial. The martyr's
children placed an empty box in front of her tomb.[1]

THE NUMBER 44 CONTEMPORARY COUNTERREVOLUTIONARY CASE
IN CHANGCHUN CITY, JILIN PROVINCE

Shi Yunfeng, a worker at the Changchun Number 1 Optical Instruments
Factory, was only 26 when he was executed.

Beginning on October 29, 1974, ten work units throughout Changchun
received anonymous leaflets over a three-day period. To frighten the local regime even more, at noon on November 5, a slogan was put up on a
traffic-police post in the center of the city.

The leaflets and slogans declared nothing but the truth. "Even the
leader of the Party is a common Party member. Oppose 'blind loyalty'!"
"Oppose 'individual worship'!" "The CCP does not need a 'Party emperor'!" "The policy of activating class struggle every seven or eight years
is a policy leading to the destruction of the Party and the country," "The
so-called 'Cultural Revolution' is nothing but that of 'extreme leftist policy' going out of control!"

These leaflets and slogans not only spooked the Jilin Province regime, it
also frightened the small imperial palace under the Gang of Four in Beijing. In no time, the machinery of dictatorship was mobilized.

Seven days after this all began, the radical leader Wang Hongwen issued the following instructions: "These anonymous tracts are very reactionary. . . . The Public Security Ministry will assist Jilin Province and
Changchun Public Security Bureau to investigate the case." The document was also signed by Jiang Qing, Zhang Chunqiao, and Yao Wenyuan.

Wang Huaixiang, the first Party secretary of Jilin, was a typical political
sneak. He determined that the person involved must be a veteran cadre.
If Wang could crack this case, he would not only be able to use it to get at
the veteran cadres whom he detested but he would also be able to deliver
the case as a gift to the small imperial palace in Beijing. And so he issued
instructions to establish an exceptionally large investigation group: 300
detectives from the provincial public security units and 1,652 special-case
groups established in each and every unit of Changchun. Altogether 6,600
people were involved.

The "Number 44 Contemporary Counterrevolutionary Case" was soon
solved. The culprit was not an old cadre, but a low-level worker named
Shi Yunfeng. Wang Huaixiang was very disappointed. More instructions

arrived from the Public Security Ministry. The case was only half complete. More investigation was needed. Wang was thrilled. He immediately arranged the next stage of the movement with himself as the commander in chief. Eventually two abettors *(jiaosuofan)* were uncovered, one at the level of a deputy head of a department *(chu)* and the other at the section *(ke)* level. Although their ranks were rather low, they both had been intimately involved.

During March and April 1975, two articles were published, entitled "On the Social Basis of the Lin Biao Counterrevolutionary Clique" and "On the Overall Dictatorship of the Bourgeoisie," by Yao Wenyuan and Zhang Chunqiao, respectively. Wang Huaixiang was more than thrilled by all of this and secretly celebrated his arrest of the "abettors." He also arranged to summarize the principles regarding the emergence of the "newborn bourgeoisie" and "political abettors" by citing the Number 44 Case. Wang was attempting to provide fresh evidence for the new theory propounded by the Gang of Four. But the two low-level cadres had merely exchanged some ideas with Shi Yunfeng and did not know about the slogans and leaflets. The Public Security Bureau was reluctant to act, and considerable controversy broke out over the definition of "abettor." Wang Huaixiang, although he admitted that the two cadres were not "direct abettors," he insisted on accusing them of being "counterrevolutionary abettors." Only by doing so could he invoke the new formula of a newborn bourgeoisie at the front of the political stage and that of the bourgeois class in the Party at the back stage. And only by doing so could this case be used to prove the correctness of the theory of overall dictatorship. Thus, Shi Yunfeng and three other people were paraded throughout various units of the city for criticism.

Not surprisingly, Wang Huaixiang's efforts were not in vain. In May 1975, the regime in Beijing demanded a summary of the experiences involving the Number 44 Special Case. In September, Jiang Qing herself invited Wang to make a privileged tour of the left-wing showpiece, Dazhai agricultural brigade in Shanxi Province. From then on, Wang's status in Jiang Qing's eyes increased dramatically, and he was instantly promoted.

Wang Huaixiang attempted to uncover even more dirt on this case and thus continued the investigation right up to the collapse of the Gang of Four. After the smashing of the Gang in 1976, Wang feared that his end was also near. At the time Shi was convicted, Wang ordered that all materials on the Shi case be destroyed in order to protect himself. One must bear in mind that when Wang compiled the materials, Shi had been accused of "attacking Chairman Mao and reversing the verdict on Liu Shaoqi." Wang, the frightened rat, planned to desert his sinking ship and jump onto another.

The always submissive Public Security Bureau sentenced Shi Yunfeng to death. On December 17, 1976, the regime announced the death sentence to Shi, leaving him two days to appeal. Only two days to appeal for such a major case. How vicious! His desire to live inspired Shi to complete a 1,000-word letter of appeal. But since his heavy handcuffs made it impossible for him even to hold a pen, he had to ask his cellmate to complete the document. It was all in vain, of course, for without a trial his appeal was turned down. These people were so lazy that they did not even try to act out a trial. The reason was simple: The Party is the court. The death penalty as decided by the first Party secretary of the province could not be altered.*

Shi Yunfeng's mother, Jia Xiuyun, rushed to the gate of the provincial committee on a stormy night. Holding her son's letter of appeal she tried to stop every passing cadre vehicle, but no one paid any attention. Hopeless and helpless, she threw her two arms into the air and screamed, "Please save my child! He opposed the Gang of Four. Why is it that the Gang has been smashed, and he is still to be killed?!" Every passerby shed tears.

On December 19, 1976, sentencing day arrived. In the morning, it was announced that Shi's appeal had been rejected and that the execution would soon be carried out. Shi Yunfeng yelled "unfair." The director of the municipal Public Security Bureau then proposed, "The criminal has a good attitude and should not be executed." The director then reported the case to the Party secretary of the city judiciary body who all along had held a different view about this case. He in turn reported the case to the secretary of the provincial Political and Legal Committee:

"The criminal has appealed. The execution should not be carried out."

"Do not allow him to appeal!" the provincial secretary retorted.

"The criminal continues to appeal. The execution should not be carried out," the city secretary shot back.

"Use necessary measures!" The provincial secretary ended the argument.

The provincial secretary of the Political and Legal Committee was a pal of Wang Huaixiang and felt that something was out of the ordinary. So he asked Wang for instructions. For Wang, Shi Yunfeng had to be executed so that his political position in demonstrating his firmness in supporting Chairman Mao would be protected.

---

*Direct intervention by CCP leaders in the legal system in China is a common political abuse that continues to this day.

At the public declaration of Shi's death sentence, the secretary of the provincial Political and Legal Committee issued the following order over the phone in the name of Wang: "The plan must be carried out. Measures must be taken to fulfill the implementation of the plan."

Shi was immediately stuffed into a prison vehicle. Yet he still yelled out, "Provincial supreme court, provincial supreme court. I have confessed. Why wasn't I treated leniently?!" According to the traditional practices followed by the imperial courts, if a criminal kept yelling "unfair," the action was stopped and a new trial would be ordered. Shi Yunfeng's cries of "unfair!" only hastened the efforts of the dictatorship machinery to implement fully the "necessary measures": The rope was tightened around his hands, procaine was injected into his throat, cotton balls were stuffed into his mouth, and surgical threads sealed off his lips. He could neither move nor speak. All he could do was vent his anger with his eyes while facing the dark gun. Gun shots rang out across the frozen landscape. A pioneer of ideological liberalism had fallen at the dawn of the smashing of the Gang of Four.

Many years later, people came to the realization that it was not really a dawn.[2]

THE ZHAO JIANMIN CASE

This is a spy case neither large nor small. In the beginning of 1968 at a meeting in the Jingxi Guest House [a military hostel in Beijing], Kang Sheng, an "adviser" to the Central Cultural Revolution Group, pointed straight at Zhao Jianmin, Party secretary of Yunnan Province, and said, "You are a traitor."* Zhao immediately protested. But without the slightest bit of evidence, Kang Sheng attempted to use his power to suppress Zhao. "This accusation is based on my forty years of revolutionary experience," Kang claimed. "It's my intuition." Kang challenged Zhao to swear his innocence on paper. Zhao had no other alternative, and so he wrote, "I am not a traitor. The CCP can investigate me as it pleases." Immediately following this incident, an unprecedented political movement began in Yunnan accusing Zhao of being a traitor and a spy. Kang Sheng's intuition that Zhao was a traitor ultimately brought about the persecution of a great number of cadres in Yunnan. More than 10,400 cadres ended up being persecuted to death because of the Zhao Jianmin case.

---

*Mao Zedong's top security boss, Kang Sheng, had a long history of ferreting out "spies" in the CCP, all the way back to the notorious "rescue movement" during the Yan'an period (1936–1945).

YINLANG SEAL THEFT CASE

On December 3, 1968, a strange case occurred at the Yinlang Railway Station located in the heart of Daqing, the site of China's famous oilfield: The public seals for the "Revolutionary Committee" and "political work team" disappeared from the double-locked drawer of the head of the local Revolutionary Committee, Han Laiyu. Acting out of his sense of obligation, Han immediately reported the incident.

The Revolutionary Committee of Sa'ertu railway district immediately concluded that this was a case involving a newborn counterrevolutionary group opposed to the red political power and they dispatched a special investigatory team to the Yinlang Railway Station.

After an initial meeting over the matter, everyone went to dinner except for Han Laiyu, who paced the floor in his room. Without breaking through the door and into the drawer, how could the seals be stolen overnight? He kept pacing and, to his surprise, he discovered one of the seals, a bit broken, lying under his bed. He immediately reported it to the special investigation group and asked if the mass meeting that was scheduled for that evening should be held as planned. "The meeting will be convened as planned," he was instructed. "But don't let anyone know about the recovery of the seal." Why, Han wondered, should the meeting be held, if the seal has been found? The reason was simple. The special investigation group had not really aimed at recovering the lost seals. Rather, it was out to get "counterrevolutionaries."

Slogans such as "Reveal the 'December 3' counterrevolutionary case until our death!" "Protect the red political power with our life!" and so on were heard throughout the meeting hall. Yet there were some people at the rally who were still able to think rationally. Zhang Zhicheng, a gatekeeper, declared, "Perhaps the rats did it. It is said that they make a habit of sharpening their teeth by chewing on things." Before Zhang had even finished, he was pushed to the center of the assembly hall and bombarded with accusations. "On what basis can you say that this act was committed by rats?" "How do you know that rats like to sharpen their teeth?" "Perhaps it was you who did it!" It was too late for the poor Zhang, under such heavy attack, to express regret over his suggestion. But others in the crowd remembered what he said.

On the next day, three workers went to the office to search for the rat hole and easily discovered it. One of the workers stuck his hand in the hole and pulled out a big pile of rotten cotton, pieces of paper, and so on. To get at the rats' nest they dug into the hole and lo and behold! they found the other seal, broken. Surrounding the seal were broken pieces of wood and paper, along with traces of red ink from the seal. Since both seals had now been retrieved, wasn't it time to conclude the case?

More traces of rats were immediately discovered in Han Laiyu's table, including some rat feces next to the medicine bottle in the drawer. The special investigation group, however, decided to ignore all the facts. Instead, they declared that the criminal was the escaped capitalist roader, Han Laiyu. Evidence: He possessed both the time and conditions to commit the crime. He had also created a false site and had attempted to blame the rats in order to save himself. Of course, Han did not accept this accusation. Nonetheless, he was subject to criticism, put under surveillance, and prohibited from working. Yet ruthless physical torture and a false arrest did not force Han into submission.

While Han was undergoing this ordeal, new events occurred at the railway station: Work garments, candles, and other items were all being nibbled at. These new discoveries were immediately reported to the special investigation group in order to demonstrate the blatant activities of the rats and to save Han. But members of the special group, with nerves constantly sensitive to the vagaries of class struggle, immediately came to the conclusion that the evidence had been doctored just to save Han. Thus, those who had contacts with Han were themselves forced to participate in the "study group." A "brutal counterrevolutionary gang" headed by Han Laiyu consisting of six members was concocted.

Han Laiyu kept appealing and, in 1969, when the case was reinvestigated, his label was reduced from "counterrevolutionary" to someone who had committed "serious mistakes."

Throughout, Han Laiyu was never submissive. In May 1972, the Qiqihar railway branch began yet another investigation. This one involved a serious examination of the rats. The work team interviewed the epidemic prevention stations in both Qiqihar and Baicheng and learned that the rats were gnashers. Since their teeth grow so quickly, any failure to sharpen them can be fatal. In addition, the new investigation team learned that rats possess a great capacity for moving things and are able to pull things whose weight is three times their own body weight into their holes. Moreover, rats are good at climbing, so climbing onto the top of a table would be easy for them. The special group also interviewed people at the Tianjin Seal Factory, who noted that the soybean oil and castor oil used to prevent the seals from cracking were the two kinds of oils most favored by rats.

The special group also sent the two seals along with the broken pieces of wood, the paper, and half of the candle allegedly nibbled on by the rats to the highest units of authority—the Institute of Animal Research and the Institute of Agriculture and Forestry of the Chinese Academy of Sciences—for further examination. The researchers tested rats from Daqing and proved that rats from that area had indeed nibbled at the seals. The

Institute of Agriculture and Forestry also compared the remnants of the seals with the broken slivers of wood and proved that they were one and the same. Using microscopic analysis, the Public Security Office of the Qiqihar railway branch also discovered the presence of rat hair in the red ink.

Was that enough? No way. For none of this evidence proved that Han Laiyu had not simply doctored the site. Were the rat feces next to the medicine bottle in his drawer not a human creation? To answer this question, the special group attempted to place one piece of rat feces on the surface of the glossy bottle to prove that a human being could not have left the rat droppings there.

These serious scientific experiments were far from complete: How could it be proven that the rat feces had in fact been left by the rat? To answer this question, the group started a new experiment. They placed a rat in a big glass bottle and watched it day and night. On the third day, an invaluable picture appeared: when the rat relieved itself, the feces stuck to the surface of the bottle. The experimenter carefully opened the bottle to obtain the evidence.

This entire case directed at Han was by all means a farce. The process of overthrowing the farce continued to demonstrate a high level of scientific investigation. Despite the evidence that rats had nibbled at the seals, since the drawer was locked, how was it that the seals had ended up in the rat hole? The group then examined the structure of the table and found that the back of the drawer was not closed off, so that a 50 millimeter crack exposed the drawer to the surface of the table. Since the diameter of the seal was 38 millimeters, the rat had clearly been able to pull the seal out of the drawer.[3]

*   *   *

Conclusion: The rats were counterrevolutionary!

Long live the rats!

THE RED BICYCLE CASE
OF THE CHINESE ACADEMY OF SCIENCES

On August 24, 1968, a woman scientist named Zhang Bin, who often rode a red bicycle, was suddenly arrested at her home and immediately incarcerated in the infamous Qincheng political prison outside of Beijing.

Who was Zhang Bin? During the Nationalist period (1912–1949), she was a student majoring in chemistry at Furen University (now Beijing Teachers' University). Later, she went to the United States for advanced studies in organic chemistry and received a Ph.D. Out of a sense of patriotism, she and her husband (Lin Tongyi, a professor of mechanics) returned to the mainland in 1955 and were assigned to work as associate researchers at the Institute of Sensitization Materials of the Chinese Academy of Sciences.

After her arrest, this naive scientist thought for sure that it was all a mistake. After considerable thought, she concluded that perhaps because she had been overseas for so many years the Party was merely testing her, and she was ready for the test. Many days passed, but she was given no reason for her incarceration. Instead, she was confronted by an armed prison guard, and a damp, dark prison cell less than three square meters in size, which was infested with rats, lizards, and spiders.

Even the most cultivated person has limits to his or her patience. Zhang Bin finally became outraged. "Why did you arrest me?" she demanded to know. That question brought her nothing but vicious beatings. Because of her "uncooperative attitude," her handcuffs became heavier and heavier, and the heavy manacles were kept on her back even when she slept and went to the bathroom. When her ration of cornbread fell onto the floor, she had to crawl with her entire body to get it into her mouth. Any trace of resistance and the guards would throw her down on the floor and beat her face. Sometimes, they hung her up by her feet and tied her arms together. They called this "weighting" (*chengtizhong*).

The guards also tried to get her to admit to being a spy and a counterrevolutionary. Zhang Bin was outraged. "You accuse me of being a counterrevolutionary. What's your evidence?" she cried. "I do in fact oppose your kind of 'revolution'!" Zhang Bin's protest spread to the highest authorities, surprising the VIPs in charge of special cases. One day, Zhang Bin was told that the leader would come to see her. The leader was a vicious-looking woman in her fifties, who was accompanied by a big crowd. She was Liu Shuyan, the wife of the radical leftist Chen Boda, who was also consultant to the Central Special Case Investigative Group, headed by Wang Dongxing, Mao Zedong's personal bodyguard. With a cold smile, Liu said sarcastically, "What a miserable state you are in today. You big shots with degrees! What prestige do you have now?" With another cold smile, Liu left.

During the seven years and four months of her imprisonment, Zhang was subjected to two separate "interrogation" trials. The prolonged inhumane mental and physical torture finally caused her to lose her mind. Zhang Bin was diagnosed as schizophrenic in 1972. She was sent to a mental hospital—one that specialized in persecuting political prisoners—the Beijing Stability Hospital.

On November 8, 1973, the Third Office of the Central Special Case Investigative Group released Zhang Bin on grounds that "no evidence for spying" had ever been presented. Her sudden arrest and then unexpected release was befuddling. What crime had Zhang Bin committed? It was a question everyone was anxious to have answered, but no one dared to ask.

On December 30, 1978, ten years after her arrest, Zhang Bin was finally rehabilitated, and the reason for her imprisonment was revealed. During those years, Chen Boda, Xie Fuzhi, and Guan Feng, among others, concocted an "international spy ring." Although Zhang Bin had nothing to do with it, someone revealed that among the people who had close contact with the so-called spy group was a woman riding a model 26 red bicycle. The public security system quickly deployed detectives all over Beijing to follow any "woman riding a red bicycle." Unfortunately, Zhang Bin did in fact ride a model 26 red bicycle and became an immediate suspect. Later it was discovered that the culprit was a woman named Cai Suwen. However, the Public Security Bureau also accidentally discovered that Cai's brother-in-law was Liu Yuanzhang of the Institute of Mathematics of the Chinese Academy of Sciences and that, unfortunately, Zhang Bin was Liu's sister. Putting all these people together, Chen Boda and company formed the membership of the "international spy ring" on the spot. As Chen Boda wisely determined, "Zhang Bin is American stuff, not a good thing. Liu Yuanzhang is double material, studying in both Japan and the U.S. Arrest them all for me." Thus began the case of the wrongly accused.[4]

*   *   *

It seems that in China, one should never ride a red bicycle. But no one knows if it is safer to ride a black, white, or a green bicycle.

THE SONGTAO FLATULENCY CASE

This case occurred in Niulang District of Songtao Miao* Autonomous County in the eastern plateau region of Guizhou Province. On the night of January 18, 1976, a young man named Long Zhengyun was arrested and subjected to interrogation. There was only one question: "Why did you set out to plan a murder?" Long Zhengyun refused to answer, but the interrogation continued into the next day. Long Baoyin, head of the commune armed police office, demonstrated his viciousness by slapping the suspect several times and then hanging him from the ceiling. Immediately, Long

---

*The Miao are a Sino-Tibetan minority that in 1982 numbered around 5 million. China has over 100 autonomous counties that are similar in organization to the autonomous regions.

Zhengyun's face became pale and he began sweating like crazy. Finally, when Long Zhengyun could tolerate the torture no longer, he started accusing his father, Long Decan, his uncle, Long Niancan, and his cousin, Long Maoyun, of planning to "kill people." Long Baoyin immediately arrested these three and hung them up, too, in order to force confessions out of them. These three victims then accused Long Maoyun's uncle Wu Xianbao of "planning to mobilize 2,000 people to riot and to kill."

This sensational case of an "anti-CCP riot" was immediately reported to the higher authorities. But perhaps owing to the absurdity of the case, it was never dealt with.

Two months later, the Tiananmen incident burst forth on April 5, 1976, in Beijing.* Shi Mengming, Party secretary of Songtao County, gave a mobilization speech advocating "an immediate start of a movement to oppose any reversal of verdicts on rightists and to investigate mass counterrevolutionary activities." Long Wenfei, Party secretary of Niulang District, got the message right away and immediately thought about the closed case just mentioned. He issued the accusation that "Deng Xiaoping's feet have stepped into Niulang." In order to "smash the Xiaoping village," a ruthless "searching out of counterrevolutionaries" (*zhuicha fangeming*) movement broke out in Niulang District.

Long Wenfei ordered his pal Long Baoyin to use lynching devices to force people to confess. A forty-five member "counterrevolutionary gang" that planned to "carry out a riot involving 7- to 8,000 people in July or August" was uncovered. Long Wenfei then visited the Qixin brigade where things were all quiet and attempted to establish a model of "expanding the victorious results of searching out counterrevolutionaries." A few armed militia beat up farmer Qin Haicheng and forced him to confess. They put the victim in a barrel and rolled it over night and day until the victim's feces and urine seeped out. Qin Haicheng, during the ruthless lynching, accused fifty-six people of being counterrevolutionaries— thereby surpassing the number accused in Niulang brigade. Thus, Long Wenfei held another mass rally for the whole district and passed on the unique wisdom that "the candle does not light itself unless you have lit it; counterrevolutionaries will not confess on their own unless you force them to do so."

Long Wenfei knew that the campaign would bring him a bright future. In the past, he had been a paragon of virtue in "learning from Dazhai in

---

*A first burst of democratic fervor that was crushed by the state militia controlled by Jiang Qing and that led to Deng Xiaoping's purge (his third) from the CCP's top leadership. See Ruan Ming, *Deng Xiaoping: Chronicle of an Empire*, tran. Nancy Liu, Peter Rand, and Lawrence R. Sullivan (Boulder: Westview Press, 1994).

agriculture" and "changing heaven and earth." Now he had become famous throughout the county as an expert in searching out counterrevolutionaries. With the support of the county Party secretary, Shi Mengming, Long Wenfei established an elaborate organization to search out counterrevolutionaries. Groups to search out counterrevolutionaries were set up at the district level, in five communes, and in twenty-eight brigades. A militia office and investigation teams were formed under these groups. The militia engaged in patrols, carried out arrests, and interrogated victims night and day; and investigation team members slept during the day and carried out their ruthless lynchings at night. The total number of people in both work groups numbered 435. Their self-made lynching tools consisted of, among other things, chains, locks, whips, clubs, and hammers. The methods of physical torture numbered more than fifty and included flying hammer with oil, bats climbing on the walls, duck splashing water, flying miller putting out a fire, five horses quartering the dead body, hanging up the pigs, rolling dragon holding on to a post, cutting feet tendons, and many more.

Long Zhengyun's father, Long Decan, underwent continuous ruthless torture largely because he failed to implicate other members. The victim finally smashed a rock against the side of his own head while calling out "Long live Chairman Mao," "Long live the Chinese Communist Party" and collapsed to the floor. The two militiamen, instead of helping the victim, attempted to kill him by pressing a wood stick down his throat, and when that didn't work, they buried the victim alive.

Long Maohe, a son of the 78-year-old farmer Long Yingpin, was also threatened with lynching because he failed to hand over a list of counterrevolutionaries. His father, in order to save him, confessed that he had burned the list and so he was beaten to death.

With these ruthless lynchings, counterrevolutionary organizations popped up everywhere: "Underground Communist Party," "Restoring the Village Gang," "Democratic Party," "National Army," "Xiaoping Village," "Commander in chief," and so on and so forth. According to statistics compiled on various villages, including Niulang, Shaba, Yinyan, Muzhai, and Daxing, thirty-six counterrevolutionary riot gangs and 1,300 members of counterrevolutionary groups connected to more than a dozen districts, five counties, and two provinces were uncovered.

Soon after the searching out counterrevolutionaries movement began in Niulang District, the public security units at both the prefecture and county level suggested on numerous occasions that the movement be stopped. The county Party secretary, Shi Mengming, reiterated, "The direction of the movement is okay. If there are any problems, I accept all responsibility!"

With support from Shi Mengming, Long Wenfei became even more cruel. He blatantly attacked the public security units at both levels. "They aim at protecting class enemies and do not engage in class struggle."

The terror in Niulang became increasingly vicious. Long Wenfei and others secured weapons from the county and dug a trench in front of the district committee building and set up machine-gun emplacements on top of the building to frighten the locals. In the meantime, Long also illegally declared martial law and issued the following demands: "Counterrevolutionaries must confess before a certain date; travelers outside the district must return by a certain date; all visitors must report; everyone must seek permission to leave their place of work; curfew begins at 8:00 P.M.; and anyone out after 8:00 P.M. will be shot by the militia." Long Wenfei also blatantly announced at a meeting that "wrongly killing one hundred is better than letting one guilty person escape."*

The next day, Teng Jiuxian, head of the armed police at Yinyan commune, telephoned Long and said, "A counterrevolutionary attempted to escape and so I shot him in the rice paddies with my machine gun." Long immediately spoke up in praise of old Teng. "You have certainly done a good deed!" he declared. "Secretary Shi of the county has instructed us not to be afraid of the deaths. We must carry out our work."

Conspicuous and indiscriminate killing began from that point. Every day people would hear such reports as "killed while escaping," "committed suicide out of guilt," and so on. The success of the revolutionary deed was measured by the number of deaths. Within one month, the death toll reached thirty. There were also eighteen people who were slated to be killed, but in the end the plan was not carried out. After a death occurred, no one was allowed to cry, to speak, to collect the body, to take off the bloody clothes, or to bury the victim in a coffin. A few four elements types were ordered to throw the bodies into a pit.

What was behind this incident in which more than 1,300 counterrevolutionaries were uncovered, resulting in thirty-two deaths and 263 casualties?

Let's return to the chilly day on January 18, 1976, when Long Wenfei ordered a group of young men to change the course of a stream that ran in front of the district office building in order to establish a Dazhai-like model. Darkness fell. The workers started a fire and everyone was sitting around the fire resting. Suddenly, someone loudly passed gas, which caused everyone to laugh like crazy. After a small inquiry, everyone pointed to a timid-looking young man named Long Zhengyun and ac-

---

*A common adage voiced to justify harsh punishments and tough measures.

cused him of passing gas. The mockery and ridicule made Long cry. The young lads continued to make fun of Long. "You are in your twenties, old enough to get a wife," they chided him. "Shame on you! Don't cry, don't cry. How about if we mate you with the hunchback girl!" More hearty laughter followed.

A bit drunk, and finding this public ridicule intolerable, Long Zhengyun blurted out, "You are making fun of me. I am mad. I am going to kill two of you!"

Two young men, having realized that Long was from a landlord's family, sensed that there was something wrong with Long's remark about killing and threatened to report it to the authorities. Whenever the son of a landlord publicly threatened to kill someone it was considered to be a serious act of class revenge. Someone tried to calm the young men. "Come on, Long was just kidding," they said. "Cut it out." The two young men reported it anyway.

That is how the tragedy just described befell the people of Niulang. Such ruthless lynching and killing with so much bloodshed stemmed from nothing but the flatulence of a single, timid person at the end of one fine day.[5]

THE ANTI-LIN BIAO CASE ON HAINAN ISLAND

Guan Minghua, a female physician's aide at Yacha Farm, Sha County, of the Li-Miao Minority Autonomous Region in Hainan, was only thirty-seven years old when she was killed.

It was mere happenstance. At a meeting called to criticize the "Three Family Village"* held on the farm at the beginning of the Cultural Revolution, Guan Minghua happened to fall asleep due to extreme fatigue from working late the previous night. Suddenly, she was awakened by a loud shout. "Guan Minghua, stand up!" she heard somebody scream. "You fell asleep at a meeting criticizing the 'Three Family Village.' What is your attitude during this political movement?"

Guan immediately stood up and explained, "I went out to help deliver a baby last night." But she was interrupted. "Stop making excuses!"

Accusations were immediately thrown at her, including the fact that she had once admired Deng Tuo's works. Guan Minghua was now

---

*The name of a column published during the early 1960s in the Beijing municipal Party theoretical journal *Frontline (Qianxian)* by a leading journalist, Deng Tuo, that leftists accused of propagating anti-Maoist tracts. The attacks on Deng Tuo and other literary figures in Beijing inaugurated the Cultural Revolution.

dubbed a "little black-gang member" who wore the same pants as the "Three Family Village."

After the criticism, Guan lost her position as a physician's aide, and she was sent down to the agricultural production team to do manual labor under surveillance. One moment of sleep had resulted in disaster.

Yet her troubles were far from over. Soon after New Year's Day in 1969, Guan was arrested on suspicion of being a spy and was interrogated at the local public security office. During her illegal detention, Guan was subjected to various threats, scoldings, and more interrogations. Guan's political history was clean, however. At the age of eighteen, she had volunteered to work in Hainan and on several occasions she had been voted a model worker. There was no way to find fault with her. After torturing her for three months, the authorities were forced to release her. When she returned home to the farm, Guan discovered that the contents of her house had been confiscated. She found this hard to bear and wrote a few big-character posters in which she criticized a certain leader on the Revolutionary Committee at the farm. Finally, those who had wanted to persecute her found a fault. First they accused her of attacking the newborn Revolutionary Committee and opposing the red political power. Later, when the farm was converted to a production brigade, the leader Guan had criticized became the deputy regiment commander, so the accusations against Guan became more serious. "Attacks on the production brigade approved by Chairman Mao and supported by Vice Chairman Lin Biao" and "attacks on the proletarian headquarters" were two of the accusations leveled against her.

During the period when Guan had been incarcerated at the Number 4 contingent, in addition to being criticized, interrogated, and beaten, she was also forced to engage in heavy manual labor. One day, after returning home from the labor site, she wrote the following line in her diary. "The golden-yellow sun is suspended above the sheltering forests, sending forth golden sunshine." This led to a new accusation.

"What do you mean by the golden-yellow sun?"

"The sun at dusk is golden-yellow," she responded.

"Reactionary! Chairman Mao is the reddest sun. How dare you use a golden-yellow sun to allude to Chairman Mao. What do you mean by 'suspended above the sheltering forests'?"

"I saw that the setting sun was above the sheltering forests."

"Reactionary to the extreme! Chairman Mao is the never-setting sun. How dare you use the setting sun to allude to Chairman Mao!"

"I did not attack Chairman Mao. The sun rises and sets."

The accusation was confirmed. Guan had written in her diary about "Mao Zedong Thought going down hill." This was a blatant example of "Opposing Mao Zedong Thought."

Guan Minghua settled into a prolonged meditation. Why were the "three loyalties" and the "four devotions" emphasized during the Cultural Revolution? Why were the common people forced constantly to voice their loyalty, dance the loyalty dance, and wear the loyalty buttons? Why was Mao Zedong being mystified? Why were the common people being accused of criminal offenses for mere slips of the tongue or for a bit of recklessness? Lin Biao! Lin Biao possessed dangerous ambitions! In this way, Guan linked her own persecution and the sufferings of the people and country to Lin Biao.

One time when Guan was forced to confess, she bravely defended Liu Shaoqi. The interrogator cunningly forced Guan into a corner. "Vice Chairman Lin stated at the 1969 Ninth Party Congress that Liu Shaoqi aimed at seizing the power of both the Party and state," he declared, "while you claim that Liu Shaoqi was entrusted by Chairman Mao. Who is right? Vice Chairman Lin or you?"

Guan Minghua's resentment and anger toward Lin Biao finally burst forth. "I am right! Lin Biao is wrong!"

How dare Guan Minghua oppose Vice Chairman Lin! The counterrevolutionary hat was finally firmly placed on her head.

During the period when she was waiting to be sentenced, Guan Minghua, despite the pain from the physical and mental torture, wrote more than 10,000 words in her diary and submitted an application to join the Chinese Communist Party. She also wrote two articles entitled "A Warning to Vice Chairman Lin to Surrender" and "A Letter to the Revolutionary Masses of the Eighth Regiment." She also declared, "Lin Biao is a time bomb buried beside Chairman Mao, a Khrushchev-style opportunist and conspirator"; "Many people have seen through Lin Biao as a wolf in sheep's skin"; "A revolutionary fire is burning all over the country"; "Lin Biao's day of doom is approaching!"

The commander in chief of the PLA Guangzhou Headquarters held a meeting to criticize Guan Minghua and sentenced her to death so that they could present Guan's head to Lin Biao to show their loyalty.

On the morning of March 12, 1971, the murderers announced Guan Minghua's death sentence at the prison that had been illegally established at the production brigade where she had formerly worked. Guan Minghua was extremely weak, but her mind was still strong. "Kill me? Do it! History will prove that I am right," she declared.

She put away some things to leave to her husband and children. Dressed in her favorite flower-patterned blouse and with combed hair, she calmly walked to the execution ground. In Hainan, where the method of using a tube to block the throat was not employed, the murderers stuck a thick bamboo stick down Guan's mouth. Fearing that Guan would spit it out, they then affixed the bamboo stick to an iron wire that was wrapped around the back of her head, so that at the execution grounds Guan was unable to shout out "Down with Lin Biao." The onlookers called to witness the execution saw that while everyone else was shouting "Long Live Chairman Mao," Guan's head was raised in honor, but when everyone shouted "Vice Chairman Lin Forever Healthy," she immediately lowered her head. The three evil gunshots felled a heroine who had dared to persist with a different point of view.[6]

On the ground, silence was frozen in terror.*

THE NEW INNER MONGOLIA PEOPLE'S PARTY CASE IN BALIN, INNER MONGOLIA

In May 1968, Kang Sheng, Jiang Qing, and all the new aristocrats in the Party slandered Ulanfu as an "organizer of a 'New Inner Mongolian People's Revolutionary Party.'" This referred to the fact that during the period of liberation in the 1940s, the CCP had sent Ulanfu to establish a CCP branch in Inner Mongolia. In order to make the branch acceptable to the locals, it was decided that the CCP participation would remain confidential and instead the name "Inner Mongolian People's Revolutionary Party" would be used as a cover. After the territory was won, the CCP did not tolerate other political groups sharing its cozy bed, and the New Inner Mongolian Party began to haunt CCP leaders. Once an attack on the Party began, the Revolutionary Committee in the Inner Mongolia Autonomous Region immediately followed suit without reservation. They posted announcements ordering Party members of the New Inner Mongolia Party to come out and register within three days; otherwise, they would be treated as enemies of the people. From that point on, disaster befell the vast Inner Mongolia grassland. In no time, work units were smashed, factories stopped production, and herds of fat, strong cattle and sheep were left unattended. Numerous Mongolian yurts were flattened for purportedly having served as intelligence posts. Illegal interrogation houses and prisons sprouted up everywhere. The once beautiful and peaceful grassland trembled in the red terror.

In October 1968, a wave of uprooting and eliminating the New Inner Mongolian Party swept the grassland. The August 1 brigade located north of the Zhaowuda region had a mixed Mongolian and Han population. One day, Song Zhenting, deputy Party secretary of the brigade, held a meeting of movement activists to uncover enemies. Out of nowhere,

---

*The CCP claims that Lin Biao subsequently attempted to assassinate Mao Zedong in 1971. He died in a plane crash on a furtive escape to the Soviet Union and was then denounced in various political campaigns as a "swindler."

they accused a certain Monk Wu of serving as the head of the Inner Mongolian Party. After enduring days of the "torturing eagle" *(aoying)* style of interrogation, Monk Wu was finally forced into confessing that he had organized the Black Line Horse Detachment under the New Inner Mongolian Party and had planned numerous conspiracies. Following Monk Wu's confession, a poor and lower-middle peasant named Li Shuyou was pushed onto the stage to be criticized.

"Li Shuyou, just honestly confess your participation in the reactionary New Inner Mongolian Party!"

The interrogation was led by a fellow named Xiu Fu who harbored old hatreds against Li Shuyou. Li was hung from the ceiling, but, sweating all over, he still declared, "I did not join the party."

"Bastard!" Xiu Fu began to curse. "Monk Wu confessed that he recommended you to join the party!"

"Never." Li Shuyou's voice became weaker.

Xiu Fu was outraged, shouting at the people in the hall. "What shall we do to him since he has refused to confess?"

"Give him a hand!" Five or six young lads shouted as they approached Li Shuyou and slapped him. When Li's body was covered with blood and he could no longer tolerate the torture, he admitted to joining the "party." He had also recommended his wife to join. In addition, he confessed that Monk Wu had committed adultery with his wife.

More and more innocent people fell into the disastrous quagmire. Soon, Li Shuyou's wife, Yu Xifeng, who was eight months pregnant, was also pushed onto the stage to be criticized.

Ye Guojun, the deputy head of the uncovering enemies detail, said with glee, "Yu Xifeng, today's meeting is held for you. Confess your problem."

"I only worked and never participated in any organization."

"Your husband has admitted everything. Dare you remain stubborn? If you don't confess today, do you think you can bear the physical punishment?"

"Even if I cannot bear it, I cannot lie!"

"It seems that your skin is tight! If you do not confess, we will give you a chance to loosen up! Beat her!" Ye Guojun shouted to the crowd of hooligans.

Ye Guojun's younger brother and elder sister pulled off Yu's clothes and slapped her a few times. Ye Guojun then pulled Yu Xifeng's hair and kicked her in the stomach. Yu Xifeng screamed in great pain and collapsed. The thugs did not show a bit of sympathy to this woman who was about to give birth and continued with the beating and kicking. The still-disgruntled Ye Guojun pointed to a girl at the meeting. "Are you a revolutionary?" he demanded to know. The girl was Yu Xifeng's niece. She stood up and looked at Ye Guojun hesitantly.

"If you are a revolutionary, then you must fight." Ye Guojun threw the whip in front of the girl. "Beat her!" he ordered. The girl held the whip in a trembling hand and was startled, bereft of any courage.

"Stop farting around. Beat!" Yu Guojun ordered loudly. The girl ground her teeth, held up the whip, and beat. After two strokes, she threw the whip away, knelt down in front of Yu Xifeng's feet, crying, "I've betrayed you! It was against my conscience!" Ye Guojun was in a bad mood. He glared through angry eyes. "Pull her out!" he commanded. Two militiamen immediately rushed to the stage and pulled the girl outside. On the next day, Yu Xifeng suffered a miscarriage.

The villagers united and bailed Li Shuyou out for a few days so that he could take care of his wife at home. The entire family was reunited in tears. Soon, the seven-day deadline set by Xiu Fu passed. The militiamen went to Li's home. "You did not return to the prison on the seventh day," they told him. "You have one out—to die!" Then the news came that more people had been arrested, and that Monk Wu had committed suicide. Everyone's hearts were broken upon hearing the news. The children held Li Shuyou's legs. "Dad, Dad," they pleaded, "you cannot go back there. They will beat you to death!" They had no one to turn to. The whole family held each other in tears.

On the night of November 28, 1968, the interrogation room at the August 1 brigade of Wulan Taohai commune was well lit and it permeated with steam. They were waiting for Li Shuyou to arrive so that they could torture him. Soon, the militia arrived and informed the audience that all four members of Li Shuyou's family had hanged themselves. Li Shuyou and his fifteen-year-old son hanged themselves with a single rope, as did Yu Xifeng (a Mongolian) and their ten-year-old daughter. The four bodies hung from the ceiling without any movement, just like four exclamation marks. Li Shuyou's two eyes remained open and full of eternal hatred. The innocent faces of the children were glistened with tears.

The death of the Li Shuyou family did not restrain these murderers. Xiu Fu not only denied the villagers a funeral, he even prohibited people from buying grass mattresses in which to wrap the bodies. The villagers had to cut in half the Lis' old bed mattress in order to wrap up the two adults. The two children were merely covered with some yellow soil. Li's property was also confiscated, including the house, a rubber-wheeled cart, and some trees. Even the donkey and the dog were slaughtered and eaten by Xiu Fu and Ye Guojun to "celebrate the victory."

Between October 1968 and May 1969, sixty-three people out of the 120 member households in the August 1 brigade were accused of being members of the New Inner Mongolian Party. Among the accused, fourteen were persecuted to death and sixteen people were permanently physically handicapped. Ten years later, the verdict of the spurious case of the New Inner Mongolian Party was reversed.

Statistics released after the Cultural Revolution revealed that the New Inner Mongolian Party case led to the investigation, criticism, and imprisonment of 346,000 people. (Mongolians constituted 75 percent of the victims.) At one time, there were so many people in prison that Inner Mongolia was short of prison space and some people had to be transferred to Tangshan city in Hebei Province, to be incarcerated. Eighty-seven thousand one hundred eighty people were permanently impaired. Sixteen thousand two hundred twenty were persecuted to death.*

The tragedy of the Li Shuyou family was merely a drop in the bitter sea of this concocted case.[7]

THE HITCHHIKING CASE OF QINGHE, XINJIANG AUTONOMOUS REGION

On August 15, 1960, Bayimola (a Uygur),[†] deputy head of the Industry and Agricultural Department of Qinghe County, Xinjiang Autonomous Region, who had been sent to a cadre training program, was ordered over the phone by the A'letai Prefecture to report immediately to the prefecture committee to be assigned to a new position.

Early the next morning, Bayimola carried his luggage to the side of the road and prepared to hitch a ride. He had no luck until sundown. All of a sudden, two policemen, escorting a pair of prisoners, walked to the roadside, put down their luggage, and gazed off toward the road's horizon. Bayimola became very excited. Companions! If a special vehicle comes by to pick these guys up and is headed in the direction of A'letai, he thought, then surely I can ask for a ride.

At about six o'clock, a truck came from the direction of A'ertai. When he spotted the two policemen and their prisoners, the driver pulled up and parked the truck on the side of the road. The prisoners and the policemen got on. The anxious Bayimola threw his luggage onto the truck and got on too. The policemen gave him a wordless look and told the driver to move on. Bayimola was very happy. It seemed to him that his method was very effective. Don't ask anything, just get on the vehicle; if questioned, then explain.

The truck stopped at the entrance of the A'letai Public Security Bureau. The policemen and prisoners jumped off the truck. Bayimola also got off and carrying his luggage headed in the direction of the prefecture committee office.

----

*See W. Woody, *The Cultural Revolution in Inner Mongolia: Extracts from an Unpublished History* (Stockholm, Sweden: Center for Pacific Asia Studies, Stockholm University, 1993).

†Uygurs are an Altaic-language minority group in China's northwest, which in 1990 numbered over 7 million.

Suddenly, he heard someone shout "Freeze!" When Bayimola turned around, a policeman rushed toward him and pulled him by the collar. "Where are you going!"

"To the Organization Department of the prefecture Party Committee," Bayimola replied.

"No way!" the policeman shouted harshly.

Bayimola was confused. He had forgotten how to speak the unfamiliar Mandarin Chinese and tried to explain his situation in his native Kazak dialect. The policeman could not understand what he was saying and punched Bayimola in the chest. "What are you mumbling about!" he shouted. Bayimola was ordered to follow the prisoners. He did not know what to do. If he followed the prisoners, it would seem like an admission that he himself was a criminal. If he did not follow, however, how would he deal with the vicious policeman, since he could not explain the situation to him in Mandarin? "Walk!" the policeman commanded. Bayimola humbly turned around and followed the two prisoners toward the prison gate. From then on, he was a prisoner.

But he was not that worried, because he thought that once he explained everything, all would be okay. It took a lot of effort for him to find a prison guard who spoke Kazak. After begging the guard for a long time, Bayimola was able to get him to listen to his explanation. The guard, upon hearing the story, smiled sarcastically. "Explain it to whomever arrested you," he said. Bayimola thought that the guard did not quite understand, and so he followed him into an office to continue his explanation. At last, Bayimola had only one simple request. He asked the guard to telephone the prefecture Party Committee.

The guard became impatient and started cursing. "Stupid Ass!" he bellowed. "Be honest with yourself. No matter who you are, county director, or governor, once you enter this gate, you're a prisoner."

Bayimola could not restrain himself anymore and pounded on the table. "Show me the arrest warrant," he shouted. "I've never seen a public security person like you."

"I've never seen a prisoner like you. Get out of here," replied the guard.

In September 1961, Bayimola was sent to a labor camp in Fuhai. After a year of muddleheaded prison life, Bayimola, who was only in his thirties, was all wrinkled. His failing eyesight had filled him with frustration and resentment.

"What kind of prisoner is he?" the camp director asked.

"A political prisoner perhaps."

"Did you bring his materials with you?"

"No."

"Another prisoner without a registry. There are quite a few here." The director was annoyed.

"Just put him here," the guard said somewhat unhappily.

In April 1962, the public security department and the court of A'letai Prefecture sent a work team to clear up leftover cases at the labor camp. They found that in Bayimola's file, other than a few letters of appeal, there was nothing. After reading the file, the members of the team started chatting among themselves.

"Too weird, too weird. Is it possible? What a slander and insult to our public security departments!"

"I've read a lot of novels. But I've never heard anything more weird than this!"

"Perhaps this guy made it up to destroy the reputation of our public security departments?"

After the discussion, they wrote "hold for investigation" in the file. Satisfied that they had completed their task, they left.

Half a year later, a bureau-level deputy director came down to inspect the work. Upon hearing Bayimola's story, he ordered the camp leader to investigate. The director immediately had a talk with Bayimola and asked him to write a letter of appeal as soon as possible.

By this time, Bayimola had already been in prison for two years. All he wanted in the whole world was to regain his freedom as soon as possible. He sat down and recalled all he could to find a way to save himself. He finally came up with a quirky strategy. He decided to confess.

Bayimola had uttered some truths during the 1957 Anti-Rightist Struggle and Anti-Rightist Tendency Movement and had been accused of being "anti-Party," "opposed to agricultural cooperativization," "engaged in ethnic separation," and so forth, and so on. In addition, years earlier he had become a "bandit" and had subsequently been subjected to reform. Although he had lost his Party membership and cadre position, he had been sent to receive training at the cadre training program. There were two choices for people coming out of that program. One was to refuse to confess and to go to prison; the other was to confess to everything and be released and assigned to a job. Two years later, when Bayimola came out of the program, he was assigned to work at the Party Organization Department of the prefecture Party Committee. That was because he had admitted to everything and was thus granted generous treatment. Recalling those events, Bayimola wrote a confession, admitting to all his various crimes. After reading the confession, the prison director wrote, "Bayimola's crime is not light, but due to his good attitude and earnest work at the camp, I suggest that he be sentenced to six months of labor." The materials soon were returned without even being verified. Thus, Bayimola had finally registered himself and had become a real "prisoner."

After Bayimola had been mistakenly sent to prison, his family members dared not receive his monthly salary from the county office. Two years after the Public Security Bureau had announced that Bayimola was a prisoner in labor camp, the county committee ordered the financial department to eliminate Bayimola's name from the payroll. At that same time, the county committee decided to send the five members of Bayimola's family to the countryside. His eldest daughter was expelled from the Communist Youth League, the second daughter was kicked out of school, and the youngest daughter and son were deprived of any rights to attend school in the future. The sixteen-year-old eldest daughter and the fourteen-year-old third daughter were forced to marry early in order to reduce the financial burdens on the family.

After Bayimola's release, no work unit would offer him a job. Having no other choice, he had to stay at the camp to be employed. In July 1976, he was finally allowed to become a peasant in his home area of Qinghe County.

In May 1978, Bayimola began appealing his case. After more than one year of "passing the buck" (all of the cadres involved in the Bayimola case had already been promoted and were desperately afraid of being held accountable for any possible wrongdoing), Bayimola saw his case finally reversed on June 6, 1979. Bayimola was also promoted to head of the Qinghe County Husbandry Bureau.

When the truth was revealed, the results were dramatic. People could not help but wonder who should be held accountable. Perhaps the public security unit should have come first for arresting and imprisoning Bayimola without following any legal procedures. The Party Organization Department should also have been held accountable for not searching for the missing cadre. The county executive committee should also have been held accountable for not probing into the reason why one of its own residents was imprisoned and for sending his family members down to the countryside. The great pity was that none of these units were willing to accept any responsibility. On the contrary, they all demanded that Bayimola himself be held responsible for the following three reasons: (1) his punishment served him right because he hitchhiked in a vehicle he knew nothing about; (2) he had been too honest and naive in deciding not to argue and fight on his own behalf; and (3) at the end of 1962, Bayimola had confessed his guilt; therefore, what had been wrong with sentencing him?[8]

Naturally, Bayimola, who suffered wrongly for nearly twenty years because of having hitched a ride on the wrong vehicle, had neither the ability nor the interest to argue over who should be held accountable for his case. He said, "Today, the Party has restored my political life by assigning me an important position. Frankly speaking, I never expected this to happen. I am fifty years old this year and I will try my very best to devote myself to the four modernizations."

In China, one would be better off not hitchhiking at all.

NOTES

1. Zhang Shushen, "Songs of Righteousness" *(Zhengqige)* in Zhou Ming, chief editor, *Pondering the Course of History (Lishi zai zheli chensi)*, vol. 3 (Beijing: Huaxia chubanshe, 1986), p. 220.

2. *Jilin Daily*, April 22, 1980.

3. Li Yaokun, "The Stolen Seal" *(Dao yin)*, in *Spring Breezes into Rain (Chunfeng huayuji)* (Beijing: Chunzhong chubanshe, 1981), vol. 1.

4. Jie Ting, "The Disaster that Ensued from Riding a Red Bicycle" *(Qi hongzi-xingche yinlai de henghuo)*, in ibid.

5. Ombudsman Office, Guizhou Provincial CP, "Years in a Miao Village" *(Miaoxiang fengyun)*, in ibid.

6. Li Shifei, et al., "After Rehabilitation" *(Zhaoxue zhihou)*, in *Southern Daily (Nanfang ribao)*, March 28, 1980.

7. Fu Baotong, "Beacon Fire in the Dark Night" *(Heiyeli de fenghuo)*, in *Spring Breezes into Rain*, vol. 2.

8. Ombudsman Office, Xinjiang Autonomous Region CP, "The Weird Prisoner" *(Qiguaide qiufan)*, in *Spring Breezes into Rain*, vol. 2.

Epilogue:
A World in Equilibrium

Marx once stated, "The critique of religion is the prerequisite of every critique."[1] Marx destroyed the Heaven in Faramita even as he intended to establish heaven on earth. He criticized spiritual religions, but created a vulgar, worldly religion. He destroyed the withering flowers decorating religious shackles but failed to get rid of the chains restraining humankind. Instead, he put fresh flowers on them. Only by removing these flowery chains can humankind breathe freely and establish our own unholy home full of humanism. Only by so doing can we say when the new sun rises every day, "I belong to this world. This world belongs to me."

However, in today's reality, we do not have the right to utter such words proudly, for we have yet to get rid of the flowery chains around our necks. We can take the beautiful flowers off the chains, but we cannot put the chains on other people's necks. Our hope is not to eliminate a ruthless totalitarian power that employs violent politics just so we can establish the rule of a new totalitarian system in place of the old one. The history of struggle against totalitarianism that has now lasted for thousands of years should make us more mature and enable us to break the vicious cycle from chaos, to suppression, to insanity, and to move toward a healthy form of existence—equilibrium.

On May 30, 1974, during the insanity of the Cultural Revolution, Mao Zedong met with the renowned Chinese-American physicist and Nobel Prize winner, Li Zhengdao.

"Why is 'symmetry' (duicheng) so important?" Mao asked rather earnestly.

"What surprised me was that so soon after I met Mao Zedong, he directly posed a question about physics," Li Zhengdao noted.

At that meeting, Li Zhengdao was the only guest. Between their two couches was a tea table on which there was a pile of paper, a few pencils, and a cup of green tea. Li Zhengdao picked up a pencil and placed it on the paper and flipped the pencil in Mao's direction with his finger. Then Li flipped the pencil back a little bit. The pencil first rolled toward Mao then back to Li. "In that movement, there was not one static moment, but the entire process was symmetrical," Li explained.

Mao was very interested in this demonstration and he continued to inquire whether physicists had used the principle of symmetry to formulate their fundamental concepts of the universe. Li then explained how Einstein had developed his theory of relativity based on the dual principles of balance *(pingheng)* and symmetry.

What is the principle of balance? And why was Mao so interested in it? It is a scientific method employed to explore new things, starting from the notion that things in the universe must exist in a balanced state. Modern science has developed the method of symmetry to a high stage. Li Zhengdao's Nobel Prize was won for his explanation of such symmetry. Naturally, Mao was very interested in it. The dialectical unity in Marxism actually emphasizes separation, contradiction, imbalance, and disequilibrium instead of unity, tension, balance, and equilibrium. Thus, in the social and political realms, it opposes cooperation, reform, and peace; instead it focuses on class struggle, revolution, and violence. Symmetry? How can the nature of the world be a static symmetry? Had modern physics, post-Marx, overthrown the core of dialectics *(bianzhengfa)*, the unity of opposites?[2]

I am sure Li Zhengdao profoundly understood Mao's intentions, and thus his demonstration was marvelous. The pencil rolled over and rolled back. Li Zhengdao persisted in explaining the principles of a scientist: symmetry. And Mao also understood the core of the demonstration. What he mainly focused on however was the fact that the pencil was "moving" continuously, which was extremely important to him. Movement, contradiction, social turmoil were not negated. *Ca suffit!*

The previous description came to me like a lightning bolt from the sky. The core problem of dialectical materialism, I realized at once, was its imbalance and disequilibrium.

Equilibrium is the necessary condition for things to exist. Humankind must cautiously maintain the balance of the things they need. Eating serves the purpose of maintaining the balance of energy and water in the human body; sexuality serves the balance between the collection of sexual energy and its release; the protection of forests and animals serves the purpose of maintaining ecological equilibrium. International military surveillance serves the purpose of maintaining military equilibrium; the invisible hand of Adam Smith's *Wealth of Nations* serves to maintain the balance between production and sales.

Humankind has often tried its best to destroy the internal balance and that, in turn, has led to self-destruction. Depriving enemy troops of water and food is a way of using the disequilibrium between energy and water of the body; fright and abuse that result in psychological abnormality use the psychological disequilibrium; destruction of the internal balance means elimination. The socialist revolution advocated by Marxism called for the elimination of the bourgeois class, along with anyone holding different views, thereby causing a serious imbalance of classes and politics; to eliminate private ownership thereby upsets the balance between the forces and relations of production; suppression and one-party rule create a disequilibrium of power. Such disorder produces more disorder, which eventually leads to a vicious cycle. This is the reason no socialist country has been able to escape the situation whereby class struggle becomes more and more severe. This is also revealed in Mao Zedong's pitiful summation that to bring order out of chaos "class struggle must occur every seven or eight years." (As the common people have added, "each struggle lasts seven or eight years.") Thus, we can make the following deduction. Communism itself is the self-destruction of human society.

*   *   *

My friends, it's time to say good-bye.

I thank the reader wholeheartedly. You have tolerated stinking corpses and the smell of blood, holding back the desire to vomit, and followed me in completing this long journey with scarlet memorials at our side. Now we have come to a complete understanding that no matter what language we speak—Mandarin Chinese, Zhuang, Mongolian, Tibetan, Russian, German, or English—language is basically irrelevant. We can communicate through our eyes. From your eyes, I can tell that you have one last wish; from my eyes, you can also tell that I have the same wish.

We wish that all this should be known in the future. We hope that, just as in Auschwitz, Buchenwald, and Nanjing, a memorial—a scarlet memorial—will be erected in Guangxi.

There should also be built a huge memorial hall in which all the violence and ruthlessness from communism, capitalism, state socialism, militarism, racism, colonialism, totalitarianism, and feudalism will be revealed so that our offspring will remember it. (The ruthlessness and violence of communism reaches the climax of all violence and ruthlessness, and the cannibalism in Guangxi was the zenith of ruthlessness and violence toward humankind.)

We hope that on the 10,000 granite stones outside the memorial there will be carved the names, birth dates, and death dates of the victims. And inside the hall will be carved the names of all those cannibalized.

And we hope that on the plaza in front of the memorial these words will be etched in stone: *NO, NEVER AGAIN!*

As for myself, I have finally unburdened myself of this heavy cross that I have carried for a long time. I finally have achieved salvation for my own soul.

Tears stream down silently. All of a sudden, I remember a poem my dear wife, Bei Ming, composed while in prison after June 4, 1989.

PHOTO 5.1   Zheng Yi during his internal exile in
China, during which time he wrote *Scarlet Memorial*.

The death penalty has been announced
The prayer has been completed
Inhale deeply for the last time
Close your eyes and wait for the miracle after the gunshot

October 1990 to July 1991, written while on the run in my motherland

NOTES

1. Karl Marx, "Introduction: Critique of Hegel's 'Philosophy of Right,'" in
Marx-Engels Selected Works, vol. 1, pp. 1–2.
2. Hai Lude et al., editors, *Mao Zedong Upfront (Shenghuo zhongde Mao Zedong)*
(Beijing: Hualing Publishing House, 1989), pp. 310–311.

Glossary of Participants

Chen Boda: Deceased in 1975, Chen served as political secretary and ghostwriter to Mao Zedong during the Yan'an period (1937–1945). During the early 1950s he was involved in CCP propaganda work and was vice president of the Marxism-Leninism Institute in Beijing. In 1956 he was appointed to the Politburo and became deputy director of the Propaganda Department; he served as editor-in-chief of the *Red Flag (Hongqi).* A radical during the Cultural Revolution, he headed the Central Cultural Revolution Group with Jiang Qing until he was purged in 1970.

Chen Manyuan: Born in Mengshan County, Guangxi Province in 1911, Chen Manyuan joined the Red Army in 1929. In 1949 he became the deputy commander of an army corps in the Fourth Field Army of the People's Liberation Army. In 1949 Chen was also appointed chairman of the Guilin Municipal Military Control Commission. In 1950 he became a member of the Standing Committee of the CCP Central-South China Bureau. In 1955, he was appointed first secretary of the Guangxi Provincial CP, and in 1956 he became an alternate member of the Eighth CCP Central Committee. In 1968 during the Cultural Revolution, Chen was branded a capitalist roader and purged. He was rehabilitated in 1974 and in 1982 became a member of the Central Advisory Commission. He died in 1986.

Deng Xiaoping: Born in 1904 in Sichuan Province, Deng was the eldest son of a landowner and in 1920 traveled to France as a work-study student where he also joined a Chinese socialist youth organization. Upon returning to China, in 1924 he entered the CCP and assumed his first position as an instructor at the Xi'an Military and Political Academy. In 1929 he helped organize communist military forces in Guangxi Province and became a political commissar. During the 1945–1949 Civil War, Deng was a member of the Second Field Army in the Crossing the Yangtze River and Huaihai battles. In 1952 he was appointed a vice

Works consulted in preparation of this glossary include *Who's Who in the People's Republic of China,* 1st ed., ed. Wolfgang Bartke (Armonk, NY: M. E. Sharpe, 1981), 2d and 3d ed. (Munich: K. G. Saur, 1987 and 1991); Wolfgang Bartke, *Biographical Dictionary and Analysis of China's Party Leadership, 1922–1988* (Munich: K. G. Saur, 1990); and Ruan Ming, *Deng Xiaoping: Chronicle of an Empire,* tran. Nancy Liu, Peter Rand, and Lawrence R. Sullivan (Boulder, CO: Westview Press, 1994), from which several entries have been borrowed, courtesy of the authors.

premier and in 1956 a member of the Politburo Standing Committee and head of the Party Secretariat. He was condemned in the Cultural Revolution for having previously criticized the personality cult of Mao Zedong and for his "liberal" policies on agriculture. He first appeared after the Cultural Revolution in 1973 as a vice premier and in 1975 was reappointed to the Politburo Standing Committee only to be dropped again in 1976 following the April Tiananmen demonstrations. Deng reappeared in July 1977 and assumed all previous posts, plus PLA chief of staff, and in 1981 he became chairman of the Central Military Commission. In November 1987 he retired from all posts, except the Military Commission, a position that he finally yielded in November 1989.

Hu Yaobang: Born in 1915 in Hunan Province, Hu became a Red Army soldier at the age of 15 and in 1933 engaged in youth work for the central Party leadership in the Jiangxi Soviet. During the Civil War (1945–1949), he served in the Political Department of the Second Field Army and later in the Southwest China Military and Administrative Council, both of which were organizations dominated by Deng Xiaoping. In 1957 he headed the then recently reorganized Communist Youth League. He was later attacked during the Cultural Revolution. Hu Yaobang reappeared in 1972 and in 1977 became a member of the CCP Central Committee and the director of the Organization Department. In 1978 he entered the Politburo and headed the Propaganda Department and then in 1980 became general secretary of the Secretariat. He was appointed the third and last chairman of the CCP until this position was eliminated in 1982. Hu remained general secretary until his dismissal in early 1987. Hu Yaobang's death in April 1989 sparked the student demonstrations that culminated in the June Fourth 1989 Beijing massacre.

Jiang Qing: Mao's wife and later member of the so-called Gang of Four, Jiang Qing was born in Shandong Province under the name of Li Yunhe. In the 1930s she was a film actress in Shanghai where she was also a member of the CCP underground. After divorcing her first husband, Jiang Qing traveled to Yan'an in 1938 where she met Mao and, despite reservations of the Central Committee, married the chairman after he secured a divorce from his third wife. Although Mao initially promised that Jiang Qing would stay out of politics, Jiang Qing became active in 1965 when Yao Wenyuan (a later cohort in the Gang) directed his acid pen at the drama *The Dismissal of Hai Rui from Office*, which, Yao suggested, was a veiled attack on Mao. During the Cultural Revolution, Jiang Qing assumed a prominent role in the Central Cultural Revolution Group led by Chen Boda, and in 1967–1968 she egged on Red Guards to launch vicious assaults on the Party and army. With the purge of Chen Boda and the demise of Lin Biao in 1970–1971, Jiang's influence waned as she focused increasingly on foreign policy. In October 1976, she was purged with the other three members of the Gang (Zhang Chunqiao, Yao Wenyuan, and Wang Hongwen) and in 1981 was sentenced to death (with a two-year reprieve) for her role in the Cultural Revolution. She committed suicide in 1991.

Kang Sheng: Born in 1899 to a family of well-off landlords, Kang Sheng was one of the most important CCP leaders involved in intelligence and security and also liaison with foreign communist parties. In the 1930s he was an underground Party operative in Shanghai and then went to Moscow where he studied Soviet security techniques and was CCP representative to the Communist International. Returning to Yan'an in 1937, Kang Sheng was reinstated as a Politburo member and headed the growing security apparatus, including the Social Affairs Department or secret police and was also a top official at the Party School. During the early 1940s, Kang promoted the notorious "rescue campaign" aimed at ferreting out alleged KMT spies and "Trotskyites" in the CCP, but which ended up purging many innocent intellectuals. In the late 1950s, Kang was involved with Deng Xiaoping in the growing dispute with the Soviet Union over ideological and other issues and at the same time strongly defended Mao's Great Leap Forward policies. Kang's political star rose considerably in 1962 when he was appointed to the Party Secretariat headed by Deng Xiaoping. During the Cultural Revolution he served as a critical advisor to the radical faction of Jiang Qing and became a member of the Politburo Standing Committee. Kang died in 1975.

Li Jingquan: A veteran of the 1934–1935 Long March and a political commissar in the Second Field Army of the PLA, Li Jingquan was appointed chairman of the Military Control Commission in 1950 in Chengdu, Sichuan Province. In 1952 Li became the first secretary of the Sichuan CP, and from 1961 to 1967 he served in the same capacity on the Southwest Bureau of the CCP Central Committee. In 1956, he became a member of the Central Committee at the Eighth Party Congress and from 1958 to 1967 served on the CCP Politburo. Li was also a member of the National People's Congress, China's nominal parliament, until he was purged from all posts in 1967. He later became a member of the CCP Tenth and Eleventh Central Committees. Li Jingquan retired in 1982 to the Central Advisory Commission and died in April 1989.

Lin Biao: The "closest comrade in arms" during the Cultural Revolution of Mao Zedong and his constitutionally designated successor, Lin died in 1971 during an alleged attempt to assassinate the chairman. Lin was a major military leader during the 1945–1949 Civil War when on one occasion his siege of the northeast city of Changchun led to the deaths of several hundred thousand people. After spending considerable time for medical treatment in the Soviet Union, Lin became a marshal of the PRC in 1955 and the minister of national defense in 1959. He emerged as an important political figure in 1964 at a PLA Political Work Conference and was canonized as Mao's official successor in the 1969 Ninth Party Congress constitution. Lin and his entourage maintained an uneasy alliance with the radical faction surrounding Jiang Qing.

Liu Binyan: After joining the underground CCP in the 1940s in Tianjin, Liu Binyan worked with the *Beijing Youth Daily* in the early 1950s and later with the *People's Daily*. He was branded a rightist in 1957 for his scathing criticism of bureaucratism and was sent to labor on a state farm. After returning to work in the early 1960s, he was denounced again in the Cultural Revolution and then rehabilitated yet again in 1979. In 1985 he was elected vice chairman of the All-China Writers' Association. In 1987, during the antibourgeois liberalization campaign, he was expelled from the CCP. In 1988 he traveled to the West, remaining in exile after the

June 4, 1989, crackdown in Beijing. He was denounced in November 1989 in the *People's Daily* as the "scum of the Chinese nation." Liu's written works include *People or Monsters?* and *A Second Kind of Loyalty.*

Liu Jianxun: A veteran of the Shanxi Province "Dare-to-Die" corps in the 1930s, Liu Jianxun became the first secretary of Guangxi Province in 1957 and served from 1958–1961 in the same post of the reconstituted Guangxi Autonomous Region. In 1958 he also became an alternate member of the CCP Central Committee. He served as first secretary of Henan Province from 1961–1966 and from 1971–1978. Liu Jianxun disappeared in 1978 due to "grave errors and crimes" and he lost his last remaining post as a deputy from Henan Province to the National People's Congress in 1980.

Liu Shaoqi: A native of Hunan Province, Liu emerged as the first heir apparent to Mao Zedong in the 1950s. He replaced Mao as state chairman in April 1959 in the political fallout over the disastrous Great Leap Forward. Author of "How to Be a Good Communist," Liu's political star rose throughout the early 1960s as he supported a substantial loosening of state controls on the economy, especially agriculture, to help China recover from the Leap. Liu was attacked very early in the Cultural Revolution as "China's Khrushchev" and as "the Number One Party person in authority taking the capitalist road." He was replaced as Mao's heir by Lin Biao and was formally expelled from the CCP in October 1968. He later died ignominiously in a solitary cell.

Liu Shuyan: Wife of Chen Boda (his third), Liu Shuyan was born in Sichuan Province in 1922 and joined the CCP in 1938 at the age of sixteen. During the revolution, she engaged in underground Party work and mobilization of workers and youth. During the Cultural Revolution, she generally supported the leftist politics of her husband until his purge in 1971.

Mao Zedong: Chairman of the CCP from 1935 until his death in September 1976, from 1958 onward Mao generally ceased attending Politburo meetings. Like the bodies of Lenin and Ho Chi Minh, Mao's body is preserved in a crystal sarcophagus. Mao's body lies in the memorial hall in Tiananmen Square, Beijing.

Ou Zhifu: A member of the Zhuang minority, Ou Zhifu served in the Red Army during the 1930s and in 1941 became a regiment commander in the Eighth Route Army. In 1949 he was identified as a division commander in the Fourth Field Army and in 1950 became a deputy commander (and, in 1952, commander) of the 48th Army. In 1958 Ou Zhifu became commander of the Guangxi Autonomous Region Military District and was promoted to major general. In 1964 he was elected to the National People's Congress and in 1968 was appointed vice chairman of the Guangxi Revolutionary Committee, until 1972. In 1969 he also became deputy commander of the Guangzhou Military Region.

Qiao Xiaoguang: After serving briefly in the Hunan Province CP, in 1952 Qiao Xiaoguang was appointed secretary-general of the Guangxi Province CP and director of its Organization Department. From 1956 to 1961 Qiao was China's ambassador to North Korea, and from 1961 to 1965 Qiao was secretary of the Guangxi Autonomous Region CP. In 1966 he became the region's acting first secretary. In 1972, Qiao was appointed to the Standing Committee of the Guangxi Autonomous Region CP, and from 1977 to 1985 he served as its first party secretary. From 1977 to 1987, he was a member of the CCP Central Committee. In 1983 he was forced to make a self-criticism of his own factional practices, and in 1987 he joined the Central Advisory Commission.

Tao Zhu: A graduate of the Kuomintang's Whampoa Military Academy in 1926, Tao Zhu emerged as a major military leader in central and northern China throughout the 1930s and 1940s and at the same time was a key figure in the central Communist Party leadership. From 1951 to 1952, he served as acting secretary of Guangxi Province and in 1953 headed the CCP Central Committee's South China Sub-bureau. From 1953 to 1965, Tao served as the first secretary of Guangdong Province and in 1966 became director of the CCP Propaganda Department and a member of the CCP Secretariat and Politburo. In 1967 he was branded a counterrevolutionary revisionist and purged. He died in 1969 and was posthumously rehabilitated in 1978.

Ulanfu: Born in Suiyuan, Tumd Banner, and educated in Moscow, Ulanfu was an ethnic Mongolian who organized Communist forces and a base area in Inner Mongolia. In 1945 Ulanfu became a member of the CCP Central Committee and in 1949 was appointed secretary of the Inner Mongolian Sub-bureau of the CCP Central Committee. From 1955 to 1967, he served as first secretary of the Inner Mongolian Autonomous Region and was a member of the Eighth Central Committee. In 1967 he was labeled a ruler in an independent kingdom and purged. In 1973 he was rehabilitated and reappointed to the Central Committee and became director of the CCP United Front Work Department and a member of the Politburo. Ulanfu died in 1988.

Wang Dongxing: Since the 1930s, a member of various guard units for CCP leaders, including Mao Zedong, Wang Dongxing in 1955 was appointed vice minister of public security. During the Cultural Revolution he was appointed director of the General Office of the CCP Central Committee and became a member of the Central Committee at the 1969 Ninth Party Congress. In 1973 he was promoted to the Politburo and in 1977 became a vice chairman of the CCP and a member of the Politburo Standing Committee. As commander of the security forces in Beijing, Wang played a key role in the arrest of the Gang of Four. In February 1980, he was removed from all Party and state posts but was made an alternate member of the Central Committee in 1982. In 1985 he joined the Central Advisory Commission and was effectively retired and reportedly was put under house arrest.

Wang Huaixiang: A major general in the Korean War (1950–1953) and from 1962 to 1967 a deputy political commissar in the Jilin Military District, Wang Huaixiang was appointed to the Ninth (1969) and Tenth (1973) Central Committees. In 1968 he became chairman of the Jilin Province Revolutionary Committee (until its abolition in 1977) and political commissar of the Jilin Military District. Wang Huaixiang disappeared in 1977.

Wei Guoqing: A member of the Zhuang minority, in the 1920s Wei Guoqing initially joined the Kuomintang but in 1929 switched to the Communist side. Wei took part in the 1934–1935 Long March and in 1946 became a major general and a deputy political commissar in the Third Field Army. In 1954 he contributed to the Vietnamese defeat of the French at Dien Bien Phu in Vietnam by directing Chinese-supplied artillery. After serving as mayor of Fuzhou city in Eastern China, in 1955 Wei became governor and Party secretary of Guangxi Province. In 1956 he was made an alternate member of the CCP Central Committee, in 1958 he became chairman of the Guangxi Autonomous Region, and in 1961 he became its first Party secretary. In 1967 Wei Guoqing became political commissar of the Guangzhou Military Region. In the same year, he was accused by Red Guards of suppressing the Cultural Revolution in Guangxi. However, Wei was absolved of any wrongdoing by Party leaders and in 1968 became chairman of the Guangxi Revolutionary Committee and ordered that "mass trials" be held, which resulted in thousands of deaths, some by cannibalism. In 1971 he was appointed first secretary of the reconstituted Guangxi CP. In 1974 he became a member of the Standing Committee of the National People's Congress. From 1977 to 1982, he served as the director of the General Political Department of the PLA. Throughout the 1980s, Wei Guoqing served in various posts in the National People's Congress and remained a member of the CCP Politburo and Central Committee until 1985 when he resigned all posts.

Xie Fuzhi: A veteran military man who joined the Red Army in 1931, in 1949 Xie Fuzhi became an Army commander in the Second Field Army and a member of the Chongqing Military Control Commission. From 1953 to 1959, he was political commissar of the Yunnan Military District and the Kunming Military Region. From 1959 to 1972 he was minister of public security, and from 1964 to 1972 he served as political commissar of China's public security forces. In 1969, Xie became a member of the CCP Politburo and a member of the CCP Central Military Commission. From 1971–1972, he served as first secretary of the Beijing Municipal CP until his death in March 1972. In 1980, Xie was posthumously expelled from the CCP because of his ties to leftist political factions.

Zhang Chunqiao: A guerrilla fighter during the 1940s, Zhang Chunqiao in the early 1950s became managing director of the People's Liberation Army *Liberation Army Daily* in Shanghai. In 1959 he was appointed to the Politburo of the Shanghai Municipal Party Committee and director of its Propaganda Department. In 1966 he was deputy head of the Cultural Revolution Small Group under the Central Committee and helped initiate demonstrations by Red Guard *zaofanpai*. Zhang headed the Shanghai People's Commune, which later became the Shanghai Revolutionary Committee. In 1969 Zhang became a member of the Central Committee and the Politburo. In 1975 he became a vice premier and director of the PLA General Political Department. In October 1976 he was arrested as a member of the Gang of

Four and in 1981, like Jiang Qing, was unrepentant at his trial and was sentenced to death with a two-year reprieve.

Zhao Jianmin: A veteran of the Korean War (1950–1953) and in 1949 member of the Guiyang Municipal Military Control Commission, Zhao Jianmin served as Party secretary of the Shandong Province CP from 1955 to 1960. A critic of the 1958 Great Leap Forward instigated by Mao Zedong, Zhao disappeared until 1963 when he was appointed Party secretary of the Yunnan Province CP. In 1968 he was branded a renegade and purged until his rehabilitation in 1978. In 1980 Zhao was appointed vice minister of the 3rd Ministry of Machine Building and in 1982 became a member of the Central Advisory Commission. In 1984 he participated in a "rectification" (i.e., purge) of the Xinjiang Autonomous Region CP.

About the Book and Author

This compelling book provides a meticulously documented account of officially sanctioned cannibalism in the southwestern province of Guangxi during the Cultural Revolution. Drawing on his unique access to local archives of the Chinese Communist Party and on extensive interviews with Party officials, the victims' relatives, and the murderers themselves, Zheng Yi paints a disturbing picture of official compliance in the systematic killing and cannibalization of individuals in the name of political revolution and "class struggle."

The treasure-trove of evidence Zheng Yi has unearthed offers unprecedented insights into the way the internecine, factional struggles of the Cultural Revolution reached a horrifying level of insanity and frenzy among the ethnic Zhuang people of Guangxi. Profoundly moving, acutely observed, and unflinchingly graphic, *Scarlet Memorial* is a shining example of a genre of investigative reporting that courageously and independently records obscure and officially censured historical events, revealing hidden dimensions of modern Chinese history and politics.

Zheng Yi (which means "justice") is one of China's foremost novelists and journalists. His works include *Old Well (Jaojing)*, which was later made into an acclaimed film. A leader of the 1989 Tiananmen Square protests, he spent over three years as a fugitive from the Chinese government before escaping to Hong Kong. He now lives with his wife, Bei Ming, in the United States.

Index

191